Forms of Folklore in Africa

Forms of Folklore in Africa

Narrative, Poetic, Gnomic, Dramatic

Edited by Bernth Lindfors

Illustrated by Adebisi Akanji

University of Texas Press, Austin & London

International Standard Book Number 0-292-72418-7 (cloth);
0-292-72419-5 (paper)
Library of Congress Catalog Card Number 76-050961
Copyright © 1977 by the University of Texas Press
All Rights Reserved
Printed in the United States of America

The essays in this volume were published in *Research in African Literatures.*

Contents

Dramatic Forms

Preface

BERNTH LINDFORS

All the essays in this volume were published in *Research in African Literatures*, a journal founded in 1970 to encourage serious study of African oral and written literatures. In its first seven and a half years, *RAL* has been fortunate in attracting contributions from folklorists in Africa, Europe, and America who have made interesting new observations based on extensive field work and thorough library research. This book provides a sample of their pioneering scholarship.

It also affords a selective rather than an exhaustive introduction to a vast field. No single collection of essays could adequately cover the full range of traditional expressive arts found in the diverse cultures of a continent as huge and complex as Africa, but most of the major genres of African folklore and several of the largest ethnic groups (Yoruba, Xhosa, Kongo, Berber) are represented here. The survey extends from Morocco in the north to Zululand in the south, from Guinea in the west to Kenya in the east. Several essays discuss texts from a wide variety of cultures, while others concentrate on materials collected from a single ethnic group—sometimes that to which the writer belongs. The result, we hope, is a book of sufficient breadth to interest the general reader yet of sufficient depth to be of use to the professional folklorist.

Students of folklore should find these essays particularly instructive, for they demonstrate a variety of approaches to the study of oral literature. In addition to conventional descriptive and analytical efforts, there are attempts to synthesize data drawn from thorough surveys of printed sources as well as to construct new theories of oral performance based on original firsthand research. Studies boldly comparing traditions of aesthetic expression which are not often examined together (e.g., weaving and poetry, oral and written tales, African and European drama) stand side by side with investigations offering fresh perspectives on such familiar touchstones in African folklore scholarship as trickster tales, tone riddles, and ideophones.

We wish to thank all the contributors to this book for allowing their essays to be reprinted. We are also extremely grateful to Adebisi Akanji for providing the entertaining illustrations.

Introduction:
Folklore in African Society

What is folklore in Africa? What does the African know about the narratives and poems of his culture? How does he conceive of them and what does he perceive in their forms and themes? How does he use them properly in society and what do they mean to him? The answers to these questions may vary from one African society to another. Presently we attempt to learn to ask the questions which might enable us to understand the folklore of an African society the way the members of the community do.

The forms of folklore, as speakers delineate and recognize them, have cultural symbolic meanings. Texts, framed into genres and performed in socially defined communicative situations, acquire significances beyond the literal meanings of their constituent words. Ritual songs, for example, which abound with repetitions and obscure terms, are rendered meaningless outside their verbal or social contexts; or, in other cases, their transition from one context to another involves a transformation of meaning. Genealogies and legends function towards the promotion of social stability because they are symbolic expressions of political power and historical truth; parables are effective in settling personal disputes due to their capacity to symbolize moral truth, and tales and riddles can entertain because of their inherent ability to unsettle reality. The defining features of forms and genres are hence capable of communicating in society the symbolic meanings of a category of expressions, or of a single text.

Since these defining features distinguish folklore genres from casually formulated information, and since they also differentiate between various forms of speaking, they have the ability to communicate the meanings inherent in these respective forms. For the demarcation of genres to be culturally communicable, they need to be conceived and perceived as distinct verbal entities; such a recognition has to be linguistically expressed, and validated both by the text itself and the social context of its performance. Consequently the attempts to discover the principles of folklore communication in each culture in Africa must begin with the identification and analysis of the cognitive, expressive and social distinctive features of folklore forms. The cognitive features consist of the names, taxonomy and commentary by which a society labels, categorizes and interprets its forms of folklore within a wider system of discourse; the expressive features are the styles, the contents and the structures which characterize each genre, and the social features are the constituents of the situational contexts of each folklore performance. The ethnographic study of folklore in Africa should uncover the principles of folklore communication in each culture and language.

I. COGNITIVE FEATURES

The need for the study of the names and classification systems of ethnic genres in Africa has long been recognized, yet such awareness has not resulted in any methodological ethnographic descriptions. As early as 1948 Margaret Green pointed out that "we need to discover what literary 'genres' occur, particularly those recognized by the people themselves, and, if possible, what is their relative importance. We need also to discover what literary forms occur within these 'genres.' If there is drama, for instance, does it use prose or verse or both?"[1] She abides by her own proposal with a preliminary description of Igbo genres, but other students of African folklore, though sympathetic to her plea,[2] have failed to heed her counsel. Instead they entangle themselves in a futile attempt to synchronize African with European literary taxonomic systems.

Melville and Frances Herskovits, for example, who clearly recognized that the classification of verbal forms of "each society must be studied in terms of its own particular orientations,"[3] tried, and partially succeeded in eliciting indigenous taxonomy but were still confounded by its ambivalence and ambiguity. "Narratives overlap even in the two major divisions [*hwenoho* and *heho*], and Dahomeans themselves are hard put to it to give a categorical answer if asked to designate the type to which certain tales belong. This applies especially where the *heho* is of the type *we would describe* as a fable, or as a parable. Indeed, a parable has been named by one informant as falling into the proverb group."[4] (my italics)

In an attempt to inductively formulate a cross-cultural classification system for prose narratives based upon indigenous taxonomies, Bascom proposes to consider myth, legend and folktale as three categories which are widely recognized. Myth is sacred, its events take place in the remote past and its major characters are gods; legend could be either sacred or secular, its actions occur in the recent past and its principal figures are human; in contrast to both forms, the folktale is secular, its actions could take place at any time and any place, and its dramatis personae are either human or non-human beings. However in the process of fitting the Yoruba bipartite classification of prose narratives into this tripartite system, Bascom bends the Yoruba indigenous taxonomy rather than his own construct, considering the *itan* as a compound class of myth-legend, rather than examining the features the Yoruba perceive in this form as a verbal entity.[5] The principles underlying indigenous categorizations are rooted in cultural thought, language and experience. The differences in names of genres, in classes of verbal behavior, and in their symbolic meaning reflect essential cultural concepts. Deciphering their significance may provide us with the key for understanding folklore communication the way its speakers do.[6]

a. *Generic Names.* The names of folklore forms reflect their cultural conception and significance. The semantic components of such terms constitute sets of features which the speakers of a language regard as the primary qualities of each verbal form. These are the characteristics of a genre which signify the symbolic meaning of a given form in a culture. For example, the Jabo people of Liberia emphasize the component of antiquity in their name for the proverb, *da' di kpa* "to take old affairs,"[7] while the Hausa people of Nigeria stress the element of wisdom in their term for the genre, *karin magana*, "wise saying."[8] While the uses of proverbs in both societies are similar, the ideational reasons for their practices are quite distinct. The Jabo settle conflicts by evoking the sanction of tradition and antiquity; in addition, the archaism which proverbs convey has an ornamental value in discourse and poetry. The Hausa, on the other hand, apply to similar social and verbal contexts the notion of wisdom. No doubt, it is quite possible that the etymological meanings of terms, or their original semantic components, may become obscure; also use, performance and symbolism can infuse them with wider connotations. For example, the Sandawe of Tanzania name their riddles *tántabule*, a term which is not only applicable to stories and the songs within the stories, but is also associated with birds. The imagery of fowl, the actual names of birds, and allusion to them appear also in the formulaic procedure of riddlings Similarly it is said of the songs in the stories "that they fly like birds." It is this close semantic association between riddling and birds which underlies the taboo of riddle playing during the planting season. "Birds would come and eat up all the seeds"[9] of those who break this prohibition. Thus the names of genres could reflect their meaning in imagery and indicate their association with the cultural belief system.

b. *Taxonomy of Genres.* The categorization of forms is a statement of their relations to each other in terms of inclusion and exclusion. All genres that share a certain feature in common are included in a single category, and the other forms in the system which have other qualities are excluded from the previous class and form other groups. The bases for ordering verbal forms into categories are the distinctive features of each genre, and the cluster of these features signifies its symbolic meaning. There are three ways for designating the category of a form: cognitively, by naming it, pragmatically by performing it in particular contexts, and expressively by formulating it in a distinctive language which is peculiar to the genre. This last method of designating the generic qualities of texts will be discussed later, together with the description of the expressive features of folklore. If the taxonomic system of verbal art is coherent and culturally valid, each expression must have stylistic, thematic, and contextual correlatives which will justify its inclusion in one class or another.

Obviously, at present it would be impossible even to attempt any conclusive definition of the taxonomic principles by which African peoples order their folklore. The information currently available permits only the illustration of the problem with a few isolated cases. For example, the overriding feature of all the verbal forms of the Limba people of Sierra Leone is their source as the speakers themselves perceive it. In Limba terms, all their stories, proverbs, riddles, and metaphors come from previous generations, from "the old people" (*bebɔrɔ be*); hence they categorize all these forms in one class—*mbɔrɔ*. Naturally, on a pragmatic level they distinguish between the various folklore forms and perform them in different social contexts: stories are told on occasions of entertainment, proverbs in contexts of persuasion and argumentation.[10]

In contrast, the expressive features serve as the fundamental principles for classification of folklore for the Nyanga people of Zaïre. Although they apparently do not have terms for prose and poetry, there is a general recognition that forms with rhythmic language belong to one class and those with prose sentences to another. Within each of these general categories the Nyanga identify several genres by name, form, context, and theme. For example, they have two terms for prose narratives: *uano* and *mushíngá*. "The first is a tale in general, the second a tale where the supernatural element, produced by the intervention of divinities, celestial bodies, monsters, and forest specters, stands in the foreground."[11] Other types of Nyanga prose narratives are *nganuriro*, "'true stories' about partly imaginary, partly real events" told mainly by men who open the narration with the first person formula "I (we) have seen . . .";[12] *mwanikiro*, meditations expressed in a concise style; *kishámbáro*, discourses on a serious public affair uttered by the elders or political leaders; *ịhano*, instructions and teaching of the youth about customs and behavior, often introduced by the formula "we are accustomed to do . . ."; and finally *kárịsị*, the epic narratives of the Nyanga, which are few in number and are known to only a small number of people. The poetic genres are neither fewer nor less varied in terms of their distinctive features.[13]

Not surprisingly, in several African societies features of performance rather than of content or attitude serve as the distinctive marker between genres of folklore. For example, the Bini of Nigeria, the Gbaya of Cameroun, and the Lamba of Rhodesia and Zaïre all distinguish between tales with and without songs. In Benin tales including songs are *okha*, while those without them are *umaȓamwẹn*. Although it is permissible to sing during the narration of *umaȓamwẹn*, the songs are not an integral part of the plot; the contrary is true of the *okha* in which the hero of the tale finds himself in a situation in which singing is appropriate or even necessary and desirable. The storyteller then starts singing and the listeners respond in chorus.[14] Similarly the Gbaya recognize two narrative genres—*to* and *lizang*. There are several expressive features in which these forms differ. "The *to* 'tale' is a narrative of from less than a hundred words up to six thousand words, relating one episode or a series of episodes about human characters and birds, animals, and water creatures. A *lizang* 'parable' is an object lesson drawn from nature or a short narration of human experience from which a lesson is drawn. The only distinguishing feature between the tale [*to*] and parable [*lizang*] may be a song. Almost invariably there is one song in a tale, and in a long tale there may be up to ten or more, but in a parable [*lizang*] there are no songs."[15] Similarly Clement Doke comments that "Lamba folk-lore is classified by the natives in two ways, according to the mode of recitation. First and foremost comes the prose story, called *Icisimikisyo*. The other, which, for want of a better term, is translated as "Choric Story", is variously called by the natives,— *Ulusimi, Icisimi, Akasimi* and *Akalaŵi*. This is a prose story interspersed with songs. The stories are mostly recited by the women and girls . . ."[16]

In addition to performance, the actual social use to which a verbal form is put can also serve as a distinctive taxonomic feature. For example, the Haya people of Tanzania differentiate between proverbs in terms of their effect in the context of speaking. "An *enfumo* is a proverb used to bring together the opinions of speaker and hearer. The speaker tries to effect an agreement between the hearer and himself. An *omwizo*, on the other hand, may be used by the speaker to signal that there is not a peaceful relationship between the interlocutors. In sum, an *enfumo* draws the speaker and the hearer together, an *omwizo* drives them apart."[17] According to Seitel, a single proverb in two distinct situations can be considered as *enfumo* and *omwizo* respectively. In other words, what is categorized is not just a verbal expression but a social situation as defined by proverb use.

Similarly, the Bini people distinguish three forms of proverbs, albeit in their system there is a correlation between content and category. Not every kind of expression would be appropriately used in different social situations. The three Bini proverb genres are *ere*, *ivbe*, and *itan*. *Ere* refers, directly or indirectly, to events and personalities in Benin traditional history, and has a moral intent in its application in conversation. For example, the proverb *n'o gha yi n'agbon, e da eho ahianmwẹn n'utioya*, "He who [fulfills] his life [goal], should not heed the bird that cries 'danger'," is an *ere*. It alludes to an episode in a famous battle in Benin history. The bird mentioned in the proverb is said to be prophetic. "If it cries *oya o, oya o*, danger or disaster is ahead, if *oliguẹguẹ, oliguẹguẹ* one's errand will be lucky. If it cries persistently *oya o* in front of a man, he will return rather than continue on his way . . . When (Ọba Ẹsigie) went to war with his brother Aruanran, the *ahianmwẹn n'utioya* cried *oya o* on the road, but the Ọba killed the bird and did not give heed to its cry."[18] The second proverb genre is used in admonition or as an offense, and has no metaphorical or referential meaning aside from the immediate contextual situation. Statements such as *ebiebi o r'owa okhu* "darkness is the home of evil," or *arhunmw'okpa i bi ma* "one person cannot form a crowd" illustrate the *ivbe* genre. While the previous two types of proverbs have rhetorical utility, the third form, *itan*, has mostly esthetic value, functioning as linguistic ornamentation in formal discourse. Singers and storytellers employ *itan* in their songs and narratives and public speakers intersperse their speeches with it. An example of such a proverb is *a ma mien n'o rho omwan, a ghi tobo'mwan*, "If nobody praises one, he should praise himself."[19]

These examples of the various possible generic distinctions demonstrate the complexity of the problem. We have not been able to establish a logical, consistent and coherent system of inclusions and exclusions in either case, but the failure is our own. The systematic formulation of the paradigm of features of each genre, requires a thorough research of a folklore, a culture and a society. Only then would it be possible to view the forms of verbal art the way native speakers do. In a way, the taxonomic system of a genre is a representation of a cognitive map of the communicative competence of folklore. That is, it is a verbal statement of the cultural, linguistic and folkloristic rules for the appropriate use of folklore in society.[20]

c. *Commentary.* In addition to naming and speaking folklore, people appear to talk about it, making exegetical statements or in other cases even making proverbs about proverbs, jokes about jokes. In other words, folklore forms are, in and of themselves, the subject of folklore, much the same way other aspects of culture, society and nature are. Although such statements would be even less systematic than taxonomies of genres, they do provide glimpses into the thoughts of the speakers about the forms available for their use. Alan Dundes suggests considering these ideas as "metafolklore."[21] Examples of metafolklore in Africa are the Yoruba proverb *Owe l'esin oro; bi oro ba sonu owe l'a fi nwa a* "A proverb is like a horse: When the truth is missing, we use a proverb to find it,"[22] and the Igbo proverb "proverbs are the palm-oil with which words are eaten."[23] Both statements not only illustrate the value proverbs have in African speech, but also reflect the use and the significance of the form. While the Igbo statement points to the esthetic value of proverbs, the Yoruba suggests a regard for the proverb as an expression of truth. Both, however, are only isolated examples and could not even hint at cultural differences between the Yoruba and the Igbo in regard to proverb use. Yet comments such as these, and other statements about verbal art forms as expressed in narratives, songs, riddles and metaphors offer a native exegesis of the symbolic value of genres and instruct children in the significance of folklore types and their proper social use, thus contributing to the formation of cultural ideas about folklore.

II.   EXPRESSIVE FEATURES

The names and taxonomy of folklore genres and the commentary about them constitute abstract knowledge about the style, themes, structures, and uses of the forms of verbal art. In the social reality of folklore communication and performance, they serve as an ideational reference point, a cultural system of order to which new experiences are related, and by which they are interpreted. This abstract knowledge is also a source of ideas which enables speakers to generate folkloric expressions anew, uttering them in appropriate situations with adequate ability. But the translation of these abstract thoughts into dynamic verbal communication requires the utilization of expressive features which would enable the formulation of meaningful folkloric communication. Such features are inherent in the texts spoken in society. They identify a particular expression as belonging to a generic category and communicate ideas in culturally recognized terms. The expressive features of folklore enable speakers to differentiate it from other modes of verbal communication, and to state their intent, attitudes and purpose in implicit rather than explicit terms.

The most obvious and clearly recognized expressive feature is rhythmic language. The words of songs have a musical basis which marks them off from conversation; recitations have a pattern of accents and beats which differentiate them from informative and informal speech. Hence rhythm distinguishes poetry from prose. But in addition to this basic indication of the nature of expressions there are some other features which signify their meanings; they are the opening and closing formulas and the distinct styles, themes and structures of the texts. No doubt it is possible to regard the first of these—the phrases that open and close folkloric expressions—as one of many stylistic features, as Gordon Innes has done.[24] Nevertheless, however much these formulas are stylistic devices, they also function as markers of transitions from and to conversational speech and as indicators of the symbolic meaning of a particular expression. Hence, they have a unique position and function in the process of folklore communication.

a. *Opening and Closing Formulas*. In situations where changes in the rhythm, pitch or intonation of speech do not function as indicators for the transition to folklore, both speakers and listeners require verbal markers which distinguish the speaking of folklore from non-folklore.[25] Opening and closing formulas serve this need. They frame the expressions, setting the boundaries between formal generic expressions and whatever type of verbal exchange precedes and follows them. Such phrases are not so much part of the narrative text as of the verbal interaction between the speaker and his listeners. They signal the nature of a tale and enable the listeners to prepare an attitude of belief, disbelief or humor toward a forthcoming narration. In the folklore of African societies opening and closing formulas occur mostly in association with riddles, epics and prose narratives.[26]

The opening formula of a riddle ensures the challenger the agreed participation of the potential responder and differentiates it at the same time from other forms of questions. These phrases function, hence, as defining features of the riddle genre in the contextual situation.[27] The following Sandawe riddling illustrates that exchange:

1. C :	*Tántabule*	[Here is] a riddle.
2. R :	*Tánkwetá*	Forward with it
3. C :	*Ríorío*	*Ríorío*
4. R :	*Láfa thwií*	The bird of the fig-tree
5. C :	*Tántabule*	[Here is] a (the) riddle
6. R :	*Tánkwetá*	Forward with it
7. C :	*Tsí khoo n!ũsets'e'e*	My house has no mouth
8. R :	. . . .	(*No reply, or wrong one*)
9. C :	*Húmbuko séé*	Give me a cow
10. R :	*Humbuú*	Here is [your] cow
11. C :	*Hapú húmbũs' n/ĩge !'okai, tsí khoo n!ũsets' éi: Di'a*	As for your cow, I have eaten it. If my house had had no mouth: An egg[28]

The dialogue in the first four lines is an opening formula which precedes any riddle. The closure of the game, lines 9–11, marks an exchange in which the responder is unable to solve the riddle; in other cases the answer itself serves as a closing formula. In some cultures, however, the presentation of the solution requires a formulaic reply as in Berber riddles:

MZ+R8 A5 TTc NN, LXIBIT TAR IMI
UR A5 TTc NN ITTINI R+BBI XS TIJLIT
I riddle it you, a storage jar without an opening
God will not tell you otherwise than that it's an egg[29]

The opening formula relates directly to the genre it introduces. The rhetorical function of the opening phrases is to define the text generically and to socially permit the expression of its unique qualities. Thus in the recitation of a long historical epic like the Sundiata, the epic of Mali, the singer has to establish his authoritative knowledge of this intricate, multi-episodic narration, and to state the legitimacy of his performance. Hence the singer devotes the opening of the recitation of this epic to the presentation of himself:

> I am a griot. It is I, Djeli Mamoudou Kouyaté, son of Bintou Kouyaté and Djeli Kedian Kouyaté, master in the art of eloquence. Since time immemorial the Kouyatés have been in the service of the Keita princes of Mali; we are the vessels of speech, we are the repositories which harbour secrets many centuries old. The art of eloquence has no secrets for us; without us the names of kings would vanish into oblivion, we are the memory of mankind; by the spoken word we bring to life the deeds and exploits of kings for younger generations.
> I derive my knowledge from my father Djeli Kedian, who also got it from his father; history holds no mystery for us . . .[30]

In the absence of parallel texts from Mali it is impossible to determine whether such a presentation is formulaic in the strict sense of the term—that is, a verbatim repetition of the phrases—or whether it establishes the authority and legitimacy of the singer in the presence of his audience, stating his rights to the epic narrative.

The opening formulas of short narratives enable the examination of their relations to the stories, their performance and their listeners. They define the tales in each society generically as fiction and distinguish them from reality. In cases in which the text contains phrases which violate social etiquette, the opening formula disavows any serious intent. For example, Rattray notes that the Ashanti of Ghana, precede tales containing obscenities with a disclaimer as an opening formula: *Ye' nse se, nse se o*, "We do not really mean, we do not really mean (that what we are going to say is true)."³¹ However, even nonobscene narratives have distinct fixed openings such as *Ye se*, "they say," and *Oba bi*, "certain woman." The closing formula of the tales is *M'anansesem a metooye yi, se eye de o, se ennye de o, monye bi nni, na momfa bi mpene*, "This, my story, which I have related, if it be sweet, (or) if it be not sweet, some may take as true, and the rest you may praise me (for telling it)."³²

The significance of the opening and closing formulas in narrative performance in establishing contact between the storyteller and his audience is even more apparent among the Hausa of Nigeria, where, Skinner notes, the story usually begins *ga ta ga ta nan* "see it, see it here," to which the audience can reply *ta je ta komo* "let it go, let it come back" or *ta zo, mu ji* "let it come, for us to hear." The traditional finish is *Kungurus kan kusu*, probably "the rat's head is off." *Bera*, the commoner word for "rat," sometimes replaces *kusu*, and *kungurus* (an ideophone, perhaps to be rendered by "chop-chop") has the variants *kunkurus* and *kurungus*. Other endings, less common, are "I ate the rat, not the rat me"; "it wasn't because of Spider that I made it up— I was making it up in any case." However, when tales are written down, not performed, as most of the narratives in Skinner's volume are, the rhetorical need the opening phrase fulfills disappears and "the initial and final formulas are often omitted, or something more mundane or Muslim inserted by the scribe. So we have, for the beginning, often merely 'a tale' or 'another tale' and for the ending, *haza wassalamu*, 'this with peace', the normal epistolary ending, or even the Arabic *tammat* (rendered 'finis')."³³

In other societies the opening formula takes on an aspect of address. Hence it varies according to the social composition of the listeners. Although such a rule is not rigidly imposed, Benin tales told to children open with the phrase *okh'okpa siensiensien*. The first part of the phrase is literally "This is a story," but the last word has no meaning outside the context of storytelling. Such a phrase would be inappropriate for an adult audience who should be addressed with the phrase *okh'okpa ke do re*, "A story is coming," followed by a presentation of the principal characters. In both social contexts the phrase *evba no okha nan ya de wu*, "here the story dies" signifies the end of the narration.³⁴

In singing there is no need to distinguish expression from conversation by opening and closing formulas; the metric language and the music serve that end. Yet in some cases artists use them as a signature to identify the singing with their personality. In his study of Yoruba Ijala singers, Babalola illustrates such a use of identity-establishing-phrases by two different artists. One usually begins his performance by exclaiming *Haa ! e e e e e !*; on the other hand, his friend starts with the phrase

> *Mo gbé ṣe èmi dé,*
> *Enu ni tií yọ, 'ni*
> Here I am with my usual trouble-making
> This leads one into calamity.

Such phrases may be followed by "introductory formulas," which singers use at the very beginning of their chants. For example

> *Ibà ni ng ó f'ojó óní jú orin èmi d'ọla*
> Only chants of homage to my superiors shall I perform today.
> Tomorrow I shall perform my entertaining chants.

Or,

> *Ng ó re'lé . . . .*
> I shall now proceed to the house of so-and-so.
> i.e., I shall now chant a salute to the lineage of so-and-so.

The closing formulas serve the Ijala artist to indicate the end of his turn in the performance and invite the next singer to take over from him. For example

> *Eyun-ùn téléngé l'ónà ibèun*
> That has gone away nicely along that road.
> *Ẹ gbè m'l'éle.*
> Take over from me in vigorous chant.[35]

In conclusion, both in prose and in poetry such formulas are performance markers, signals which indicate to the listeners the intent and purpose of the speaker and provide breaks in the flow of narrating and singing which enable others to introduce their stories and songs.

b. *Style*. The text and performance features which distinguish folklore from everyday language, and folklore communication from conversational speaking, comprise the stylistic qualities of verbal expressions. On the one hand they represent measures of deviation from standard communication, but on the other hand they reflect attempts at approximation of ideal norms of performance for each genre. While there is a personal style in the delivery of folklore, it is subject to the cultural constraints and conception of excellence in narrative and poetic performance.[36] Hence the esthetic ideas a society has about folklore are expressed in stylistic terms.[37] Singers and storytellers are able to reproduce such ideas by phonic, verbal, and mimetic means. The first relate

to the physical production of sounds, the second to the selection and
syntactic orders of words, and the third to the dramatic and visual
presentation of the text. Not all three types of stylistic features occur
simultaneously in the same performance of a single genre. In fact it is
quite possible that dominance of, say, phonic features, would preclude
any possibility for mimicry and gestures; on the other hand all three
means of stylization might be present in the same situational context,
occurring sequentially to each other, or simultaneously.

The Zulu praise singer "recites the praises at the top of his voice
and as fast as possible. These conventions of praise-poem recitation,
which is high in pitch, loud in volume, fast in speed, create an emotional excitement in the audience . . ."[38] The phonic stylistic features of
the singers among the Bahima of Ankole are similar,[39] except in the
case of the Zulu praisers mimicry has a larger share of the performance.
"The professional praiser at court accompanies his recitation of the
chief's praises not only by walking but by leaping about with gesticula-
tions as the excitement increases. He suits the actions to the words, the
words to actions; the performance is indeed dramatic. Movement, both
visible and audible, is the essence of praise-poem recitation."[40] Available descriptions suggest phonic changes among some Bantu peoples,
even in storytelling, though they occur to a lesser degree than in the
recitation of praises. Among the Akamba people, for example, "a person
should be able to vary his voice, according to the story (or part of the
story) he is telling. If he is describing hunters stalking their animals,
his voice will naturally be gentle and quiet; whereas if it is a raid and
the clamour of fighting, he will raise his voice and make it rather
rough."[41]

Verbal and mimetic features are more common in narrative performance. Although Finnegan notes that Limba narrators use tone in an
exaggerated way for narrative effect, and also may change the tempo
and rhythm of speech for the same purposes, the main features of narrative style are repetition of words and phrases, parallel phrasing and
listing.[42] Actually the last two features are variations on repetition, involving the recurrence of themes, and things or events of a similar type.
The mimetic features involve dramatization of the actions described,
using formalized gestures, "the representation of eating by making as
if to take a ball of rice in one's right hand; the click and downward
sweep of a hand to indicate anger or beating; putting a hand to one's
mouth to express extreme astonishment; pointing by pushing out the
lips and moving the head; or pushing the elbows slightly out from the

body to suggest chiefly dignity and pride.''[43] Otherwise, the actual vocabulary and syntax of Limba narration are much the same as those of everyday language.

In the examination of the style of Gbaya narrative performance Noss singles out the predominance of the use of ideophones as a stylistic feature. He finds it the "most pervasive, and in that sense the most important"[44] feature in narrative description. For example, describing rabbit visiting the lion, the narrator says: "He takes some eggs, fashions himself a great bell, and goes to hide in the reeds *Mɛk Mɛk Mɛk Mɛk Mɛk Mɛk*, where Lion sends his underlings for water. Soon Fox comes along *kirik kirik* and begins to wash out his water pot *hokoro hokoro*. At that, *Gbévévévévévévé*! Rabbit rings his great bell. . . ."[45]

In an attempt to discern the verbal features of historical, not fictional Tonga narration, Jones and Carter have identified four distinct characteristics: staging, overlapping, repetition and synonymous expressions. The first of these terms refers to minute segmentation of the action, particularly noticeable in journey descriptions. For example:

Tweenda, twiinka mutala, twaa kusika kumbal'aaLwizi
We traveled, we went through, and we arrived near the Zambezi.

The second feature, overlapping, "is the mainstay of the Tonga narrative, the technique which accounts for the major proportion of redundancy. In essence it is the use of lexical material from a preceding part of the utterance, generally that immediately preceding, to initiate a new structure." For example:

baa kumujata. Bamane kumujata
then they caught her. When they had finished catching her . . .

or

twaa kusika kumigodi. Tukasike kumigodi
we arrived at the mines. When we had arrived at the mines . . .

The third stylistic feature, repetition, appears as stem reduplication, repetition of a whole word or word-complex, and of a whole phrase or sentence. These could be a nominal repetition which indicates an intensification of meaning as in *akati-kati* "right in the middle"; adverbial repetition which also functions as an intensifier as in *Abatuba bafwa abanji lobo-lobo-lobo-lobo* "the whites died in very great numbers"; and finally, repetition of the entire verb-form signifying continuation of action, for example, *Tweenda, tuya bweenda, tuya bweenda* . . . "We traveled, we kept on and on traveling . . ." Co-occurring with all cases of repetition is the foregrounding of the phonic feature of speed and loudness which appear in the recitation of praise or heroic poems among Bantu peoples.

The fourth feature of synonymous expressions is not as frequent as the previous three yet is found, with some variety, in Tonga narration; for example, *Twazubuka. Twaya kutala* "We crossed (the river). We went over." Jones and Carter distinguish three types of synonymity, the elaboration, such as *inzala yanjila. AmaTebele baul'eezilyo* "Famine entered. The Matebele lacked food"; the negative opposite, *batujata toonse, taakwe wakazwa pe, taakwe wakapona pe,* "they caught all of us, no-one got away, no-one was saved"; and finally a synonymity which involves a repetition of lexical elements with change of grammatical form, as for example, *Isike buyo muJanisbeg, nedyakasika* "When it had arrived in Johannesburg, when it arrived. . . ."[46]

The co-occurrence of phonic and mimetic features becomes more apparent in the actual context of storytelling. In these situations two stylistic aspects of storytelling characterize narrative performance in many African societies: active audience participation and dramatization. The telling of a story is often a dialogue between the narrator and his listeners, the former unfolds the events and the latter respond vocally in affirmation. Such an exchange may be solely verbal, melodic or both. In Mende society, for example, "direct questions may be addressed to the audience, which they answer, and a storyteller may seek assurance from his listeners that they are following the story."[47] Among the Limba the narrator may nominate a friend designating him "as the answerer (*bame*), to 'reply' (*me*) to the narration. . . . Once appointed, this 'answerer' must then interject phrases like 'yes' (*ndo*), 'mmmm', 'fancy that' (*woi*), 'really!' (*ee*) at appropriate moments, and react quickly with laughter, exaggerated amusement, or dismay at events related in the story."[48] Thus the chosen friend represents the audience as an active participant, helping out in carrying out the narrative performance.

Choral singing in response to the storyteller, which occurs in the narrating situation, is also a form of audience participation. It appears to be a prominent feature of storytelling in many African societies. Thus, speaking and singing occurs in repeated sequence. The songs are part of the plot and are introduced by the narrator as the voice of the main character. The choral response makes the audience participate in the process of storytelling as well as in the narrative plot itself. Storytelling is hence characterized by alternations between speaking and singing.[49] While singing brings the audience into unison with the narrator, his own increased mimicry sets him apart, making him a focus of visual, not only verbal, attention. In the narration of the Mwindo epic, dramatization of action occurs simultaneously with singing and speaking.

"Episode by episode, the epic is first sung, then narrated. While singing and narrating, the bard dances, mimes, and dramatically represents the main peripheries of the story. In this dramatic representation, the bard takes the role of the hero."[50] The degree of incorporation of mimetic features into narrative performance is dependent on cultural conceptions of public behavior and circumstantial conditions. In Benin, for example, storytellers, both amateurs and professionals, minimize the dramatic features of their performance since an outburst of emotions and movements contrasts with the Bini notion of dignity, respect and self-composure. In other societies the artist's musical accompaniment of his narration imposes understandable limitations on his freedom of movement. Still, the mimetic features of performance are an integral part of narration in many African cultures. Among the Mende, for example, dramatization is one of the features distinguishing between fictional and nonfictional tales. "There is a difference in style of delivery between nonfictional and fictional narratives; the former are delivered as historical narrative, with little attempt at dramatization; they usually contain little, if any, direct speech and no songs, and are not heightened by audience participation." In contrast, in the delivery of fictional narratives "the use of direct speech . . . is found extensively in tales, and . . . [it] gives scope for the skilled narrator's dramatic gifts. Some narrators will adopt a different manner of speaking for each protagonist . . ."[51]

In sum, phonic, verbal and mimetic features, in different relationships to each other, define stylistically the performance of various forms of verbal art. The correlation between style, content and attitude has not yet been properly analyzed in a sufficient number of African societies to allow for effective generalization. It is quite possible, for example, that the explanation for the lack of dramatization in Benin storytelling is erroneous. It should be attributed not to cultural values of public behavior, but to the attitude toward the narratives. The Bini people do not have separate categories for fictional and nonfictional narratives, and hence they might relate to all stories with the seriousness history demands. In any case, whatever the explanation might be, the observations Innes makes in regard to storytelling in Mende society do indicate that the absence or occurrence of stylistic features have symbolic meanings to the speakers and listeners.

c. *Content*. The very selection of themes as adequate for folklore expression depends upon cultural rules of communication and is indicative of the conception the members of the community have of the subject. Not all cultural knowledge and sociohistorical experiences are the proper topics for songs, narratives, riddles, or proverbs. Folklore does not present the entire gamut of cultural ideas and actions of a society, but selected domains of themes which are deemed suitable for particular genres of expression. The particular view a culture has of the subject determines its qualification for inclusion. The division of knowledge and experiences into thematic domains is directly related to cultural conceptions of nature and society. For example, among the Nyanga the demarcation of the animal world in general as an appropriate thematic domain for folklore does not reflect the totality of ideas about the symbolic significance of animals in any given culture:

> The dramatis personae in the tales are animals—all kinds of animals, but particularly the Duiker antelope, the turtle, the hunting dog, and the leopard. It is striking, however, that the most sacred animals, like the pangolin, the hornbill, the flying squirrel, the dendrohyrax, the bongo antelope, and the potto, are *never* included in these stories.[52]

Similarly, the tortoise, the spider and the chameleon are the most common animal characters in Benin prose tradition. Other creatures like the elephant and the vulture appear with somewhat lesser frequency. But the cow, and probably other domestic animals, such as the goat, chicken and dog, which are part of Bini daily experience and appear in several folkloric genres—proverbs, praise names, epithets—do not appear as personified characters in folktales. They lack the mythical dimension possessed by the chameleon, tortoise and spider, who were once human courtiers in the palace of *Ogiso*, the mythic dynasty of rulers in Benin tradition. As punishment for their unethical conduct in the court, they were incarnated in animal form.[53]

Thus, the selection of themes for folklore depends upon their symbolic value in culture. Those subject matters which have religious and political meanings occur in the verbal and social context of appropriate expressions, such as rituals, praise songs, and epic narrations. The themes of entertaining and instructive expressions should be free of any religious constraints. In general the thematic domains of folklore in Africa do not differ from those the world over. Human relations, historical events, natural and supernatural beings and forces, recur in narratives and songs, proverbs and riddles. In the presentation of events and characters there is a great emphasis on the marvelous and the extraordinary, the outstanding and the unique. The incorporation of human and animal figures in prose and poetry transforms them into symbols for the culture, which are then repeated in traditional expressions with a constant meaning, creating a language of folklore for each culture.[54]

d. *Structure*. The thematic domains of folklore in each society are culturally defined. The formulation of narrative plots out of this substance is also subject to principles of creativity and existing conceptions of narrative and poetic forms. The transformation of a theme from an aggregate of events into a coherent story involves adherence to an order of episodes and relations between actions and characters which are considered acceptable and appropriate within the folkloric system. No doubt such structural ideas often become normative patterns which are only approximated. The social circumstances in the storytelling situation and the narrative abilities of the speaker affect the content and the structure of the narrative, but even these changes follow rules for social verbal behavior, or can be understood in terms of accidental events.

Actually, the idea that tales and songs, proverbs and riddles follow communicable structural principles is a theoretical statement about the nature of creativity and performance; its validity needs demonstration and its explanatory power should be evaluated in comparison with other approaches which attempt to account for folkloric abilities. In a series of articles Harold Scheub has recently developed a rival approach to the study of African folktales.[55] Dealing with the *ntsomi*, a genre of "fabulous story, unbelievable, a fairy tale," of the Xhosa people in Zululand in the Republic of South Africa, Scheub emphasizes the uniqueness of each narration. "The performance of a *ntsomi* at a certain time and in a certain place is a unique evanescent phenomenon; it cannot be repeated, it will never be recaptured. The artist will never again create a particular image in that particular way."[56] In order to analytically deal with such an ephemeral text and theoretically explain its performance Scheub proposes three key terms: *core-cliché, core image,* and *expansible image*. The core-clichés are phrases, songs, sayings, with which the artist unfolds the core images he recalls from memory. "The artist has many core images in her memory, but she does not of course recall all of them at once. These images are discontinuous mental pictures, usually revealed in the easily remembered core-clichés which are placed in a linear continuum only during performance. With a broad theme (which determines the general direction of the entire *ntsomi*-tradition) governing the shape which the conflict and resolution will take in performance, the artist seeks to select those core images from her repertoire which are appropriate to the work she is in the process of creating. She recalls core images by means of a complex, free associational cueing-

and-scanning process which enables her to arrange and rearrange the many images and image-segments of tradition into a variety of *ntsomi*-performances."[57] Core images have the potential of expansion through repetition, elaboration and modification, thus becoming expansible images which "can be expanded as often as the performer desires, and it is in the repetition of the image that such performances achieve their esthetic force . . . at the very core of *ntsomi* composition lies this expansible image."[58]

As the speaking of language involves the constant creation of new sentences, so the performance of folklore always requires the generation of new narrative ideas and metaphoric relations. Yet it is also reasonable to assume, in continuation of the analogy to language, that the narration of tales is not a whimsical, accidental mental activity in which "storytellers merely link the core-clichés together, repeating them as often as necessary to push the plot forward to its denouement."[59]

Perhaps "as often as necessary" is the key phrase which reveals the deficiency in Scheub's explanatory theory of performance and creativity. What are the dictates of this necessity? What are the rules to which a narrator has to adhere in order to fulfill the "necessary" requirements of storytelling? No doubt some of these rules are social and situational. The composition of the audience, whether it consists of children or adults, and the nature of the communicative event, whether the occasion is festive or pensive, are factors contributing to the process of storytelling. But at the same time the verbal artist, either professional or amateur, does not create within a cultural mental wilderness. Like sentences, tales have form and structure, even though their analysis has not yet achieved the precision linguists have accomplished in the description of the syntax of language.

One of the most recent of these studies, and the most pertinent to the present discussion, is the essay by Denise Paulme, "Morphologie du conte africain."[60] Like other students of narrative structures she assumes that tales are not conglomerations of episodes and characters, accidently related, but that there are coherent, even though not immediately apparent, relations between the episodes and the characters of a tale, and that the progression of the plot follows the internal logic of the narrative. Furthermore, the narrators themselves also have distinct models in their minds about the relationship between characters and actions that should obtain in a story.

For analytical purposes she proposes to consider the basic unit of a tale an elementary narrative action of the order "the hero meets an old woman," or "the father gives a horse to his son." She terms such a unit a "proposition." A series of such propositions is a "sequence." On the basis of these two terms she offers the following: A narration consists of a series of sequences which are connected with each other in time, or in which a relation of cause and effect obtains.[61]

Accordingly, Denise Paulme discerns within the corpus of African narrative seven structural types in which the relations between the sequences are qualitatively distinct from each other.

Type I: Ascendency (Lack–Amelioration–Lack Liquidated)
There is a narrative progression of improvement. Setbacks are possible and likely, but they do not change the essential movement toward the elimination of the lack.

Type II: Descendancy (Normal Situation–Deterioration–Lack)
In these tales the deterioration is triggered by a violation of an interdiction; the sequence that follows results in a permanent negative condition.

Type III: Cyclical
The cyclical structure combines the sequences of the first and the second type. The narration starts with lack, rather than with a normal situation, and progresses toward improvement and achievement of a normal situation, but then the hero violates an interdiction and lack is restored.

Type IV: Spiral
The progression toward improvement in this type of structure suffers setbacks, but the next round of amelioration is markedly better than the first one. The sequence starts with a lack, and as in Type I it is liquidated through amelioration. However, later, usually due to the action of an enemy, not the hero, lack is restored or impending; the hero overcomes his adversary, improves his condition, and eliminates his opponent.

Type V: Mirror-Image
This structural type involves two heroes who take symmetrical series of tests, yet their actions are in inverse relationship to each other, and could be described in moral terms as good and bad. The positive character is rewarded whereas the negative one is punished.

Type VI: Hour-Glass
As in the previous structural type, there are two heroes in these narratives; however, their courses of action are not parallel but opposing each other. Whereas the hero starts from lack, his opponent begins with a normal situation. Their courses of action converge, and, after this contact, the consequence is a normal situation for the hero and a lack for his adversary.

Type VII: Complex
The sequences of this structure are actually similar to the hour-glass structure, albeit the amelioration of the hero and the deterioration of his opponent do not occur simultaneously but in succession. In other words, the narrator changes the central character of his story, focusing on a positive figure in the first part of the narration and a negative character in the second part.

The validity of this typology of narrative structures may be subject, no doubt, to further tests of verification, and its application to the corpus of Xhosa narratives that Scheub recorded would be of particular interest. Yet the question whether such structures really exist in the narratives themselves, or whether they are just constructs formulated by insightful, or shortsighted, folklorists misses the main issue of the relevance of structures to communication of folklore. The problem with which we are concerned is whether the listeners and the narrators can perceive the forms and conceive of the existence of such narrative structures.

Out of my own research it is possible for me to contribute an anecdote which would suggest an affirmative answer to this question. While I was talking with Mr. Aigbe, a professional storyteller in Benin, I asked him whether he could create new stories, or did he tell only traditional narratives. "I can compose new stories," he answered. "How do you go about it?" I asked. "Very simply," he answered. "Let's assume I am telling a story about you. I would first learn the names of your father and mother, the name of the town where you were born, the names of the places to which you traveled, the names of the people you met, and then I would tell the story of your life, how you were poor in the beginning, how you worked hard and suffered greatly, how you studied and then came to Benin. Finally, I would end the story telling how you succeeded in your studies and became famous and very wealthy." Although I am still waiting for the fulfillment of the last stage of this narrative, his answer demonstrates not only a concern with accuracy and detail, but also the narrative model which he has in his mind, one which is similar to the "Ascendancy" type which Paulme proposes.

III. SOCIAL FEATURES

In the actual communicative situations the rules of folklore use, the set of behavioral prescriptions and expectations become the social features of verbal art forms. The cognitive system discussed earlier reflects the abstract principles which govern the use of folklore in society, but it is the actual manipulation of forms in personal interaction and the ability to modify rules pragmatically which demonstrate the dynamics of folklore in society, and the interplay between principles and necessities. For example, in Yoruba society the speaking of proverbs is a prerogative of older people. "Yoruba etiquette dictates that a younger person's use of a proverb in the presence of an older person must be marked by a prefatory apology. The standard politeness formula runs something as follows 'I don't claim to know any proverbs in the presence of you older people, but you elders have the saying . . .' "[62] Similarly, Benin professional storytellers "seldom visit the king's compound, as there is a superstition that anyone who tells a story to the king with an akpata (a musical instrument) will shortly die."[63] However, proper prayers and adequate charms can avert this danger.

Thus, in addition to the abstract rules of folklore communication which the cognitive system may reflect, there is another set of pragmatic rules which outlines the actual range of possibilities for folklore communication in society. The meaning, interpretation and understanding of tales, songs, proverbs and riddles in their social use, are affected by the adherence to, or deviation from, these rules by the speakers. Since the process of folklore takes place in social situations, it is necessary to discern the perceptible attributes of the communication as the members of the community perceive them. Thus the variables that affect the position of a community member in his society, such as age, sex, and status, become also the features that define the appropriateness of an expression to a situation. They reflect the range of expectations the listeners might have of the performer. The temporal and spatial features, as they define a communicative event[64] and delineate the boundaries of the situation, indicate the meaning and the relevance of folkloric expression to a situation.

a. *Social Position*. The age of speakers has a direct bearing upon the forms which they know and are able to use properly and which the cultural rules permit them to employ. Children's songs, for example, are generically defined in terms of age. As members of the community mature, they grow out of the repertoire of children. The following Yoruba verse

Iya lonigbowo mi.	Mother is my helper
Ontuju mi ni kekere.	(She) cares for me during youth.
Ehin re lofi pon mi	(She) carries me on her back
Iya ku ise me	Mother does well for me.
Mi yio ki' ya mi ku ise	I will greet my mother
Pelu teribamole	With great respect
Emi koni ko 'se fun (i)yamimo	I will not refuse work for my mother again
Iya-o ku-ise mi o	Mother thank you.[65]

is strictly a children's song in content, rhythm, and form, and would not be sung, except as a possible recollection, by an adult. There are, naturally, social, and sometimes even political, circumstances by which adults are asked to recall their childhood verses. Ayodele Ogundipe, for example, tells that during the civil war in Nigeria, tongue-twisters, a genre enabling children to acquire verbal dexterity, was used as a marker of tribal identity. Soldiers asked not for her identification cards but for the recitation of the Yoruba tongue-twister

Mo ra dòdò ní Iddó
Mo jè dòdò ní Iddó
Mo fi owo dòdò r' ómò òní dòdò ní idodo ní Iddó
I bought fried plantains at Iddo
I ate fried plantains at Iddo
I wiped my hands on the naval of the fried plantain seller at Iddo.[66]

In many African societies the riddle is the child and youth form par excellence.[67] It serves as a verbal instructive device within the peer group enabling young people to acquire the cultural conception and categorization of the natural and social world around them. In terms of age, riddles and proverbs are in an inverse relationship to each other. While riddling is a verbal game that children play, proverb saying, hardly a game, is the exclusive right of adults. Moreover, children may be spoken to with proverbs, but rarely utter them themselves, at least not in the presence of adults. A Fante maxim states clearly this use of proverbs; "A wise child is talked to in proverbs."[68] Among the Akan, Boadi notes, "It is common for an adult to use a proverb when talking to a child but the reverse is unusual."[69] The use of proverbs in and of itself could become a symbol of age. Their instructive value, their association with eloquence, experience and wisdom make them inappropriate for a child to employ. Furthermore, the esthetic quality of a proverb may be associated with age, as is the case among the Akan. Boadi notes that proverbs with imagery which is considered too ordinary, uninteresting and lacking in correctness would be inappropriate for adults. For example, he suggests that if an adult spoke the following proverb *s woamma wo y nko antwa nkron a, wontwa du*, "If you do not allow our neighbor to cut nine, you will not cut ten," "he would be judged an incompetent speaker. Very likely, he would receive evaluative comments such as *n'ano ntee*, "His lips have not dried up yet."[70] In other words, competence in proverb speaking is associated with age.

Another form which is age-bound is the fictional narrative. As in the case of riddles, in some societies it is inappropriate for an adult to indulge in matters which are imaginary and have no realistic substance. Herskovits comments in that regard about the attitude toward animal tales in Dahomey: "Animal tales are for children who need instruction embodied in the morals appended to these tales, not for those grown old in experience . . . stories . . . about animals, constitute a major technique for giving children a moral and social education, and the storytelling contests held by the children are among the most vivid experiences of their life. Obviously, then, in Dahomean thought, such tales are not for the adult. He is concerned with the lives of the gods . . ."[71]

The cultural designation of fictional tales and riddles to childhood has also, as we shall later see, parallel temporal features in the time restrictions imposed on both genres, and in their occurrence in the same communicative events in sequence with each other, the riddles preceding the tales. In some cultures these common denominators are cognitively marked, as with, for example, the Sandawe who have a single name for riddles and tales and the songs within the tales, *tántabule*.[72] Age, hence, serves as a distinctive feature for a series of genres. The association between them may either be in terms of content or context, and together they constitute a paradigm of forms of a given age.

Sex is another feature which distinguishes folklore performances and becomes a basis for two paradigms of verbal genres. The significance attributed to sex as a distinctive feature of types of verbal art differs from one society to another; yet in variable degrees of complementarity, there are forms and subjects which the members of a community associate with one sex and not another. Storytelling, for example, is mostly a women's function in several, though by no means all, southern African societies. While among the Xhosa "the Ntsomi-performer is a woman,"[73] among the Thonga "storytellers are of all ages and of both sexes."[74] In West Africa, among the Limba of Sierra Leone, Finnegan comments that "stories can be and are told by anyone of whatever age or status," but apparently this is a reference to a social ideal; in reality "in general women do not often tell stories. This may be, in part, related to the fact that the men, though they work very hard at times, generally enjoy a more complete leisure at certain seasons and at the end of the day, whereas women are always occupied with cooking, cleaning, or tending children. The men usually sit around more in groups, and make more of a formality of speaking or handing out the palm wine. At another level, it is understood that it is a specifically masculine quality to be able to 'speak' well and thus make effective use of rhetoric, parable, or illustration, whereas a woman is expected to sit and listen, clap to show her respect and appreciation, or join in the chorus of the songs."[75]

No doubt, cultural values, work patterns, ideas about speech and folklore, and the respective conceptions of the roles of men and women in society, could offer partial explanation for the association of forms with one sex only. However, since other African societies share similar values and ideas, and yet consider storytelling the art of women, not men, or of both, this explanation is insufficient. Other factors should be considered. The subject matter of the tales, their audiences, contexts, and consequently styles, might differ in each case. Thus, hypothetically, it would be possible to assume an African society in which women tell stories to children, whereas men narrate them to other men. Each context allows for a different thematic range. Unfortunately, so far the available information is insufficient to draw any generalizations.

However, as far as songs are concerned, there are slightly more details. Since much of African singing occurs in ritualistic occasions, celebrations of rites of passage, and meetings of voluntary associations, and in those events sex functions as a principle for social congregation, there are songs which are distinctly related to women and others which are associated with men.

For example, the context of wedding ceremonies provides ample opportunities for women to perform in various capacities. Among the Wolof, Judith Irvine reports, the co-wives are supposed to compose poems insulting the bride and her relatives and to a lesser extent the groom and his kin. The poems are recited in a loud voice, to the accompaniment of drumming and suggestive dances in front of the bride's hut. Women of noble caste, however, are usually ashamed to recite these poems themselves and so they hire *griot* women to do some or all of the recitation for them. Poems are successful when they include mention of specific events or incidents of which people have not previously heard.[76]

As part of the first marriage ceremony among the Hausa the girls sing the following song:

> The great hunt was a good hunt,
> The great hunt brought meat,
> In the great hunt we caught—
> (The great hunt was a good hunt)—
> We caught, we caught
> Ten hares, ten ground-squirrels,
> Ten buffaloes, ten gazelles,
> Ten elephants, ten antelopes,
> And ten hyenas—we caught them.
> The great hunt was good.[77]

The praise singers among the Hausa may be of either sex, but there is a correlation between the singers and their audience; "With the sole exception of female eulogists who sing praises for kings only, female *maroka* (praise singers) confine their attentions to women, and males address theirs to men . . . the institution of praise-singing is developed more elaborately in masculine Hausa culture."[78]

Like age and sex, professional status as a verbal artist defines the nature of folklore performance. Several African societies recognize professional singers and narrators. Often these "men of words" accompany men of action, the political leaders, from national kings to local chiefs, and heads of regional societies. Their social role defines the subject matter of their folkloric performances. They are the reciters of heroic poems and praise songs (the last term actually refers to a generic category and does not reflect, in all cases, the actual content of the songs). The cognitive category of praise permits criticism and presentation of social demands. The alliance with political authorities underlies the selection of themes professional reciters have to learn and perform. They unfold military victories and political achievements of their patrons, past and present, and are able to recite long narrative epics relating the adventures of earlier cultural heroes.

The term *griot*, by which these professional bards are known among the Malinke, the Wolof and the Bambara, actually encompasses a variety of speakers and singers, each of whom has his own social position and his own repertoire of tales and songs. These differences are social, cultural, regional, and in most cases well recognized by the people by name and performance expectations. However, the common denominator of all of them is the ability, and cultural permission, to exercise the power of words in order to obtain personal gain. They accomplish this goal by entertainment, by praise and often by abuse, appearing in specific culturally prescribed occasions or, in other cases, claiming recognition by drawing public attention.[79]

b. *Time and Space.* The demarcation of an occasion for folklore performance, either by professional speakers or by common members of the community, is subject to temporal and spatial constraints. Each communicative event has its own distinctive features. Riddling and storytelling, for example, occur during the evening hours in a central place. These temporal and spatial constraints are imposed on these forms of folklore communication practically throughout Africa, functioning even among the Berbers in Morocco where they are connected with the belief system. "He who tells riddle during the daytime, his children will suffer from ringworm."[80] Similar restrictions are imposed on riddling among many Bantu peoples.[81] Blacking explains this rule for riddling economically:

> The Venda game of riddles often forms part of the evening's entertainment for young people, especially during the season of *mavhuyahaya* (June to September), when the crops have been brought in and cattle roam freely over the fields without any need for herdboys, when there is plenty of leisure, and food to eat and beer to drink. Riddles may not be asked during the hoeing and planting season, *tshilimo* (October to January), when people work hard and are tired at the evenings; if children try to stay up late and play riddles during *tshilimo*, their elders send them off to bed, reminding them that there is work to be done early in the morning. Riddles should not be asked by day; otherwise contests may take place at any time during the right seasons, when young people are sitting together.[82]

Finnegan's description of the temporal constraints on storytelling among the Limba implies a similar economical reasoning.

> Stories are most frequently told in the evenings, after the sun has set. There is not an explicit rule that stories should not be told

in the daylight hours, but in practice people are then normally occupied, especially at certain points in the farming year, and at these times it would be considered unsuitable to spend time during the day in storytelling. But, especially in the relative leisure of the long dry season, there are frequent light-hearted gatherings when the day's work is finished. The most popular time is at full moon when people go to bed late, but at other times too stories are told either under the stars, or, since people like to see as well as hear the narrator, by the light of a paraffin lamp or blazing fire.[83]

Economic factors might well be the cause for such a constraint, but in the course of social folkloric performance, the evening has become an integral feature of riddling and storytelling activities, distinguishing them from forms of verbal art. Similarly, these two as well as other genres are subject to spatial designation.

Not every location is appropriate for performance. In ritualistic and ceremonial occasions, the singing of songs is automatically restricted to a space defined for these purposes, such as a shrine or any area which could be an extension of it. The various songs which are associated with cults are performed in conjunction with worship of deities and consequently are confined to the locations which are marked for religious services, rites of passage, or annual rituals. But spatial distinctions extend also to genres which are devoid of any religious associations. Storytelling, for example, in the traditional society of Benin City takes place in the central room in the house, the *ikun*. The compound population congregated in this central location and indulged in verbal entertainment.[84] In villages both in Benin society and in other cultures in Africa, the public square serves as the location most appropriate for narrations. The principle of centrality must be operative in the designation of a location as suitable for public narration. The spatial prerequisite for the performance of folklore forms, particularly those which require some time duration, is the definition of a place as a public domain. Such a designation may be temporary, by inviting people to join in a celebration in a private or permanent place, as in the case of a shrine or a village center.

While storytelling and riddling have definite temporal and spatial features, the time and place for proverb saying is situational. Except for their use in the ornamentation of discourse and in the employment of the "proverbial mode" in recitations,[85] occasions of conflict, tension and argumentation are the most appropriate for proverb use.[86] Litigation is probably the classic situation of formal verbal conflict. Within the context of the court, hence, proverb use functions to establish precedents and basic principles of wealth distribution and liability. For example, a Tswana maxim which states *Lentswe lamoswi galetlolwe* "A dead man's word is not transgressed" is "used especially when an eldest son who has been formally disinherited lays claim to the estate after his father's death."[87] Similarly in Tswana the principle of equality of men before the law is expressed proverbially: *Garelebe motho, releba molato* "We look not at the person, but at the offense."[88] Other descriptions of the use of proverbs in court conflicts, such as Messenger's description of litigation among the Anang of southeast Nigeria, demonstrates that the proverb's esthetic value could combine with its legal function, and court speech, which is rich in proverbs, can serve the purpose of the orator through its esthetic appeal rather than through mere proof of innocence or guilt.[89] Even the educational contexts of proverb use are actually situations of conflict since they instruct the young in reaction to their violation of social rules.

The social features of folklore are not merely background for a text or supplementary information which elucidates and explicates obscure references and describes performing situations. They are integral components of folklore communication. They have symbolic significance for both speakers and audience and affect the perception and conception of an expression much the same as the words themselves do. The ideas, beliefs, and attitudes that members of the community bring with them into a communicative event of folklore are an essential part of the verbal statement that a speaker makes. In the study of folklore we may discern various levels of analysis and construct complicated models[90] but all these would be of no avail if they did not bring us any closer to understanding the narratives, the songs, the riddles and the proverbs the way the people who speak them do.

NOTES

[1] M. M. Green, "The Unwritten Literature of the Igbo-Speaking People of South-Eastern Nigeria," *Bulletin of the School of Oriental and African Studies,* 12 (1947–48), 838.

[2] J. Berry, *Spoken Art in West Africa* (London: School of Oriental and African Studies, University of London, 1961), p. 5.

[3] Melville J. and Frances S. Herskovits, *Dahomean Narrative: A Cross Cultural Analysis* (Evanston: Northwestern University Press, 1958), p. 14.

[4] Ibid., p. 16.

[5] William Bascom, "The Forms of Folklore: Prose Narratives," *Journal of American Folklore,* 78 (1965), 3–20.

[6] A different approach is implied in Ruth Finnegan, *Oral Literature in Africa* (Oxford: Clarendon Press, 1970), pp. 108–10.

[7] George Herzog and C. G. Blooah, *Jabo Proverbs from Liberia* (London: Oxford University Press, 1936).

[8] See Clifford Alden Hill, *A Linguistic Study of* Karin Magana*: A Hausa Tradition of Oral Art*. Unpublished Doctoral Dissertation. Madison: University of Wisconsin, 1972.

[9] Eric Ten Raa, "Procedure and Symbolism in Sandawe Riddles," *Man*, 1 (1966), 392, 91.

[10] Ruth Finnegan, *Limba Stories and Story-Telling* (Oxford: Clarendon Press, 1967), pp. 25–48.

[11] Daniel Biebuyck and Kahombo C. Mateene, *The Mwindo Epic* (Berkeley and Los Angeles: University of California Press, 1969), p. 9.

[12] Ibid., p. 10.

[13] For general discussion see ibid., pp. 9–11. See also their volume *Anthologie de la littérature orale nyanga*. Académie Royale des Sciences d'Outre-Mer, Classe des Sciences morales et politiques, N.S. 36, i (Bruxelles, 1970).

[14] This and other examples from Benin, unless otherwise noted, are based on my own fieldwork among the Bini people which I conducted in 1966 under a grant from the Midwestern Universities Consortium for International Activities. For an example of an idiosyncratic taxonomic system of narratives in Benin, see my essay "The Modern Local Historian in Africa," forthcoming in *Folklore in the Modern World*, ed. Richard M. Dorson.

[15] Philip A. Noss, "Wanto and Crocodile: The Story of Joseph," *Practical Anthropology*, 14 (1967), 222. See also his essay "Gbaya Traditional Literature," *Abbia*, 17–18 (1967), 35–67.

[16] Clement M. Doke, *Lamba Folk-Lore*, Memoir of the American Folk-Lore Society, Vol. 20 (New York: G. E. Stechert, 1927), p. xiv.

[17] Peter Seitel, "Two Types of 'Proverb': An Aspect of Haya Speech," mss. p. 11.

[18] Hans Melzian, *A Concise Dictionary of the Bini Language of Southern Nigeria* (London: Kegan Paul, Trench, Trubner, 1937), p. 5.

[19] I am grateful to Ikponmwosa Osemwgie for the terminology of Bini proverbs, the explanation of their meaning, and the examples.

[20] Anthropologists who have dealt with taxonomic problems in culture have not applied their methodology to folklore genres. It is obvious from the above discussion that I assume that such an application would contribute to the understanding of the process of folklore communication. For relevant essays, see Stephen A. Tyler, ed. *Cognitive Anthropology* (New York: Holt, Rinehart and Winston, 1969); James P. Spradley, ed. *Culture and Cognition: Rules, Maps and Plans* (San Francisco: Chandler, 1972). The term "communicative competence" is used here in the way suggested by Dell Hymes, "On Communicative Competence," in *Sociolinguistics*, eds. G. B. Pride and Ganet Holms (Baltimore: Penguin Books, 1972), pp. 269–93.

[21] Alan Dundes, "Metafolklore and Oral Literary Criticism," *The Monist*, 50 (1966), 505–16.

[22] Ibid., p. 507. Also quoted in Isaac O. Delano, *Owe l'Esin Oro: Yoruba Proverbs— Their Meaning and Usage* (Ibadan: Oxford University Press, 1966), p. ix. Delano's translation differs slightly and reads as follows: "A Proverb is the 'horse' of words; if a word is lost, a proverb is used to find it."

[23] Northcote W. Thomas, *Anthropological Report on the Ibo-Speaking Peoples of Nigeria* (London: Harrison and Sons, 1913–14), III; 3. This phrase in itself caught the scholarly imagination and became part of titles of several essays about the usage of proverbs in Chinua Achebe's novels, who himself uses the proverb in *Things Fall Apart* (London: Heinemann, 1958), p. 4. See for example Bernth Lindfors, "The Palm-Oil with which Achebe's Words are Eaten," *African Literature Today*, 1 (1968), 3–18, and Austin J. Shelton, "The 'Palm-Oil' of Language: Proverbs in Chinua Achebe's Novels," *Modern Language Quarterly*, 30 (1969), 86–111.

[24] "Some Features of Theme and Style in Mende Folktales," *Sierra Leone Review,* 3 (1964), 17–18.

[25] See Dell Hymes, "Breakthrough Into Performance," in *Folklore: Performance and Communication,* eds. Dan Ben-Amos and Kenneth S. Goldstein. Approaches to Semiotics, 40. (The Hague: Mouton, 1973). Forthcoming.

[26] For a brief discussion of opening and closing formulas in Africa, see Ruth Finnegan, *Oral Literature in Africa* (Oxford: Clarendon Press, 1970), pp. 379–81, and J. Berry, *Spoken Art in West Africa,* p. 16. For a discussion of these formulas in a European tradition, see Mihai Pop, "Die Funktion der Anfangs-und Schlussformeln im rumänischen Märchen," in *Volksüberlieferung: Festschrift für Kurt Ranke zur Vollendung des 60 Lebensjahres,* eds. Fritz Harkort, Karel C. Peeters and Robert Wildhaber (Göttingen: Otto Schwartz, 1968), pp. 321–26.

[27] See Charles T. Scott, "Persian and Arabic Riddles: A Language-Centered Approach to Genre Definition," *International Journal of American Linguistics,* 31, iv (1965), 62; Lyndon Harries, "The Riddle in Africa," *Journal of American Folklore,* 84 (1971), 377–93; see esp. pp. 381–84 for a discussion of riddle opening formulas in Africa.

[28] Eric Ten Raa, "Procedure and Symbolism in Sandawe Riddles," p. 392. This particular riddle is widespread; see Archer Taylor, *English Riddles from Oral Tradition* (Berkeley and Los Angeles: University of California Press, 1951), pp. 473–77, Nos. 1132–38.

[29] J. Bynon, "Riddle Telling among the Berbers of Central Morocco," *African Language Studies,* 7 (1966), 85. Harries suggests a different transcription of the Berber text, see above p. 381.

[30] D. T. Niane, *Sundiata: An Epic of Old Mali,* tr. G. D. Picket. (London: Longmans, 1965), p. 1.

[31] R. S. Rattray, *Akan-Ashanti Folk-Tales* (Oxford: Clarendon Press, 1930), p. x.

[32] Ibid. The phrase appears at the conclusion of most of the tales.

[33] Neil Skinner, trans. and ed. *Hausa Tales and Traditions: An English Translation of* Tatsuniyoyi na Hausa *Originally Compiled by Frank Edgar* (London: Frank Cass, 1969), Vol. I., pp. xxiv–xxv.

[34] See Daniel Ben-Amos, "Story Telling in Benin," *African Arts/arts d'afrique,* 1, i (1967), 54–55.

[35] S. A. Babalọla, *The Content and Form of Yoruba Ijala* (Oxford: The Clarendon Press, 1966), pp. 57–59.

[36] For general discussions of style, particularly in language, see Thomas A. Seboek, ed. *Style in Language* (Cambridge, Mass.: The M.I.T. Press, 1960); Seymour Chatman, ed. *Literary Style: A Symposium* (London and New York: Oxford University Press, 1971); Donald C. Freeman, ed. *Linguistics and Literary Style* (New York: Holt, Rinehart and Winston, 1970); John Spencer, ed. *Linguistics and Style* (London: Oxford University Press, 1964); A. E. Darbyshire, *A Grammar of Style* (London: Andre Deutsch, 1971); Braj B. Kachru and Herbert F. W. Stahlke, *Current Trends in Stylistics* (Edmonton, Alberta: Linguistic Research, 1972); Bennison Gray, *Style: The Problem and its Solution* (The Hague: Mouton, 1969). A discussion of the concept of style in visual art is Meyer Schapiro, "Style," in *Anthropology Today: An Encyclopedic Inventory,* ed. A. L. Kroeber (Chicago: University of Chicago Press, 1953), pp. 287–312.

[37] See Jacques Maquet, *Introduction to Aesthetic Anthropology.* A McCaleb Module in Anthropology. (Reading, Mass.: Addison-Wesley, 1971).

[38] Trevor Cope, ed. *Izibongo: Zulu Praise-Poems* (Oxford: The Clarendon Press, 1968), pp. 28–29.

[39] H. F. Morris, *The Heroic Recitations of the Bahima of Ankole* (Oxford: The Clarendon Press, 1964), pp. 21, 38.

[40] Cope, *Izibongo,* p. 29.

[41] John S. Mbiti, *Akamba Stories* (Oxford: The Clarendon Press, 1966), p. 24.

[42] Ruth Finnegan, *Limba Stories and Story-Telling,* pp. 77–78.

[43] Ibid., pp. 79–80.

[44] Philip Noss, "Description in Gbaya Literary Art," in *African Folklore,* ed. Richard M. Dorson (Garden City, N.Y.: Doubleday, 1972), p. 75.

[45] Ibid., p. 76.

[46] This discussion is based on A. M. Jones and H. Carter, "The Style of a Tonga Historical Narrative," *African Language Studies,* 8 (1967), 113–20.

[47] Gordon Innes, "Some Features of Theme and Style in Mende Folktales," *Sierra Leone Language Review,* 3 (1964), 18.

[48] Ruth Finnegan, *Limba Stories and Story-Telling,* p. 67.

[49] There are many descriptions of singing in storytelling; see for example, Gordon Innes, "The Function of the Song in Mende Folktales," *Sierra Leone Language Review,* 4 (1965), 54–63; Gerhard Kubik, "Aló—Yoruba Story Songs," *African Music Society Journal,* 4, ii (1968), 10–22; Val Olayemi, "Forms of the Song in Yoruba Folktales," *African Notes,* 5 (1968), 25–32. Finnegan, *Oral Literature in Africa,* pp. 244–47, 385–86.

[50] Biebuyck and Mateene, *The Mwindo Epic,* p. 13.

[51] Gordon Innes, "Some Features of Theme and Style in Mende Folktales," pp. 17–18.

[52] Biebuyck and Mateene, *The Mwindo Epic,* p. 9.

[53] R. E. Bradbury, *The Benin Kingdom and the Edo-Speaking Peoples of South-Western Nigeria.* Ethnographic Survey of Africa, Western Africa Part 13 (London: International African Institute, 1957), p. 19.

[54] For references to narrative themes in African folktales, see E. Ojo Arewa, "A Classification of the Folktales of the Northern East African Cattle Area by Types," Diss. University of California, Berkeley, 1966; Kenneth W. Clark, "A Motif-Index of the Folktales of Culture-Area V, West Africa," Diss. Indiana University, 1958; May A. Klipple, "African Folk Tales with Foreign Analogues," Diss. Indiana University, 1938; Winifred Lambrecht, "A Tale Type Index for Central Africa," Diss. University of California, Berkeley, 1967. For studies of particular themes, see: Denise Paulme, "Le thème des échanges successifs dans la littérature africaine," *L'Homme,* 9 (1969), 5–22; G. Calame-Griaule and Z. Ligers, "L'homme-hyena dans la tradition soudanaise," *L'Homme,* 1 (1961), 89–118; Genevieve Calame-Griaule, ed., *Le thème de l'arbre dans les contes africaine.* 2 Vols. Bibliothèque de la S.E.L.A.F. Nos. 16, 20 (Paris: Klincksieck, 1969–70); H. Abrahamsson, *The Origin of Death: Studies in African Mythology* (Uppsala: Almqvist & Wiksells, 1957).

[55] "The Technique of the Expansible Image in Xhosa *Ntsomi*-Performances," *Research in African Literatures,* 1 (1970), 119–46; "Parallel Image-Sets in African Oral Narrative-Performances," *Review of National Literatures,* 2 (1971), 206–23; "The Art of Nongenile Mazithathu Zenani, A Gcaleka Ntsomi Performer," in *African Folklore,* ed. Richard M. Dorson (Garden City, N.Y.: Doubleday, 1972), pp. 115–55; "Fixed and Nonfixed Symbols in Xhosa and Zulu Oral Narrative Traditions," *Journal of American Folklore,* 85 (1972), 267–73.

[56] Scheub, "The Technique of the Expansible Image in Xhosa *Ntsomi*-Performances," p. 119.

[57] Ibid., p. 122.

[58] Ibid., p. 128.

[59] Scheub, "The Art of Nongenile Mazithathu Zenani, A Gcaleka Ntsomi Performer," p. 115.

[60] *Cahiers d'études africaines,* 45 (1972), 131–63.

[61] Ibid., p. 134.

[62] E. Ojo Arewa and Alan Dundes, "Proverbs and the Ethnography of Speaking Folklore," in *The Ethnography of Communication,* eds. John J. Gumperz and Dell Hymes. Special publication of *American Anthropologist,* 66, vi, pt. 2 (1964), 79.

63 Jacob U. Egharevba, *Benin Law and Custom* (Benin City, 1946), p. 71.

64 On the concept of "communicative event," see Dell Hymes, "Introduction: Toward Ethnographies of Communication," in *The Ethnography of Communication,* eds. John J. Gumperz and Dell Hymes. Special Publication of *American Anthropologist,* 66, vi, pt. 2 (1964), 12–25.

65 Robbin Burling, "The Merits of Children's Verse: A Cross-Linguistic Study," *American Anthropologist,* 68 (1966), 1434. For a study of child language play see Mary Sanches and Barbara Kirshenblatt-Gimblett, "Child Language and Children's Traditional Speech Play," *Penn-Texas Working Papers in Sociolinguistics,* No. 5 (1971).

66 Ayodele Ogundipe, "Yoruba Tongue Twisters," in *African Folklore,* ed. Richard M. Dorson, p. 211.

67 See Finnegan, *Oral Literature in Africa,* pp. 426–43; Ian Hamnett, "Ambiguity, Classification and Change: The Function of Riddles," *Man,* 2 (1967), 379–92; Lyndon Harries, "The Riddle in Africa," *Journal of American Folklore,* 84 (1971), 377–93; John M. Roberts and Michael L. Forman, "Riddles: Expressive Models of Interrogation," *Ethnology,* 10 (1971), 509–33.

68 James Boyd Christensen, "The Role of Proverbs in Fante Culture," *Africa,* 28 (1958), 238.

69 L.A. Boadi, "The Language of the Proverb in Akan," in *African Folklore,* ed. Richard M. Dorson, p. 185.

70 Ibid., p. 186.

71 Melville J. Herskovits, *Dahomey: An Ancient West African Kingdom* (1938; rpt. Evanston: Northwestern University Press, 1967), II, 325.

72 Eric Ten Raa, "Procedure and Symbolism in Sandawe Riddles," p. 392.

73 Schueb, "The Technique of the Expansible Image . . .," p. 120. See also his other essays mentioned in note 55.

74 Henri A. Junod, *The Life of a South African Tribe* (1912–13; rpt. New York: University Books, 1962), II, 211. It is not clear why Finnegan (*Oral Literature in Africa,* p. 375) considers narration by women as "a common southern African pattern," citing the Thonga in particular as an example.

75 Finnegan, *Limba Stories and Story-Telling,* pp. 69–70.

76 Judith T. Irvine, "Public Performance and the Wolof Griot: Verbal and Structural Sources of Power," Paper read at the 1972 African Studies Association Annual Meeting, Philadelphia.

77 Mary Smith, *Baba of Karo: A Woman of the Moslem Hausa* (New York: Praeger, 1964), p. 93.

78 Michael G. Smith, "The Social Functions and Meaning of Hausa Praise-Singing," *Africa,* 27 (1957), 27.

79 For studies and discussion of professional verbal artists, see: S. A. Babalola, *The Content and Form of Yoruba Ijala,* pp. 40–55; Biebuyck and Mateene, *The Mwindo Epic,* pp. 15–19; Trevor Cope, *Izibongo: Zulu Praise Poems,* pp. 27–28; Charles H. Cutter, "The Politics of Music in Mali," *African Arts/arts d'afrique,* 2, iii (1968), 38–39, 44–47. Eric de Dampierre, *Poetès nzakara* (Paris: Julliard, 1963). Archie Mafeje, "The Role of the Bard in a Contemporary African Community," *Journal of African Languages,* 6 (1967), 193–223. H. T. Norris, *Shinqīṭī Folk Literature and Song* (Oxford: Clarendon Press, 1968), 51–59. Domique Zahan, "Le Griot," *La dialectique du verbe chez les bambara* (Paris and the Hague: Mouton, 1963), pp. 125–48. Hugo Zemp, "Musiciens autochtones et griots malinké chez les Dan de Côte d'Ivoire," *Cahiers d'études africaines,* 4 (1964), 370–82, "La legendes des griots malinké," *Cahiers d'études africaines,* 6 (1966), 611–42. *Musique Dan: La musique dans la penseè et la vie sociale d'une société africaine* (Paris and The Hague: Mouton, 1971), pp. 191–277.

80 J. Bynon, "'Riddle Telling among the Berbers of Central Morocco," p. 99.

81 P. D. Beuchat, "Riddles in Bantu," in *The Study of Folklore,* ed. Alan Dundes (Englewood Cliffs, N.J.: Prentice-Hall, 1965), pp. 184–87.

[82] John Blacking, "The Social Value of Venda Riddles," *African Studies*, 20 (1961), 2.

[83] Ruth Finnegan, *Limba Stories and Story-Telling*, p. 64.

[84] Daniel Ben-Amos, "Story Telling in Benin," *African Arts/arts d'afrique*, 1 (1967), 54–55.

[85] Charles Bird, "Heroic Songs of the Mande Hunters," in *African Folklore*, pp. 275–93; "Aspects of Prosody in West African Poetry," in *Current Trends in Stylistics*, eds. Braj B. Kachru and Herbert F. W. Stahlke (Edmonton: Linguistic Research, 1972), 207–15.

[86] About the rhetorical use of proverbs, see: Roger Abrahams, "A Rhetoric of Everyday Life: Conversational Genres," *Southern Folklore Quarterly*, 32 (1968), 44–59; "Introductory Remarks to a Rhetorical Theory of Folklore," *Journal of American Folklore*, 81 (1968), 143–57; Peter Seitel, "Proverbs: A Social Use of Metaphor," *Genre*, 2 (1969), 143–62.

[87] I. Schapera, "Tswana Legal Maxims," *Africa*, 36 (1966), 125.

[88] Ibid.

[89] John Messenger, "The Role of Proverbs in a Nigerian Judicial System," in *The Study of Folklore*, pp. 299–307.

[90] See Alan Dundes, "Text, Texture, and Context," *Southern Folklore Quarterly*, 28 (1964), 251–65; Dan Ben-Amos, "Toward a Componential Model of Folklore Communication," in *Proceedings VIIIth International Congress of Anthropological and Ethnological Sciences 1968 Tokyo and Kyoto* (Tokyo: Science Council of Japan, 1970), II, 309–11.

Narrative Forms

The Technique of the Expansible Image in Xhosa *Ntsomi*-Performances[1]

HAROLD SCHEUB

The *ntsomi* is a fabulous story, unbelievable, a fairy tale, a seemingly insignificant piece of fantasy, endlessly repetitious. It is also the storehouse of knowledge of Xhosa societies, the means whereby the wisdom of the past is remembered and transmitted through the generations, an image of private conduct and public morality, a dramatization of values, an externalization of the Xhosa world-view. This ancient wisdom is communicated in an artistically pleasing manner, so much so that the artists and their audiences have developed an intricate set of esthetic principles, which has in its turn produced a demanding system of art criticism.

The performance of a *ntsomi* at a certain time and in a certain place is a unique and evanescent phenomenon; it cannot be repeated, it will never be recaptured. The artist will never again create that particular image in that particular way. One can make a script of the performance, but that is a shadow of the actual production. A series of images, original and often improvisatorial use of details, stylistic effects, the alchemy of performer-audience relations, the temperament of the artist—these join briefly in time and space, and then only a memory remains.

The creation of a *ntsomi* is essentially a solo performance. The focus is the performer. She has memorized no "lines"; she has a repertory of "core-clichés," and in the arrangement of the parts and the whole, she in effect writes her own script. She is her own director, her own cast of characters. She is actress, singer, dancer, mime, and the only general guides that she has are a general theme sanctioned by the tradition and her own experience. She has almost unlimited freedom to extemporize. She is called upon, usually without prior notice, to bring her intellect and imagination to the task of transforming the core-images into fresh and original productions.

In the Transkei and to a large extent in Zululand, in the Republic of

South Africa, the *ntsomi*-performer is a woman, and the finest artists are generally held to be old women. This latter generalization is not entirely true. While grandmothers, if they are not too old, are often excellent artists, girls in their teens have been found to be polished performers, and women between the ages of thirty and fifty are among the finest. Men also know the core-clichés, and they are not without effective stylistic resources. Some of the most competent artists I encountered during a recent research journey to South Africa[2] were men. If conditions are proper and if the audiences are not moved to ridicule their efforts, young and older men are capable of creating excellent *ntsomi*-productions. There is a vague division of the sexes in the oratorical arts, but the line is not drawn with absolute force. Men, for example, generally create heroic poetry (the so-called "praise-poetry"), but women are not barred from doing so (a regular visitor to the court of Chief Diliz' Intaba Mditshwa was a female *mbongi*[3] who, albeit something of a novelty, was nevertheless a poet of considerable skill). Men relate historical events, but women are among the most enthusiastic of historians. Many men insist that the performance of *ntsomi*-images is just not their forte, and that, in any case, they have put all such childish exercises behind them. Still, the men do often participate in the performances.

Performances of *ntsomi*-images usually occur during leisure hours, particularly at dusk when a grandmother, an aunt or a mother performs inside the home before the children go to bed. The children gather around the fire, or lie on their beds, the artist as usual in the center. This is an agreeable environment for the production of a *ntsomi*. There is no light except that cast by the fire, and the performer, through a skillful use of repetition and rhythm, gesture and song, almost hypnotizes the children, her movements rendered phantasmagorical as the flames and shadows created by the fire play on her face and body, and the atmosphere provides an often weird context for her vocal dramatics as well. Weaving the imaginations of the children into her creation becomes relatively easy, the spell of the performance being assisted by the physical milieu. It is at that time too that the children, having completed their tasks for the day, are most receptive to the production of *ntsomi*-images. Few performers can fail to be effective under such conditions.

But this is not the only time and place that the performances occur, nor do children alone always make up the audiences. Boys perform for each other during the long hours that they spend on the veld herding cattle. Girls, baby-sitting at home while their mothers work in the fields, develop vivid narratives of astonishing complexity early in their lives. In the cornfields, when the women take a break from their labor, performances are sometimes presented. Performances may take place at any time and in any place, if leisure time is available and if the audience is receptive.

The composition of the audience will have a significant effect on the performance. If the audience is composed primarily of children, the artist will concentrate on techniques and devices which will give the image a vividness and an animation that will delight the children. Details will be used sparingly, the attention of the performer being diverted to action and moving the narrative along with dispatch. If the audience is made up primarily of adults, and if the performer feels comfortable with them, the image will be altered, largely through the introduction of details which will deepen certain aspects of the narrative, the artist turning her attention from bold action to nuance and motivation—but without changing the basic core-clichés which are the structural keystones of the performances. This is not to say that the stylistic devices used to create *ntsomi*-images for the children will be ignored in the company of adults. They will be utilized, but they too will be altered somewhat; they will be sophisticated, and emphases will be placed elsewhere. If the audience is composed of both adults and children (which is usually the case), the artist will decide the direction in which she will take the narrative and those aspects of the core-image which she will give prominence. Alterations which are made, depending on the composition of the audience, will not necessarily be made on the structure of the core-image itself, but in its treatment. Thus, a performance before children may involve the objectification of precisely the same core-images as one before adults; but the *ntsomi*-productions will be directed in wholly different directions, with details and certain segments differing markedly. Children are not asked to leave if the performer decides to create a more serious, more complex image, but often they will become bored because they are unable to follow the narrative and will leave of their own accord. Some bawdy narratives will probably not be performed in the presence of children, but this is a matter of discretion. In any case, the children have their own repertory of bawdy *ntsomi*-images.

Setting and audience are as informal as the tradition itself. A performer does not belong to a profession. She does not normally perform publicly, but her audience, usually made up of members of the family, may be broadened to include her neighbors and friends. (The immediacy that results from the close relationship also enables the artist to overcome her first hurdle: rapport with her audience.) The artist usually does not prepare for a performance in advance, in the sense that she rehearses. She is prepared, if conditions are right (that is, if she has no pressing duties) and if the audience is sufficiently friendly and known to her, to perform anywhere and at any time. Her skill and artistry will be determined by her imagination and by these conditions. She has no need to prepare herself, since she knows all she has to know (the basic core-clichés, stylistic devices, etc.). It remains for her to arrange these elements and to present them; the external determining factors do not include rehearsals, but rather center on her relations with the audience.

The core-clichés, narrative plots and stylistic elements of the *ntsomi*-performance, all no doubt ancient and deeply rooted in tradition, are learned in no apparently formal or purposeful way. The creator of the *ntsomi* neither memorizes the narrative nor does she undergo a rigid and formal apprenticeship to "learn" plots and techniques. She has in her lifetime witnessed hundreds of *ntsomi*-productions, and her memory has distilled from those theatrical experiences certain songs, chants, sayings, characters and actions which form loosely-constructed images in her memory and which can later be recalled when she desires to construct a full *ntsomi* before an audience.

The basic element of the tradition and the center of the *ntsomi* itself is the *core-cliché* (a song, chant or saying) which, with a few related details, forms the remembered *core-image,* a distillate of the full performance which is expanded and fleshed out during the actual process of externalization.[4] The artist has many such core-images in her memory, but she does not of course recall all of them at once. These images are discontinuous mental pictures, usually revealed in the easily remembered core-clichés which are placed in a linear continuum only during performance. With a broad theme (which determines the general direction of the entire *ntsomi*-tradition) governing the shape which the conflict and resolution will take in performance, the artist seeks to select those core-images from her repertory which are appropriate to the work which she is in the process of creating. She recalls the core-images by means of a complex, free-associational cueing-and-scanning process which enables her to arrange and rearrange the many images and image-segments of the tradition into a variety of *ntsomi*-performances. She objectifies these images in performance, thus fulfilling her two central roles—that of medium, externalizing the core-images of the past, and that of artist, imaginatively selecting, controlling and arranging the materials and sources of the past (i.e., the inherited core-images) and the present (i.e., her immediate environment, the audience, the poetic use of language, her body and voice, her imagination), and giving them new life and freshness.

Building slowly, the young storyteller moves to the status of performer. She becomes so accustomed to the core-cliché, to a vast number of episodes that are often interchangeable in a variety of narrative plots that she can turn her attention from the purely verbal aspects of the craft to the performance itself, and to the extraordinary demands that the nonverbal stylistic elements force upon her. Once she has mastered a number of plot-cores and a fairly wide selection of episodes, she can become more selective in her choice of incidents and details and more artistic in their arrangement, in the blending of core-images; she plants interlocking details and clues sufficiently early in the narrative so that she emerges with a structurally tight single image (which may in fact be composed of two or more core-images). More important, she begins to add details to her narratives which provide new insights and directions, and she begins to bring the other elements of the craft into fuller, more imaginative, more wholly integrated participation in the total production. If she is finally successful, these will all become inseparable. One will not be able to treat one aspect of the performance without considering all the other aspects which are woven not into the plot but into the very fabric of the production, into the objectified image itself.

She moves, then, from a concern for plot to a conscious preoccupation with style and detail. These latter are the marks of the polished performer —the ability to juggle and order all of these artistic elements, and to emerge not with a mere plot, but with a fine work of art, a *ntsomi*-image that builds its brief life on the various tensions set up by the very nature of the performance. So confident can she become that she can begin a production without knowing exactly where she will take it. By beginning, for example, with a basic action such as a man and his wife cultivating in a field, the choices open to her are many. She can move the narrative into any number of plot situations. As she continues to shape her narrative, and as she decides the direction it will take (the further she moves into the story, the fewer the options open to her), she can begin to plant the clues and interlocking details which will bind the episodes and plots together into a single entity, so that the diverse images will have the illusion of complete harmony and union. Thus, the performer may be unaware of the direction of her total performance when she begins, but she soon begins to sort things out, to ascertain her ultimate objective, and she thus develops either a strictly episodic performance or she makes an effort to produce a more balanced production through the effective selection of images and details. During the time that she is doing this, she is also introducing and exploiting the many other aspects of her craft. She is able so to divert her attention because of her close familiarity with the plot-cores. Once the *ntsomi* is well launched, it will move forward as if of its own volition: the artist knows it well, and her tongue goes on functioning as she devotes herself to the other elements that combine to create the total performance, and returns to a concern for plot from time to time, to plant a clue or detail, constantly maintaining the basic structure of the developing image through the rhythmic use of language. Then she again allows the narrative to move along on its own for a time, so that she can concentrate on keeping the other elements of style in focus and in constant motion, working with her audience, keeping it involved, returning once more to nurse her plot, to add a few details, to move it steadily and smoothly towards its climax, or towards that difficult transitional stage when she will shift the narrative from one basic core-image to another .The early intensity that resulted from a concern to recall details and episodes from the plot-cores has now long passed, and relaxed, she can give her attention to all elements of the production.

Certain standards, while unstated, can nevertheless be deduced from analyses and comparisons of performances, variants and performers' styles. The artist is guided by these esthetic principles, standards by which her audiences judge her, by which she judges herself, which constitute the minimal traditional requirements of the *ntsomi*-form. One of these principles may be stated as follows:

Repetition is the key structural device in the artform; action is enveloped and shaped by a single *expansible image,* or by a series of such images. This structural repetition harmonizes with a thematic repetition, often given form in *parallel images.*

We shall consider the performer's use of the expansible image in this paper.

The focus of the *ntsomi*-performance is the image, and at the center of the image is the cliché. The image is objectified before an audience by means of controlled song (the rhythm of the language, blending from time to time into song) and dance (mime, body movement and gesture). The core-image is deeply rooted in song and dance, and the typical repetition of Xhosa song and dance is transferred to the *ntsomi*-form. Song (or chant, or saying) and mime, and the repetition of each, are utilized artistically in the *ntsomi*; song, given physical form by mime and rhythmic body movement, propels the developing plot forward through repetition. This basic formal movement thus duplicates the basic formal movements of dance and song as they exist outside the *ntsomi*-form. The central movement which creates the overall form of the finished *ntsomi* is of a gently swaying nature, a song or an action that repeats itself, backs up on itself slightly, then moves forward again, swaying gently, repeating itself, then inching forward to a climax. This slow, repeated, swaying motion has an incremental effect, and can be used advantageously to reveal character, depict action, create suspense and twists in the plot, all of which are enclosed within and expressed through this rhythmic form. The movement has esthetic value, a pleasing intellectual and emotional sensation of slow movement, overlapping waves, mesmerizing swaying that leads the audience almost physically to the denouement. Once the initial movement has been revealed, it is possible for the audience to participate, either physically or imaginatively, for it has the same *ntsomi* repertory as the artist, and it too sways, physically, imaginatively, sensuously, moving gently and repeatedly, until the next image is introduced, and then the same process is repeated. A beautiful form which envelops the unfolding plot, involving artist and audience, is the result, a form which is based on repetition.

Consider this song:

> Dubulihasa! Dubulihasa![5]
> You must go now, Dubulihasa!
> Because you can see
> That I'll be killed, Dubulihasa!

This brief song forms the structural focus of a performance, appearing at critical moments throughout. Aside from the repetition of the song, *structurally* there is little more to this particular narrative than transitional segments of prose linking the repeated variations of the song, each repetition moving the plot ahead, each minor change in the wording of the song assisting in the movement of the plot, that movement taking a step backward with each repetition in the sense that the villain repeats his instructions to the hapless boy at each stage of progress. Thus does the *ntsomi* "sway" slightly, just before each forward movement. The song is used fourteen times in one version of the *ntsomi,* a part of which follows. A man steals an ox from a boy who is herding cattle on the veld. The boy follows, as the thief forces the ox to travel to his home and certain slaughter. He soon discovers that the ox will not move until the boy asks it to do so.

> The man again said, "Speak, Boy, so that this ox moves faster!" The child sang,
>
> > Dubulihasa! Dubulihasa!
> > You must travel, Dubulihasa!
> > Because you can see
> > That I'll be killed, Dubulihasa!

The ox bellowed, "Mpoooo! Mpooo!"
   The man said, "Speak, Boy, so that this ox moves!"
   The boy said, at a river,
      Dubulihasa! Dubulihasa!
      You must cross, Dubulihasa!
      Because you can see
      That I'll be killed, Dubulihasa!
The ox crossed over.
   Again, the ox bellowed, "Mpooooooo!"
   The man said, "Speak, Boy, so that this ox moves!"
They were now fairly close to the home of this man.
   Again, the boy said,
      Dubulihasa! Dubulihasa!
      You must go, Dubulihasa!
      Because you can see
      That I'll be killed, Dubulihasa!
The ox travelled on, it travelled. Then, when the other cattle entered the
yard above the cattle-kraal, the ox stopped.
   The man again said, "Speak, Boy, so that this ox comes into the yard!"
   The ox bellowed, "Mpooooooo! Mpooo!"
   The boy said again,
      Dubulihasa! Dubulihasa!
      You must enter, Dubulihasa!
      Because you can see
      That I'll be killed, Dubulihasa!
The ox entered the yard. It stopped, it urinated.
   The man said again, "Speak, Boy, so that this ox comes into the en-
closure!"
   The boy spoke,
      Dubulihasa! Dubulihasa!
      You must enter, Dubulihasa!
      Because you can see
      That I'll be killed, Dubulihasa!
It entered the enclosure. The man took some ropes and came along with
them.
   He said, "Speak, Boy, so that I might snare this ox and kill it!"
   The child repeated,
      Dubulihasa! Dubulihasa!
      You must be snared, Dubulihasa!
      Because you can see
      That I'll be killed, Dubulihasa![6]

The force of this performance is its simplicity, a spare incremental repetition of song, accompanied by vigorous body movement which effectively objectifies the constant travelling motion of the characters, this in association with the more stylized, more regular movement of members of the audience, a movement which corresponds to the rhythmic frame created by the artist's poetic use of language. There is added delight when the final singing of the song twists the plot and results not in the planned destruction of the boy and his ox (toward which the preceding repetitions of the song have been directing the narrative), but to their salvation. Structurally, in this performance, aside from a brief introductory segment, the *ntsomi* amounts to little more than a single song, the repetition of which is largely responsible for the continued movement of the plot from conflict to resolution. The performer can utilize this song as she wishes, depending on how powerful (and how lengthy) she desires to make the production. Thus, in some performances of this simple *ntsomi*, the song is sung but once, the repetitions being implied (usually because the artist chooses to emphasize something else), and it may be repeated twenty times or more in other performances. The artistic excellence of this particular *ntsomi* is to be found in its physical structure: without altering the general structure of the production (i.e., the simple repetition of the song), the artist completely changes the seemingly irresistible flow of the narrative and converts apparently inevitable tragedy into escape and reunion.

The central image, the ox's refusal to move until the boy sings and requests in his song that it do so, is an *expansible image,* that is, an image that can be expanded as often as the performer desires, and it is in the repetition of the image that such performances achieve their esthetic force, though simple repetition does not, of course, guarantee a fine work, any more than the lack of a song in certain performances means that such works are lacking in esthetic value. Still, at the very core of *ntsomi*-composition lies this expansible image. Even in those productions of core-images which seem to lack clichés, it can be argued through comparative analysis that a now-discarded song once formed the nucleus.

The performance does not necessarily stop with the externalization of a single expansible image. The structure of the Dubulihasa productions is such that a single image is sufficient to insure an effective work, but even in that *ntsomi*, the artist may wish to add other core-images, also potentially expansible, to develop her creation even further. The artist has many options open to her. She may stop with the single core-image, or she may integrate an expansible image into yet another. As a result of the cueing-and-scanning process, the performer is able to bring into her production any of the many core-images in her repertory. Cues may come from any of a number of sources—from the image in the process of externalization, from a member of the audience, from the scanning process, from the active imagination of the artist.

Four versions of the popular Xhosa *ntsomi* about a bird that defecates *amasi* (curdled milk, a favorite Xhosa drink) further illustrate the use of the expansible image. The basic plot of this *ntsomi* consists of two core-images, the first (having a chant or song as its core-cliché) dealing with the bird's magical restoration of weeds to certain fields after a man and his wife have cultivated them, and the second (usually having a saying as its core-cliché) detailing the bird's fantastic ability to defecate *amasi*. These four versions suggest the effective and varied use that can be made of expansible images to create a work of art.

Version One[7]

Now for a *ntsomi*.

There were a man and a woman. They hoed in the fields. They hoed, they hoed. At dusk, they went home. After that, a bird arrived, and said,

> *Tsiro! Tsiro! Tsiro!*[8]
> *Tsiro! Tsiro! Tsiro!*
> How can you start plowing
>   when the chief has not yet plowed?
> How can you start plowing
>   when the chief has not yet plowed?
> Land, join together! Close in!
> Land, join together! Close in!
> Let it be as it was!

In the morning, they arrived. They arrived, the weeds having grown.

"Oh, Wife! Where did we hoe yesterday?"

"No, I don't know, son of my father!"

They hoed, they hoed, they hoed and hoed. They went home. The bird again came at dusk.

> *Tsiro! Tsiro! Tsiro!*
> *Tsiro! Tsiro! Tsiro!*
> How can you start plowing
>   when the chief has not yet plowed?
> How can you start plowing
>   when the chief has not yet plowed?
> Land, join together! Close in!
> Land, join together! Close in!
> Let it be as it was!

The man was disturbed by all this. In the morning, they arrived again.

They arrived, the weeds having grown.

"Oh, Wife! Where did we hoe yesterday?"

"No, I don't know, son of my father!"

They hoed, they hoed, again they hoed. At dusk, the man said, "Wife, you must dig a hole for me here in the ground. I'll expose my hand only! I want to see this thing when it comes here to the field."

So his wife dug a hole. The man got in, and he exposed his hand. The bird arrived, and went straight above his hand. It said,

Tsiro! Tsiro! Tsiro!
Tsiro! Tsiro! Tsiro!
How can you start plowing
    when the chief has not yet plowed?
How can you start plowing
    when the chief has not yet plowed?
Land, join together! Close in!
Land, join together! Close in—

He seized the bird, this man went home with it.

He arrived at home, and it said, "No! Let me go! I'm a bird that shits *amasi!*"

He said, "Please shit, that we may see!"

It produced some *amasi*. Oh, the man tasted it, he tasted it. He ate it. He said, "I've found you today!" He went home with it.

He arrived at home, and said, "Wife! I caught that thing that delayed us! that made those weeds appear here in the field!"

She said, "Oh, what is it?"

"It's a bird!"

"Where is it?"

"Here it is!" Then he said, "It shits, it shits *amasi!*" He said, "Please shit, Bird, so that we may see you do it!"

It splashed out some *amasi*.

Then the man put the *amasi* into a container. He said, "Please shit, that we may see!"

It splashed out some *amasi*. The *amasi* filled the container. The man took it.

He said, "You see, Wife, we must close it up here in the house, so that our children are fed by this bird!"

In the morning, they travelled, they went to the fields. They hoed, they hoed, they hoed and hoed.

But during the day, a child there at home called some other children. She said, "Hey! Come on and see what we have at home! There's a bird here that shits *amasi!*"

"Oh!"

"Yes!"

They came.

"Bird! Bird, shit *amasi!*"

The bird splashed it out. The *amasi* filled the dishes. The children ate it—there was hunger.

"Bird, Bird, shit *amasi!*"

It splashed it out. The *amasi* filled the dishes. They ate it.

The bird said, "Put me on the table!"

They put it on the table. It splashed out some *amasi.* The *amasi* filled the dishes.

It said, "Put me in the doorway!"

They put it in the doorway. It splashed out some *amasi.*

Then the bird flew away. Oh, the girl sat down and cried.

The *ntsomi* is ended, it is ended.

In this performance, two basic expansible images are blended to produce a full *ntsomi*-image that seems to be the model for all versions of the narrative. A chant is at the center of the first expansible image, repeated three times (it could have been repeated more often) and joined by interlocking and transitional details. The final repetition of the chant is interrupted when the bird is seized by the man. The bridge between the two images is created when the man takes the bird home with him. The second image has as its nucleus a repeated demand (saying-cliché) for *amasi*; the demand and its fulfillment are repeated five times. In the first image, the basic action involves the bird and its demands that the weeds return. Locked into that basic image is yet another, this one detailing the man's growing frustration and the resulting capture of the bird. In the second image, the basic action involves the demands that the bird produce *amasi*. Locked into this image is the bird's request that it be placed here, then there, until it finally escapes. More complex than the Dubulihasa *ntsomi,* this one requires simultaneous action in both images for the revelation of the full conflict-resolution. The structural and narrative symmetry in the two images is characteristic of the form.

Version Two[9]

There was a man who had two wives. This man possessed a bird. He said to his wives, "Don't you let this bird out!" He put it into his house, and his wives agreed. This man journeyed one day, and the junior wife said to the senior, "Let's see what this bird is like!" They went then to the house in which the bird had been placed. They arrived, and let it out.

It was this bird's habit to defecate *amasi.* They came and said, "Bird, shit *amasi!*"

It said, "Take me and put me over there above the entrance. Then I'll shit for you!"

They took it and put it above the entrance. When they had done so, it said, "Take me and put me outside in the yard!"

They took it and put it there. Then the bird flew away.

The man returned at nightfall, and when he arrived, the bird was gone. He asked his wives where the bird was, and they said, "Sir, it's gone!"

He said, "So that's the way you break my command! You let the bird out, and it flew away! Get out of here, both of you! I don't want you!"

The *ntsomi* is ended.

This brief production concentrates on the second expansible image, omitting the first altogether, except for the statement, "The man possessed a bird." The image dealing with the production of *amasi* is abbreviated to the point that it is used but once, though expansion is implied and further expansion would have been possible had it been wanted. The bird escapes, and the husband banishes his wives for disobeying his orders. In this rendering of the core-image, the artist emphasizes the husband's instructions and the punishment levied when his law is defied. The expansible image is muted, though it is still at the center of the performed image; it is diminished because of the artist's wish to emphasize the husband-wives conflict and not the *amasi* details. Had the performer expanded the image in this case, the repeated demands for *amasi* would have overshadowed the more important (to this performer) details dealing with the wives' indiscretion. It is a matter of thematic proportion, the artist achieving a thematic balance by diminishing the prominence usually given to the *amasi*-production sequence. Other details, usually minor, are brought into focus. A single core-image provides the basis of this performance, and while the versions and variants demonstrate that it has its origins in the dual core-image of Version One, the artist bends the traditional image to her own thematic designs.

Version Three[10]

A *ntsomi* said—

There was a girl. They were hoeing in the fields. They hoed, they hoed and then they went home. While they were still at home, a bird arrived. When this bird had arrived, it arrived over there in the fields, saying,

Land, close in!

Weeds! Weeds, come out!

They slept.

In the morning, they returned. They arrived, and the grass covered the field. When they arrived in the morning, this field was covered with grass!

The mother went home with the other children. The girl remained behind. She watched for this thing that, when they had hoed, continued to come and tell the weeds to come out and cover the field, so that the grass appeared. She remained there. The bird arrived, the bird arrived and the girl exposed her hand. She also exposed some kernels of corn. The bird arrived, it picked up the corn *cho cho,* just above the girl's hand. The girl seized the bird.

In the morning, her mother arrived. The girl said, "Mama! Here's the bird! I caught it! It comes and tells the weeds to come out, it says, 'Weeds! Weeds, come out!' Then I caught it! The grass was returning, and I caught this bird!"

Her mother saw the bird then, and the bird said, "I'm a bird that shits *amasi!*"

She took the bird, and when she got home, she washed the pots, she also washed the dishes. She said, "Bird, please shit!"

It produced *amasi—khiqi khiqi*! The children poured the thick milk over their boiled corn there at home.

It remained there, they kept it. The older people travelled again, they travelled, they went to hoe. They left the bird behind in the house, they shut it in.

One very small child then said to the other children, "Here's a bird! This bird shits *amasi* here at our home!"

These children put the bird above the cattle-kraal. Then the children said, "Bird! Bird, shit *amasi!*"

It produced—*khiqi khiqi*! The children took the *amasi,* they drank it. Again this bird said, "Take me and put me above the windscreen, children!"

The children put it there. The bird trotted off, the bird travelled— *prrrrrrrrrrrrr*! It left them behind there. The mothers and the girl returned. They arrived, and the bird was no longer there. The mother of these children beat them, she beat them. One of the children got up and travelled, she went and threw herself into the river. When she had thrown herself into the river, another girl came one day to the spring. When she got there, she arrived and this child was in the spring, this child who was a girl. The other girl dipped and poured, she dipped and poured the water, she dipped and poured it into the bucket. But then this girl couldn't get the bucket on her head! The other girl was quiet. When she attempted to carry the bucket, it refused to go!

She said to the girl in the spring,
   Ndende![11] Ndende, Ndende, child of my father!
   Ndende! Ndende, Ndende, child of my father!
   Come out! Help me to carry this, child of my father!
The girl in the river said,
   Your mother says, "Nyiki nyiki!"
   Her viciousness is exposed!

She beat me, she left me,
Her viciousness is exposed!
She came out and slapped her, *qha qha*! She said, "Don't tell your mother at home that I'm here!"
She went on her way. When she got home, her mother said, "Who helped you to carry this bucket, Ndende?"
"No, I carried it by myself!"
But she was overwhelmed when she tried to take the bucket down from her head here at home!
Again she returned, she returned to the spring. She dipped and poured, she dipped and poured, and the bucket refused to go on her head. She said,
Ndende! Ndende, child of my father!
Ndende! Ndende, child of my father!
Come out! Help me to carry this, Child of my father!
This child said,
Your mother says, "Nyiki nyiki!"
Her viciousness is exposed!
She beat me, she left me,
Her viciousness is exposed!
She slapped her, *qha qha qha*! and this child went on her way. Her mother sat there and watched this. She called some other people, and they came and stood around this spring so that they might see what it was that always helped this child to carry the bucket. They gathered round when she dipped, when this girl dipped. She again sang, but these people were gathered round this spring. She said,
Ndende! Ndende! Ndende, Child of my father!
Ndende! Ndende! Ndende, Child of my father!
Come out! Help me to carry this, Child of my father!
She said,
Your mother says, "Nyiki nyiki!"
Her viciousness is exposed!
She beat me, she left me,
Her viciousness is exposed!
Then she slapped her, *qha qha*!
The people came out now, they grabbed her, they seized her, they went off with her. The spring followed them, the spring followed! When this spring came to Ndende's house, her mother put an ox into it. Then the spring turned around and returned to where it belonged.
The *ntsomi* is ended, it is ended.

The artist may choose to build on the essential image, adding other expansible images to her developing performance, integrating them fully into the basic *ntsomi* with interlocking images and details so that the series of expansible images becomes a unified whole. The first two images are by now familiar, although the bird's chant in the first image is abbreviated. When the bird escapes, the children who are responsible are beaten by their mother, and one of them rushes to a river and throws herself in. This action provides the transition between the second and third images, locking the two quite securely, the motivation for the transitional details being logical and strong. The final image is commonly a part of another *ntsomi,* quite different from this one. But the artist, using the cueing-and-scanning process, finds that this borrowed image fits into this particular performance. A song forms the core of this third expansible image, an exchange between the sisters which is repeated three times. This final image has the effect of taking the audience beyond the *amasi-*production sequences, focusing on one of the guilty children and dramatically exploring her plight, detailing her adventures as they grow out of the actions of the first two images. This performance indicates the flexibility of the *ntsomi-*tradition (individual *ntsomi-*images, tied one to the other, could go on indefinitely), and it also points to the necessity of integrating additional images fully into those which precede and follow them.

Version Four[12]

A *ntsomi* goes like this—

There were a man and his wife, they had two children. One day they journeyed and went to the fields, they went to hoe. They arrived in the fields, they hoed and hoed. They returned, they went home in the afternoon. Then again the next day, they returned, they hoed, they hoed and hoed. The wife went home during the day, she went home. The man remained there, hoeing. He dug a deep hole, and he took his hat and put it over this hole. He hoed. While he was hoeing, he saw a bird sitting on top of his hat. The man seized the bird, he took it and went home with it. When he got home, he said, "My children, cook some porridge!" The children cooked the porridge, and the man said to this bird, "Bird, shit *amasi!*" The bird defecated this *amasi.* He poured the thick milk over the boiled corn for his children. The children ate, they were satisfied. The man said, "Children, tomorrow we're going to the fields again to hoe. Don't drive this bird away! Leave it alone here in the house! Then it'll shit *amasi* again. And again you'll pour the milk over your porridge!"

The man and his wife went then. The bird then bounded and flew to the door. The children said, "Bird, shit *amasi!*" It defecated some *amasi.*

The bird said, "Go and put me over there, above the cattle-kraal!"

These children said, "Will you shit some *amasi* again?"

It said, "Yes."

They took the bird and put it above the cattle-kraal. It defecated some *amasi*. Then the bird flew off, it went away. The children cried, and one of them got up and went off.

He journeyed, seeking, travelling, then meeting with some birds and asking if, "perhaps, among you is a bird that shits *amasi?*"

And these birds said, *"We* are not birds that shit *amasi!* Don't bother us!"

This child travelled on, crying. He walked, he walked and walked, travelling and asking all the birds, but never finding the genuine bird that defecates *amasi*. As he was journeying, it became apparent that evening was approaching. He saw the lights of a homestead, and he passed on to that place. He arrived, and there was a girl there.

She said, "But what are you doing here? Don't you know that my mother is a Zim?[13] Well, I'll hide you!" This child dug a hole there in the house, and she put him into it. Then she covered him up, and she sat on top of him.

Night fell, and her mother arrived. She said, "Hmmmmmmmmmmm! What's that? It smells round and juicy!"

This girl said, "No, go on! There's nothing round and juicy here!"

Well, the woman went to sleep. It was night, so she slept. Then the girl went and dug up this child. She said, "Go! Go now while my mother is still sleeping! I'll give you two calabashes." She gave him two calabashes. "One of them," she said, "contains bedbugs. The other has fleas in it. Now as you travel along the way, you should first scatter this one with the fleas. This one first. Then scatter this one with the bedbugs—when you see my mother following you!"

This child travelled then, carrying these two calabashes. Along the way, he saw this Zim coming along. When it was near, he scattered the calabash containing the fleas first. The Zim arrived and said, "Oh! Perhaps these are the fleas of my home!" It gathered them up, it gathered them up and it ate them *qwam qwam!*

The child travelled on, tense. He was now far away, and once again he saw the Zim. He poured the bedbugs from the other calabash. The Zim arrived and said, "Oh! Perhaps these are the bedbugs of my home!" It picked them up from the ground, it picked them up and ate them.

The child travelled, he travelled and came to a stream. As he crossed the stream, he saw a frog. He said, "Frog, won't you please swallow me?" The frog took the child and swallowed him. Then the frog journeyed, and as it travelled, along the way it met some boys. These boys wanted to beat the frog, but it said,

*I'*m not a frog to be beaten by you!
*I'*m not a frog to be beaten by you!
I come with Mtshotsho, son of Mvulazana!
I come with Mtshotsho, son of Mvulazana!

These children said, "Oh, Mtshotsho is that boy who journeyed when they lost that bird that shits *amasi*! What is this frog saying?"

They left it, and the frog travelled on again. When it arrived at the child's home, it stayed in the firewood. In the morning, when the man came out, he saw this frog—it was huge, its stomach was massive.

The man said to his wife, "Mabani! Please come here! See this frog! I'm going to kill it now!" His wife came out and saw this frog as the man said, "I'm going to kill it."

The frog again sang, and said,

I'm not a frog to be beaten,
For I come with Mtshotsho, son of Mvulazana!

The frog said, "First, give me some water!"

The wife went and dipped some water in the house. The frog drank it, it drank and turned and defecated Mtshotsho!

The *ntsomi* is ended, it is ended.

This performance objectifies six expansible images (see Figure 1 for a schematic representation of these images). The first image is not fully realized in this version, and is not completely motivated. The bird does not cause the weeds to return. The man digs a hole, for which no reason is given, and he places his hat over the hole. When the bird lands on the hat, he seizes the bird. It is thus not properly an expansible image, but it is doubtlessly a shortened version of the original core-image, the performer being anxious to get on to the second image. She knows in any case that her audience is thoroughly familiar with that image, and expects that it will fill in even such large gaps as exist in this part of the performance. The second image contains the repeated demands for *amasi,* and the third again deals with the quest for the escaped bird, the expansible aspects of this image being implied ("He travelled . . . meeting with other birds and asking. . ."). When an image has the function of a *transitional image* as it does in this case, the exploitation of the expansible qualities of the image is unnecessary, and the repetition need but be implied. But it is important to make the point once more that these images are in fact based on expansible images, no matter what the artist chooses to do with them.

The child, benighted, must seek a place to stay for the night. This leads to the fourth expansible image, which has as its core the saying-cliché, "Something smells sweet!" uttered by the cannibalistic mother. The child's escape provides the transition to the fifth expansible image, which is a variant of an image commonly used in another quite different narrative.

VERSION FOUR

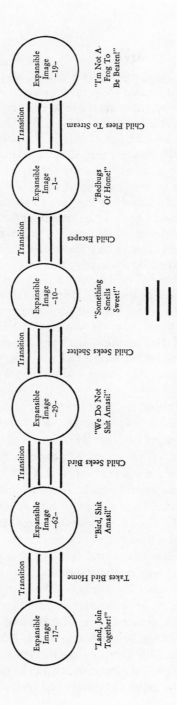

FIGURE 1

Numbers refer to an index of expansible images.

This delaying technique (the two calabashes) is used twice; in other narratives, it is used more frequently, since it is probably the most exciting of the chase-sequences available to the performer. The child flees to a stream, the Zim still in pursuit. This action provides a smooth transition to the final expansible image of this performance. The song of the frog is at the core of the image (and, like the fourth and fifth images, it has many possible applications in a wide variety of *ntsomi*-productions).

Other versions of the *amasi*-bird narrative could be mentioned, but these are sufficient to illustrate the growth and development of a production which builds on a basic set of core-images. The artist is able, because of the expansible nature of the images, to make each as long and as full as she desires; she is free to attach as many additional images to the basic set as she wants, creating a narrative that may attain three hours in length. If she is performing before a mature audience, she may objectify the basic images, giving them nuances and a depth that provide an opportunity for philosophical speculation. *Ntsomi*-performances may become so complex that the expansible nature of the images may be obscured by other details. The flexibility of the tradition is clear, and equally obvious is the important role played by the cueing-and-scanning process, by which the performer "remembers" the images and integrates them into her developing performance.

With the expansible image at the center of each of the parts that compose the finished *ntsomi*-production, other techniques are employed to lock these core-images together, both internally and externally, i.e., both within and between core-images, to provide a final and polished unity to the various elements of the performance. These techniques include the use of interlocking images and details, and transitional images and details.

Figure 2 is a synopsis of the *amasi*-bird *ntsomi*. The various actions of the narrative are labelled *a, b, c* and *d. a* and *c* refer to the basic expansible images, and *b* and *d* to the interlocking images. The expansible image, by itself, while it forms the central focus in that part of the production in which it appears, often cannot stand alone. It requires supporting details or, in some cases, supporting images. These images are "locked" into the expansible image in the sense that they tie the various repetitions of the expansible image together and mold them into a unified image. The elemental grammar of the image that is finally externalized thus consists of expansible images plus interlocking images and/or details. This is the dynamism of the plot, its movement and development: the interlocking image embraces the expansible image and carries it forward.

In the first expansible image of the *amasi*-bird narrative, the bird demands that the weeds return to the fields. As this image is repeated (and expanded), there is an incremental growth in the narrative which, in turn, can be used to create humor, suspense, pathos, etc. In this case, as we have seen, the deepening of the cultivator's frustration is achieved by means of the repeated image. The frustration of the cultivator leads to action, and this action is expressed in the *interlocking image*. Note, in Figure 2, how actions labelled *b* lock into the expansible image, *a*. "A hole was dug. The man got inside." This action occurs just before the bird sings the song the final time. The interlocking image is interrupted by the arrival of the bird and its singing. Then the song (i.e., the core of the expansible image) is interrupted, and the interlocking image reasserts itself when the man seizes the bird. It is locked into the expansible image visually and structurally, enveloping the final use of the expansible image. The interlocking image is then again interrupted, this time by the inclusion *in the first expansible image* of the first repetition of the core-cliché of the *second* expansible image—the bird's production of *amasi*. Interlocking is thus taking place within the first expansible image and between the two basic expansible images. That process completed, the artist brings the first part of the narrative performance to an end by having the man take the bird home, thus providing a bridge between the two expansible images. The digging of the hole, the hiding incident (in some versions, including the holding out of kernels of corn to lure the bird to the hole), and the taking of the bird to the cultivator's home are all a part of the same image, an interlocking image, all logically developed within a single *ntsomi*-image. But the hiding incident is developed *within* the continually developing expansible image. They cannot finally be separated, and this is why the subsidiary image is called *interlocking*. To lock the two expansible images together, the artist repeats the first *amasi*-production scene before the first image is ended. When the man returns to his home, the performer further cements the two main images together by having the man tell his wife that he has caught the bird that had made the weeds appear, thereby recapitulating the events of the first image. This apparently insignificant detail is but one of several which lock the core-images into a single image.

In the second part of the performance, the basic expansible image deals with the production of *amasi*. The second image is a direct and logical outgrowth of the first, structurally as well as thematically locked tightly into the first. The request for *amasi* is repeated a number of times; woven into the repeated request for the refreshment is a supporting or

<table>
<tr><td valign="top">

There were a man and a woman.

a   *They went to the fields.*
They hoed.
Then they went home.
When they had gone, a bird appeared.
It caused the weeds to return.

a   They returned to the fields next day.
They found the weeds there.
They hoed again.
Again, they went home.
The bird again appeared.
It caused the weeds to return.

a   They returned to the fields next day.
They found the weeds there.
They hoed again.

b   *A hole was dug.*
The man got inside.

a   The bird again appeared.
It caused the weeds—

b   *The man seized the bird.*

c   *The bird said, "I can shit amasi!"*
The man said, "Do so!" It did so.
He ate the amasi.

b   *The man took the bird home.*

THE FIRST EXPANSIBLE IMAGE

</td><td valign="top">

b   *Here is the bird that made the weeds*
return.

c   They asked it to produce amasi. It did so.
They ate the amasi.

d   *The father ordered the children never to*
let the bird out.

a   The parents returned to the fields to hoe.

d   *The children let the bird out.*

c   They asked the bird to produce amasi.
It did so. They ate the amasi.
The bird asked to be put at the door.
They put it there.

c   They asked it to produce amasi.
It did so. They ate the amasi.
The bird asked to be put *on the windscreen.*
They put it there.

c   They asked it to produce amasi.
It did so. They ate the amasi.
The bird asked to be put *in the kraal.*
They put it there.

c   They asked it to produce amasi.
It did so. They ate the amasi.

d   *The bird escaped.*

THE SECOND EXPANSIBLE IMAGE

</td></tr>
</table>

FIGURE 2   Actions are italicized the first time they appear in the narrative. They are not italicized on subsequent appearances. The two basic expansible images are labelled a and c. Sections labelled c and d include relevant details which are in addition to the basic expansible image, i.e., the image that is repeated. a, b, c and d are *all* essential to the full development of the core-image. b and d are interlocking images.

interlocking image, this one detailing the command of the father, the subsequent disobedience of the children, and the bird's steady movement toward and attainment of freedom.

The expansible and interlocking images thus combine to create the full *ntsomi;* they become almost inseparable. The supporting or interlocking image may also be seen as simply a group of related details which cluster about the expansible image and which become, in performance, a part of that image. But if the argument that the simple expansible image (with a song, chant or saying at its center and genesis) is the structurally dynamic element of each core-image is accepted, then it follows that this expansible image can structurally be separated from the core-image. What remains is the supporting or interlocking image—or, in some cases, a mere clutch of supporting details. In the anatomy of the image, the song is the central element. But the *ntsomi* is more than song; it is a performance which has as its basic tension and movement a conflict-resolution sequence. An expansible image, with the song at its core, can readily become the structural focus of a conflict-resolution movement (as in the Dubulihasa narrative), but in many cases (the *amasi*-bird *ntsomi,* for example), the repeated song *alone* is insufficient. Supporting images and details are therefore introduced into the image, but their subsidiary nature is never in doubt: the song and the image which it creates remain the center of the production.

An even more sophisticated technique of binding the various images that compose a *ntsomi*-performance into a unified whole is the use of *interlocking details*—clues and details planted in earlier images which are realized, echoed or developed in later images. In the *amasi*-bird narrative, the most effective use of interlocking details occurs in Version Four. At the end of the sixth image, the frog "drank, it drank and turned and defecated Mtshotsho." This detail effectively balances the narrative and locks the final episode to the second image (in which the bird defecates *amasi*).[14] There is a well-constructed circular movement in the performance, the final image actually locked into the opening images.

The technique of interlocking images is used effectively only by experienced artists. It represents the structural perfection of the *ntsomi*-tradition. In one Xhosa performance, Dongwana has gone after the fabulous *nabulele,* a river monster, and her mother awaits her at home, along with the girl's brother to whom she has promised a cape fashioned from the monster's skin. By skillfully lacing the account of Dongwana's courageous progress with brief but telling scene-shifts to the activities at home, the artist ties the second image to the first, and simultaneously develops a theme treating the mother's emotions. Details in this performance tone down the normally prominent adventure of the girl, and instead focus on the portrait of a miserable mother, made the more unhappy because of her daughter's dangerous quest. Interlocking details in this *ntsomi*-production effectively tie the girl's journeying to the mother's fears, making accomplished use of the scene-shift technique and the technique of interlocking details.

Sometimes the interlocking details are used to achieve results that are stark and frightening. In another Xhosa performance, a woman goes about the countryside seeking her lost child. When she is swallowed by a monster, the audience forgets about the child and concentrates on the woman's attempts to save herself. She emerges from the monster's stomach with much livestock which has also been swallowed, and on the way home. Hlakanyana, a perpetual troublemaker, offers to assist her. It is not until later, when Hlakanyana, at the woman's home, begins to feed her other children to her husband that we are reminded of the initial image, in which the woman went off to seek her child. No comment by the performer makes the connection; the emotion is evoked by the details, but they are sufficient to tie in what initially appears to be a rather isolated or forgotten opening image to the final scenes of the production. Emotions too can act as interlocking details and images.

Far more common and less sophisticated are *transitional images and details,* the bridges within expansible images and between images. The use of transitional elements to bind images together is common simply because the bridges are so obviously necessary. In addition, they are often the only interlocking elements between those images which are in any case closely aligned, so that further interlocking becomes unnecessary. Needless to say, however, the performer who avoids the use of or is unable to use interlocking materials and is wholly dependent on transitional images and details will create flabby and highly episodic productions. The performances of accomplished artists are never so flawed.

In almost all performances including two or more core-images, the transitional elements detail *travelling.* Travelling is, in fact, the basic action throughout the *ntsomi*-tradition. Since travelling is the basic action in the images themselves (emphasized by the very nature of the expansible image), then it is logical that the transitional elements will also deal with travelling, moving the central character physically from one situation or place to another. The primary action of the *ntsomi*-tradition is movement, physical movement, and it is physical movement in the form of interlocking and transitional images and details that carries the expansible image forward and creates the plot. A change in the form or direction of this physical movement means a shift from one image to another, or from conflict to resolution. Movement is vital to the tradition, action is all-important, and character is revealed not by description but through action. Similarly, theme is revealed not by interpolations or preachments, but through action.

Complete images are sometimes used as transitional elements. In such cases, they fulfill two functions, the main function being the continued development of the work of art, a subsidiary function and a structural one being its simultaneous use as a transitional device. Thus, in Version Four, the third expansible image, while it forms a part of the action of the first two images, also acts as a transitional image, linking the two sets of images that make up the performance. The first two images, locked together by interlocking details and images and bridged by transitional details, and the fourth and fifth images, also linked and locked by transitional and interlocking details, are really two closely tied *sets of images,* and these two image-sets are linked by the third image (the one in which the children go off to seek the *amasi*-bird). Not only is the third image basically a travelling image, the details linking it to the second (the child travels, seeking the bird) and the fourth (the child travels, seeking shelter) are details of physical movement. The sixth image works in precisely the same way, but it ties the fifth image to the first, i.e., it ties the second image set to the first image set. Again, the sixth image is itself a travelling image, and the details tying it to the fifth image (the child flees to a stream) and the first (the frog brings the child to its home) are details of physical movement. Thus, the *ntsomi* has been brought round full-circle, the entire set of images now brought together into a compact whole (see Figure 3).

FOOTNOTES

1. The material in this paper is drawn from my Ph.D. dissertation, *The Ntsomi: A Xhosa Performing Art,* University of Wisconsin, 1969. Copyright 1970, by Harold Scheub. The Xhosa word *ntsomi* seems more precise than "folk tale," "fairy tale," etc., and hence I have chosen to use it throughout this paper.

2. Conclusions in this paper are based on my collection of 3946 *ntsomi-* and *nganekwane-*performances by 2051 Xhosa and Zulu artists, a collection which I made in South Africa in 1967–1968 in the Transkei and Zululand. Transcriptions from tapes and translations into English are my own throughout this paper.

3. A *mbongi* (*imbongi/iimbongi*) is a Xhosa bard, creator of *isibongo* (*izibongo*), heroic poems.

4. Other efforts have been made to analyze the structure of oral traditions, most prominently the work of Lord and Parry on Yugoslav and Homeric epics, Dundes on North

American Indian narratives, and Propp on Russian narratives. My own approaches and analyses differ considerably from these works, and for that reason I have found it necessary to develop by own terminology.

See Albert B. Lord, *The Singer of Tales* (New York, 1965); Lord, "Composition by Theme in Homer and Southslavic Epos," *TAPA*, 82 (1951), 71–80; Lord, "Homer and Huso I: The Singer's Rests in Greek and Southslavic Heroic Song," *TAPA*, 67 (1936), 106–113; Lord, "Homer and Huso II: Narrative Inconsistencies in Homer and Oral Poetry," *TAPA*, 69 (1938); Lord, "Homer and Huso III: Enjambement in Greek and Southslavic Heroic Song," *TAPA*, 79 (1948); Lord, "Homer as Oral Poet," *HSCP*, 72 (1968), 1–46; Lord, "Homer, Parry and Huso," *American Journal of Archaeology*, 52 (1948), 34–44; Lord, "Homer's Originality: Oral Dictated Texts," *TAPA*, 84 (1953), 124–134; Milman Parry, "The Distinctive Character of Enjambement in Homeric Verse," *TAPA*, 60 (1929); Parry, "Homeric Metaphor as a Traditional Poetic Device," *TAPA*, 62 (1931), xxiv; Parry, "The Homeric Gloss: a study in Word-sense," *TAPA*, 59 (1928), 233–247; Parry, "Studies in the Epic Technique of Oral Verse-making, I: Homer and Homeric Style,' *HSCL*, 41 (1930), 73–147; Parry, "Studies in the Epic Technique of Oral Verse-making, II: The Homeric Language as the Language of an Oral Poetry," *HSCP*, 43 (1932), 1–50; Parry, "The Traditional Metaphor in Homer," *Classical Philology*, 28 (1933), 30–43; Parry, "Whole Formulaic Verses in Greek and Southslavic Heroic Song," *TAPA*, 64 (1933), 178–197; Alan Dundes, *The Morphology of North American Indian Folktales*, FF Communications No. 195, Helsinki, 1964; V. Propp, *Morphology of the Folktale*, Austin, Texas, 1968.

5. *Dubulihasa* is the name of the ox.

6. Performance 1910 in my collection. Taped on November 11, 1967, at about 6 p.m. in a home in Nyaniso Location, Matatiele District, the Transkei. A 50-year-old Hlubi woman was the performer, and her audience consisted of five women, also Hlubi.

7. Performance 1922. Taped on November 12, 1967, at about noon, in a home in Bubesi Location, Matatiele District, the Transkei. The performer was a Hlubi woman, about 40 years old. Her audience consisted of ten women, fifteen children and four young men, all Hlubi.

8. *Tsiro! Tsiro! Tsiro!*—a cry uttered to keep the birds from the corn.

9. Performance 1914. Taped on November 11, 1967, beneath a huge rock above the Kinira River in Nyaniso Location, Matatiele District, the Transkei. The performer was a Hlubi woman, about 35 years old. Her audience consisted of one woman, also Hlubi.

10. Performance 1781. Taped on November 9, 1967, at about 11 a.m., in a home in Nyaniso Location, Matatiele District, the Transkei. The performer was a Hlubi woman, about 40 years old. Her audience consisted of twenty women, twenty children and two men, all Hlubi.

11. *Ndende* is the name of the girl in the spring. *Nyiki nyiki*—the girl seems to be bitterly mimicking her mother, and she also uses the pejorative *unyoko* for "your mother."

12. Performance 1974. Taped on November 13, 1967, at about noon, in Nyaniso Location, Matatiele District, the Transkei. The performer was a Hlubi woman, about 50 years old, and her audience consisted of twenty women and fifteen children, all Hlubi.

13. A *Zim* is a cannibal. It has but one leg. It had two legs when it was born, a sweet one and a sour one, but its parents immediately ate the sweet leg. Still, it moves very rapidly on that one remaining leg.

14. It should be noted that, in a complex sense, there are also interlocking *thematic* details and images, and *parallel images* as well.

IMAGE-SETS. The combination of images 17 and 62, and 10 and 1 plus allied and transitional details creates, in this performance, two tightly-composed images, or image-sets, but each can also be performed as a separate image. Image 29 is closely allied to images 17 and 62, and could conceivably bring the performance to a close. In this performance, however, it acts as a *transitional image*, linking the two image-sets together. Similarly, image 19 acts as a transitional image, but locking the two image-sets together in a special way—by bringing the performance around full circle to its starting point, the equilibrium restored, the harmony which was damaged by the experiences objectified in images 62 and 1 now re-established.

PERFORMANCE 4

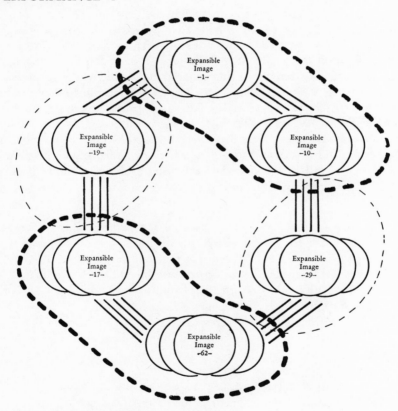

Numbers refer to an index of expansible images.

FIGURE 3

The Impossible Imitation in African Trickster Tales

DENISE PAULME

Among the numerous stories in which the African Trickster plays a role, those we shall examine here have reference to the "impossible imitation." As opposed to what usually happens in these stories— rather short on the whole—the Trickster is seen to fail for want of taking stock of his strength before undertaking a task which surpasses it. Most often it is Spider who is the Trickster figure, but other incarnations of the character—Gazelle, Turtle, or Hare—can meet the same pitiable defeat. When the Trickster's temerity does not cost him his life, he loses face and runs away disgraced. But he is known to be incorrigible, and, after a success story in which ruses and dishonesty triumph, an audience will in the course of the same evening willingly hear another story with an unfortunate outcome, different but close to the first one.

No. 1. *The elephant and the gazelle at the fishing camp* (Enenga)[1]
Elephant invites Gazelle to go fishing. They encounter a group of woodcutters who flee at the sight of Elephant. At the river, Elephant dams the current with his body; Gazelle takes in the fish. As they return, Elephant advises Gazelle not to imitate him: "You would not be successful at it."
Nevertheless Gazelle takes the chance with his wife. The woodcutters chase them; his wife stumbles and is very close to being captured. At the river, Gazelle runs the risk of being drowned as the current sweeps him away.
One must not undertake feats beyond one's strength. For once, Gazelle has not given proof of his intelligence.

No. 2. *Turtle among his kinsmen by marriage* (Mongo)
Turtle and his young sons go to see their relatives. The father-in-law points out some trees to be hewn down. The sons cut down the large trees; Turtle will set about cutting only

a Palisota, a plant which is not woody but has a fibrous stem and into which he cannot even begin to make a cut. The others, having finished their task, leave. The kinsmen and their wives come to watch Turtle, who, disgraced, runs away.

No. 3. *The gluttonous spider* (Limba)

The chief fixes the day when the villagers will go work in their field. He offers a sacrifice, has an ox killed for their meal. Spider, acting as a herald, announces the news. On the specified morning, the chief announces: "Here is a great cooking pot. Whoever is able to carry it shall receive the head of the ox." Spider is delighted; he announces to his wife: "We are going to eat the head." He offers to carry the pot. It is placed on his head; it is very heavy. Coming to a slippery rock, Spider stumbles; the pot breaks. Spider is seized and thrown against the rock; he is badly bruised. Spider runs away, takes refuge within the walls of the chief's house.

Those who are seen today on the rock where Spider was beaten are great meat lovers, like vultures.

The result of heedlessness, the imitation is not always spontaneous; it can be provoked. Then the story is longer; it presents two friends, or two who pretend to be friends, and the sequence that concerns us takes place at the conclusion: the friend who has been formerly scoffed at incites his harasser to follow his example, very often by appealing to his gluttony; the other takes the bait and allows himself to be caught. The last type of impossible imitation is the one in which one of the characters, deceived in a previous experience, takes his revenge, drawing his inspiration directly from the behavior of his antagonist: this is the plot of "The Fox and the Stork," which is found almost identically, though with different characters, among the Bantu.

Using the typology we have set forth,[2] the tales like the first model, in which the imitation is not provoked, correspond to the formula Do (failure without deception); those like the second model, in which imitation is suggested, to the formula, solely or finally, D+ (the Trickster is caught in a trap). Those like the third, in which the same deception occurs twice, belong to the category of "mirror" tales which put in opposition two deceivers, whose

	A	B
first movement is	D+	A+
second movement is	A+	D+

The adversaries A and B, each having won the first game, appear to have the same powers, without conquering or being conquered, which is not the case in the stories of the second type, in which the Trickster, if he does not die, is discredited and loses face. As a result, in all these tales, the imitation takes a different direction accordingly as the text corresponds to one or the other of these three formulas.

The tales in which the defeat is not the effect of a deception are the most numerous: 26 of a total of 62. In them the Trickster tries to improve his fortune without that improvement resulting in retribution. He fails for want of the physical power or the necessary shape.

No. 4. *Wanto and the snout of Naabareka* (Gbaya)

    In the bush, Wanto (Spider) meets the fish Naabareka, finds his snout very handsome, and asks to exchange his own for it. Naabareka objects: "You will not be able to eat." But Wanto insists and Naabareka consents.

    Wanto cannot eat; his too long snout causes each mouthful to drop. His wife tries to feed him, but she does not succeed. Half-dead of hunger, Wanto points in the direction of the spot where the exchange took place. His wife carries him there on her back.

    Naabareka listens to the wife's lament; he is overcome: "You begged and begged me. The third time I finally accepted the exchange. But God has given me my snout; it is not a gift of men. If you had died, it would have been your own fault." Naabareka returns Wanto's snout to him.

    You must listen to advice; otherwise you will die for nothing.

The deceiver is here his own victim. It is surprising to see him rush, without trying to understand anything, into an adventure destined to fail. How can one explain such irrational behavior in a character whose cunning and prudence are emphasized with delight elsewhere? Looking at it more closely, the Trickster remains true to himself and to the principle he embodies. His error is in having calculated his objective poorly. A troublemaker who finds his pleasure in unsettling things, always ready to circumvent the law or to bring to light the weaknesses of the great, almost all his adventures set forth a questioning of the established order: nothing is ever risked, the weakest is not necessarily to be believed, and it happens that deception gets the better of strength. But, if to deceive his fellow creatures remains possible, natural laws cannot be opposed.[3] Those short tales in which the Trickster, deceiving only himself, pretends to pass for another being whose attributes he does not possess would to some extent be the negative counterpart of those relating the success of the same character when he triumphs, as things turn out, over an obstacle that those who invented it believed insurmountable. Spider can pretend that he has cut down a tree, using his sexual organ as an ax (all he had to do was to send the one watching him away for a moment),[4] or that he has moistened a boulder with his sweat (a goatskin bottle did the trick, hidden under his clothes and pierced at the right moment);[5] he will never succeed by himself in obstructing the current of a river, nor will he succeed in giving birth, as in the following tale:

No. 5. *The pregnant spider* (Gouro)
      Spider argues with his wife, who reproaches him for always sending their child on errands. Spider decides to have a child: "It will be wholly mine."
      Spider asks his comrade to get him with child, but with no success. Margouillat sends him to Iroko, the grated bark of which makes his stomach swell. Spider goes into a hut reserved for confinements at the edge of the village. His stomach continues to inflate; he bursts and dies.
      His younger brother inherits his goods and Spider's wife along with them.

An analogous story of Sou, the spider of the Sara (Chad), recounts a similar lack of judgment.

No. 6. *Sou and the great bird El-Kanrin* (Sara Ngambaye)
      [After much foolishness and contrary to all prudence, Sou ate a certain bird and watched as his stomach swelled. His nephews saved him by performing an appropriate operation.]
      A few days later, Sou meets a pregnant woman. "You have eaten the bird!" He seizes her, cuts her open, and takes out twins. The woman dies, for Sou does not know how to sew her back up.
      What he sees done to others, Sou imitates erroneously.

Among all these tales in which the imitation is spontaneous, S. Thompson gives a separate place to the motif of the "Bungling Host" (J2425), which he explains thus: "A deceiver (an animal) pays visits to different animals to show off their particular abilities (frequently magical) to obtain food. He invites them in turn and tries to get his own food in the same manner. He fails and usually is very near dying."[6] In this particular form (failure without deception), the impossible imitation is less prevalent in Africa than in America. I have scarcely found any examples of it except in the western part of the continent, with Spider in the role of the bungler and with the motive the desire for grease.

No. 7. *Spider and oily Caterpillar* (Bété)
    The oily Caterpillar invites Spider. Since there is no sauce
    to go along with the rice, Caterpillar jumps into a pot of boiling
    water and jumps out immediately. The grease which coats
    him floats on the surface; the two of them have a feast.
    Returning Caterpillar's hospitality, Spider tries to imitate
    him, jumps into the fire, and is burned. Shamed, he hides on
    the roof. Hence the proverb: "It is an oily Caterpillar who is
    able to invite you to a dinner with oil."[7]

The story can be followed, always with Spider and his irrepressible desire for grease, to Chad, among the Sara Ngambaye, who attribute the adventure to Sou, the same who was unable to recognize a pregnant woman (no. 6).[8] It is found again in Burundi, with the ridiculous Leopard as the main character—a usual figure in the stories of the evil chief whom Gazelle and Turtle, the weakest of his subjects, use often as a target for their nasty tricks and whom one always takes pleasure in seeing ridiculed. Here it is the fat tail of Ram which Leopard envies and which leads him into error.

No. 10. *Ram and Leopard* (Rundi)
    During a walk, Leopard takes shelter in Ram's house. For the
    meal, Ram throws his tail over the hot cooking bricks; it broils
    and is used to season the polenta.
    A month later, Leopard invites Ram and prepares polenta.
    His wife heats up a cooking brick. Leopard sits on the brick;
    his tail catches on fire and burns. The sheep bursts out
    laughing. Leopard dies of his burns.
    The enmity between leopards and sheep originates from this
    incident.

Told with other characters, the story is no longer the same: Spider was a bungler only when he believed himself to be like Caterpillar, while, through the character of Leopard, the evil chief is accused of niggardly economizing and finds himself the object of indirect criticism.

If the story of the "Bungling Host," in the form told above, seems less prevalent in Africa than among the American Indians, we shall see that the same plot, in which the Trickster tries to imitate a partner who has shown a particular ability to secure a choice food, is found often with this important difference: the imitation is then suggested by a victim who thus has his revenge.[9]

The texts originating in central Africa in which the Trickster is the victim of his lack of forethought form a separate group, whether the unfortunate hero is Ture, the Zande spider, or, in the Ngbaka stories of the Central African Republic, his close relative To: both similarly try to imitate an example which goes beyond their powers, but, unlike the preceding examples of physical impossibility, it is no longer a matter of the operation succeeding if only it had been carried out properly: it fails because both are jealous types who try to act alone, unknown to the others and without being sufficiently prepared.

The "Misfortunes of To" wholly follow the same pattern. To is a negative Trickster; almost all his undertakings fail, as do those, for reasons appropriate to each, of Hyena of the Sudanese savanna and of Leopard in the Bantu context. The Ngbaka tell a series of short stories which set in opposition the wise one (the initiated) and the ignorant imitator: Gbaso has supernatural powers which the jealous, uncouth, and presumptuous To tries to copy without having the means to do so. The moral is constant: imitation is not always successful; one must know the whys and wherefores of things and for that one must not fear to ask for instructions.

No. 11. *To and the chickens* (Ngbaka Ma'bo)

To goes to barter with Gbaso; he finds him building a hen house. Gbaso, taking a piece of wood covered with white mushrooms, thrusts it into the hen house, where it is transformed into white chickens. Gbaso takes a few chickens, which he kills for To; he offers more of them to him. To refuses.

Back at home, To asks his mother for a piece of wood covered with mushrooms; he thrusts it into his hen house. His neck gets stuck. To's mother goes to find Gbaso so that he can free To. Gbaso says to To, "You should have let me explain it to you before trying it."

Among the Ngbaka, the purpose of the exchange in question here is to establish, between two individuals not connected by any kinship or marriage, some bonds of friendship through gifts and gifts in return that, formerly, would broaden the atmosphere of security in which one could move around. But To refuses the offered chickens. Having discovered, he thinks, Gbaso's secret, he prefers to act alone, stealthily. He fails because Gbaso was proceeding by methods required by an initiation ceremony. He at least intends to steal, and it is this intention which is punished. The point of the storyteller is even clearer in the following text.

No. 12. *To harvests some wild yams* (Ngbaka Ma'bo)
> To meets Gbaso, who is pulling up some wild yams, singing: "Touch Gbaso's penis." Gbaso offers some yams to To, who refuses them.
>
> Back at home, To tries to imitate Gbaso. He succeeds while singing "Touch Gbaso's penis," but he tries to sing "Touch To's penis" and is caught on a thorn of the yam plant. His mother has to call Gbaso to come heal him.

To call upon the supernatural is always dangerous: whoever chances it without being initiated runs the risk of seeing the powers beyond turn against him. His mother is needed to save the bungler (previously, in "Wanto and the Snout of Naabareka," the husband is saved only by his wife's intervention).

To's other mishaps illustrate the same theme. In order to get a valued food (some Landolphia fruit), Gbaso uses a supernatural process; trying to imitate him, To gets into an unfortunate situation. He loses his eyes, and only Gbaso can get him out of the fix.[10]

The two stories form a pair, the implicit message of which remains the same: one does not imitate without understanding; to do so when supernatural rituals are involved is dangerous. Gbaso, in order to grind just-roasted palm nuts, puts them in his anus. To tries to imitate him; he is burned. Here again his mother, who had taken pains to conceal a small mortar, saves him. "Why was To always wanting to go see what his friends were doing and then proceeding to try to surpass them?"[11]

To's final misadventure once more opposes wisdom and ignorance.

No. 16. *To and Gbaso go hunting* (Ngbaka Ma'bo)
> To and Gbaso leave to go hunting with their people. After the hunt, everyone is thirsty. Gbaso stamps his feet: "My father stamped his feet; in my turn I stamp my feet." Water gushes forth.
>
> A week afterward, hunting with his people, To tries to

imitate Gbaso. He begins to sing: "My father stamped his feet; in my turn I stamp my feet," but no water appears and his foot is caught. His men die of thirst. People run to call Gbaso, who says: "To has not succeeded in the imitation."

Used by an uninitiated person, the magic formula turns against the one who uses it rashly.

Almost all the tales of failure without deception with the Zande spider are drawn on the same lines. In three of them, Ture obtains through a friend's generosity a "medicine" which effortlessly procures some valued food; he thoughtlessly wastes the precious gift, gets into an unfortunate situation, and has to call for help. Also, more simply, he happens to steal the magic talisman, but, having used it, he finds himself a prisoner either in the termite's nest over which the coveted mushrooms have grown or—what comes to the same thing—because his gluttony makes him do something forbidden.[12] The lesson is therefore similar to that of To's misfortunes: one does not imitate with impunity; one must bow to the rules, know how to moderate one's desires. The storyteller sometimes adds a final sequence, in which Ture, the incorrigible, insults the one who saves him or sends his wives to be trapped as he was.

Ture, however, is a much more complex character than To. Sticking close to the mythical, this insufferable creature—who at lesser moments appears as the average human being—is shown at other times as the benefactor to whom mankind is indebted for agriculture, for water for the plants, and for fire with which to cook them. A rebel but also a civilizing hero, Ture doubtless follows his natural penchant for disorder and opposition by stealing those essential gifts which the spirits would try to hold on to; he does not think of rendering services to men; the whole point for him is in the trick thus played. Ture, feeling the need to cheat and to boast of it, does not resist the desire to break the rules. His conceit keeps him from distinguishing clearly between himself and the world around him; nothing, he thinks, is impossible for him. But, by going beyond the boundaries of the natural or social order and in so doing immediately finding his punishment, he clearly points out these boundaries.[13] A monster of egotism, Ture retreats from nothing. The story "To and Gbaso Go Hunting"—in which To, imitating Gbaso, calls upon his father's example ("My father stamped his feet; in my turn I stamp my feet")—is nothing next to the one in which Ture does not hesitate to kill his father.

No. 17. *How Ture killed his father* (Zande)

Ture meets a magician ("Bambiro"), who has brought out his medicine from a horn in his yard and is singing: "Oh ashes of my father, let some marvel appear . . . let a beautiful woman appear . . . let some beer appear." Ture asks him for his secret: "It is my father whom I have never insulted; I have always respected my father and my mother. As he was dying my father told me thus: 'Burn me to ashes, put the powder in a horn, and it will bring you much good.' "

Ture hurries to find his father; he says to him: "What a bad father you are! What good have you ever done me?" Ture kills his father, burns him to ashes, crushes them, puts them in a horn, and tells his wives to burn all their stored goods.

When Ture asks the horn for some porridge, nothing appears. After a while, a spear appears directed toward his stomach. He leaps up and runs away. His wives suffer from hunger and lack of shelter.

Through the means of the inept imitation, here pushed to absurdity (opposed to his model, a respectful son, Ture insults his father and kills him), the tale also makes use of the motif of the "Magical Objects," one beneficial—a calabash full of delicious as well as inexhaustible food—the other harmful—a whip or stick which moves by itself.[14] The origin of the objects is not usually specified; the calabash appears before even a greedy hero. Here reward and punishment both come from the father, the original source of authority, and the tale forcefully emphasizes the dangers of rebellion. The Massa of Chad tell pretty much the same story, but, no less objectionable, in it the murder of the children replaces the murder of the father, of course without results. Like Ture, the Massa Trickster (Hlo, a negative Trickster like To of the Ngbaka) takes vengeance upon his wife, whose rational behavior puts his own senseless actions into even greater prominence, as if there were need to do so.[15]

The horn of plenty and the spear of the Zande tale, the motif of the "Magical Objects" leads us into the western part of the continent.

No. 20. *Spider, the wild boars, and the old woman* (Agni)

[At the conclusion of an Agni tale] Spider, flying from his enemies, finds protection with an old woman, who says to him: "Get in my calabash; I will fight alone." The old woman refuses to give Spider up; she unsheathes her knife Faniga, which cuts

off all the enemies' heads. The danger over, Spider gets out
of his hiding place.

During the night, Spider steals the knife and leaves without
saying good-by. Upon his return home, he declares war. The knife
cuts off the heads of all his enemies, but Spider does not
know the charm which will make it stop ("Down"). The knife
kills Spider, then plants itself in the mud. This is the origin
of the sharp plant called "old woman's razor."

While, in the Zande text, riches and punishment come from the
father, one sees in the old woman of the Agni tale either an
androgynous image of a mythical and, furthermore, indifferent being,
possessor of the "calabash" as well as the "knife," or, how much more
terrifying, the evocation of the two aspects of the woman, the
ambivalent being whose "calabash"—the mother's womb, the wife's
sex—should not make one forget the terrible "knife."[16]

In this last text, even more clearly than in the bungling efforts of
To and Ture to master a magical formula or object, of which they do
not know the precise conditions for use, we shall recognize the charm
of another tale, no less widely spread than the "Magical Objects." The
motif of the "Sorcerer's Apprentice" becomes apparent when the
presumptuous novice—here the Trickster—having learned part, but
only part, of the magical formula, puts it to work; his eagerness and
his too great self-confidence undo him. Not surprisingly we find the
Agni spider once again in this role.

No. 21. *Spider and Turtledove* (Agni)

During a time of famine, Turtledove weaves a basket which
carries him through the air. He collects food, sells it, and
becomes rich.

Spider tries to imitate him and weaves a basket. He knows the
charm for taking flight but not the rest of it. He leaves, fills
his basket, but upon returning he cannot stop. The food rots;
Spider has to call for Turtledove.

"Magical Objects," "Sorcerer's Apprentice"—the mutual attraction
of these two motifs and their appearance throughout the inept imitation
are easily explained, the outcome of the action being very close if not
the same: in the "Magical Objects," the calabash and stick each obey
a charm which makes them move; the "Sorcerer's Apprentice" can call
upon only one object, but one whose use involves two formulas—one

to make it move, the other to stop it. The imprudent creature who speaks the first without knowing the second runs the risk of catastrophe.

Along the same lines as the "Sorcerer's Apprentice," an Ashanti tale tells how Spider steals a hoe from Porcupine and the lasting misfortunes which have resulted for the Africans.

No. 22. *How the hoe came to the Ashanti* (Ashanti)

Spider and his children live with Porcupine. The latter begins to clear a field; Spider asks him for part of it, and Porcupine agrees. While Spider and his children are working, Porcupine goes off to eat. When he returns, he speaks a magic charm, and by itself the hoe clears a large area. When the work is finished, Porcupine hides his hoe, but Spider has watched him.

Spider steals the hoe, but he doesn't know the charm which stops it. The hoe moves on to the sea, moves across it, and gets among the white people, who copy the model. Later they reintroduce it among the Ashanti.

Formerly, only Kotoko the Porcupine possessed a hoe.

Through the incoherent text (how did they work the land before the coming of the Europeans?), we find expressed, with the consciousness of an inferior technical ability, the need for a fable which will make that inferiority bearable: to turn appearances around, to make plagiarists of the Europeans, is a palliative which could only be an illusion. Nevertheless, it permits expression of a resentment which would be dangerous to express in a less indirect way.

The motif of the "Sorcerer's Apprentice" can be presented in a slightly different light. It is enough, observing the same roles if not the same characters, to give the most important place to the possessor of the coveted object: the master will pretend to give in to the request of the pupil who is too sure of himself, but, a prudent creature, he will give him only an incomplete formula. Therefore, on his part, a trap is set through his dissimulation. The result will tell if his mistrust was justified. As with Turtle among the Yoruba or Hare among the Mali, the Trickster is not inevitably the inept apprentice.

No. 23. *The battle between Cat and Turtle* (Yoruba)

Cat (Tiger) is the champion of all the animals; no one has been able to defeat him; all seek to be his friend.

Turtle invites Cat, who declines for a long time but finally accepts. Turtle offers him a sumptuous meal. A little later, Turtle asks Cat for his secret. "I have two powerful talismans,"

Cat tells him and tells him what they are. But he conceals the existence of a third.

Turtle successively challenges all the animals to fight and beats them all. Finally, he challenges Cat. Twice they fight to a draw. The third time, Turtle is beaten. Ever since, Turtle has always avoided Cat and fighting.

No. 24. *Untitled tale* (Bambara)

Little Hare asks the smith to make him an armband. The smith makes it; Hare thanks him. The smith then announces that he is going to forge him a small hoe which will do the work by itself if a certain charm is spoken. Hare shows off with his hoe and causes general admiration.

Big Hyena asks to borrow the hoe to cultivate a field for which, when he finishes, he will get a girl as payment. Little Hare agrees.

The hoe works, but Hyena does not know the charm to stop it; he has to continue until it kills him.

Little Hare gets his hoe back, finishes the work, and gets the girl.

The difference between the two great West African Tricksters, Hare and Spider, is very clear in these variations on the theme of the "Sorcerer's Apprentice": Spider is presented as the awkward neophyte, Hare as the initiated or at the least as the good pupil who at the first trial will find the suitable answer. Even more clearly than in the Zande tales, the initiation stands out against the background of the Bambara tale, in which the character of the smith is distinctly essential: a mysterious figure in whom the children first see one who at the time of their initiation will inflict cruel pain upon them, in the tale it is the smith from whom Little Hare gets his marvelous hoe, the reward for a completed education. Hare gives a further proof of his discretion when he gives in to Hyena's request, which nothing justifies, but, like the Cat-Tiger of the Yoruba story, keeps from revealing the complete charm. His success is in proportion to his exemplary behavior: having allowed Hyena to kill himself in fulfilling the imposed task, surely intemperately desired, he obtains the reward he has well deserved.

Without being able to affirm that it does not exist, I have not turned up any West African story in which, like Spider or Turtle, Hare himself attempted the impossible imitation. The tale of Little Hare shows the Trickster of the western savannas in his usual image: polite (he thanks the smith), deferring to the important creatures even to unctuousness, a good speaker of whom one knows one should be mistrustful but to whom one finally acquiesces, to be sorry for it too late, Hare among African Tricksters occupies a separate place which the motif of the "Sorcerer's Apprentice" brings well into the limelight.

A final variation brings us to central Africa, with Ture, the Zande Spider, in the role of the overly self-confident apprentice.

No. 25. *How Glow-worm tricked Ture* (Zande)

Insulted by Ture, who refuses the yam prepared by his wife, Glow-worm takes vengeance by showing him the site of the fires of the dead: if he absconds with a brand from it, Ture will not have to prepare torches to smoke out the termites that he covets. But at nightfall, when Ture tries to seize a brand, the fire leaps at his face and burns him. Angry, Ture sends his wife to undergo the same discomfiture. The unusual conclusion sees a compromise brought about: attacked by Ture, who tries to kill him, Glow-worm proposes a division: "I tricked you because you disdained my wife's cooking. Let us share the termites."

The tale is transcribed:

Movements	Glow-worm	Ture	Ture's wife	
1	Do	Ao		Ture insults Glow-worm's wife
2	A+	D+		Glow-worm takes vengeance by dissimulating. (He gives incomplete instructions.) Ture burns himself.
3		A+	D+	Ture repeats Glow-worm's trick with his wife
4	Do	Ao		Ture attacks Glow-worm, who admits having tricked him and proposes a compensation

Deceived, then the deceiver, if Ture does not completely win the game he does not lose it either: he will have half the coveted termites without having given himself much trouble for them. Close again to the "Sorcerer's Apprentice," we are nevertheless far from the short tales recounting an unfortunate experience resulting only from the thoughtlessness of the Trickster.

Cases in which the inept imitation is transcribed D— (humiliation because of the failures of a deception) are rare. We describe them only for the record, the imitation being in this case the act not of the Trickster (whose trick succeeds) but of a third party whose ineptness only makes the competence of his companion come out better. In a tale noted among the Kasai, the adventure is attributed to Goat, a secondary character in animal stories.

No. 26. *Leopard's wine* (Baluba and Lulua)

Kabuluku,[17] hidden in a bush, puts out his foot and trips Leopard, who is carrying a calabash full of palm wine, and enjoys the wine spilled on the ground.

His cousin Goat, whom he has told of his piece of luck, tries to do as much, but Leopard, faster than he, seizes him by the foot and kills him.

A Buma version has the same plot with a slight difference: here it is the Trickster (Turtle, not Gazelle) who suggests to Goat that they act together. Turtle escapes; Goat will pay for both.

No. 27. *Turtle and Goat* (Buma)

Turtle and Goat hide along the road and trip Leopard's sons, who are carrying wine for their father's funeral ceremony. While the young men go look for an ax to cut down what they believe to be a stump, Turtle and Goat lick up the spilled wine, but Turtle takes care to burrow underground before the return of the young men, while Goat stays where he is, is torn from his hiding place, and is put to death.

Turtle's prudence emphasizing Goat's stupidity and voracity, we find we have before us a tale parallel to the same type as those very numerous ones with Hare and Hyena, in which the latter is trapped through his shortcomings, whereas Hare, who is more skillful and above all knows enough to stop in time, extricates himself.

We have grouped under the same heading the more or less long tales of the impossible imitation in which the Trickster, having to deal with a malevolent partner, falls into a trap (D+). He is no longer the victim, as in the Do tales, of his too great self-confidence, but he succumbs, like many he has tricked, when a bait is presented. As the storyteller at least implicitly alludes to the multiple cases in which the deception of the Trickster succeeds, the tale, in the larger sense, is that of the Trickster tricked—but tricked in the frame of a well-defined action. His partner's motive, when expressed, is almost always the desire for vengeance.

We shall begin with the shortest texts, which have a single movement. One example from Nigeria will serve to illustrate.

No. 28. *Cock and Hare* (Tiv)

> Both rich and master of numerous wives, Cock and Hare are jealous of each other.
>
> Hare pays a visit to Cock, whom he finds asleep, his head under his wing. "Cock, where is your head?"
>
> "I told one of my wives to cut it off and put it on top of a stake in the yard. Thus even when I'm not there I can watch over my wives."
>
> Thus deluded, back at home Hare has his first wife cut off his head. Cock says he is grieved but, generously, offers to take all Hare's wives under his protection.
>
> "My son," Cock says to his eldest, "never lose your head over a woman. Certain ones are fickle, but, if you are clever, others will lose their heads and you will find yourself richer for it."

This story seems to be very widely diffused: H. Junod has observed it with the same characters among the Ba Ronga; Lindblom found it in Kenya with Hyena in the place of Hare.[18] Evans-Pritchard found it among the Zande with Kite in the role of the deceived creature.[19] An allusion to the habit of many birds of sleeping with their head or leg tucked under their wing, Cock's deception works through delusive advice. It will allow its perpetrator to increase his number of wives, the inconvenience of whom he himself deplores (he has to watch over them) but whom he esteems as indispensable to his prestige. The story remains close to the Do texts, especially the one (no. 4) in which Spider asks a fish, whose long snout he admires, for an exchange, which is distinctly catastrophic. The lesson is the same: everyone is unique; Spider is no more a fish than Hare is a bird; each must accept the particular condition of his birth, with its limitations. But, while the preceding tales simply showed a weak creature believing himself the equal of a stronger, here the imitation is suggested by a perfidious friend: the Tiv storyteller makes it clear in the beginning that Cock and Hare, both rich, are jealous of one another. A social background is clearly evident. Along similar lines, the Buma of Zaire tell of a deception in which Gazelle catches Leopard.

No. 31. *Nsey and Ngo* (Buma)

A chief is being sought. Nsey (a dwarf sylvacapra antelope) is proposed. Ngo, the leopard, is preferred. ("If we don't choose him, he will kill us.")

Nsey invites Ngo to his house for Sunday evening. Earlier, he had had his wife dig a hole in which he buries himself; only his head sticks out of the ground, as if he had been caught in a trap.

When Ngo arrives, Nsey's wife tells him: "My husband has left to talk to God. To do so he has cut off his head and put it in this hole." At that moment thunder is heard: "It is my husband talking to God."

Convinced that Nsey was complaining and bringing accusations against him, Ngo, back home, asks his first wife to cut off his head so that he might go defend himself. She refuses; Ngo kills her and his second wife as well. The third wife consents, saying to herself: "My friends are dead, he will kill me also."

The storm over, Nsey establishes the success of his deception. He boasts before the other animals: "I am not the chief, but I have just talked with God. Ngo, he has not succeeded in doing so."

Ever since, the children of Ngo have not gotten along with Nsey, who killed their father.

With different characters, the external design of the trap changes, as does its internal working. The Tiv story showed Cock and Hare as equals and rivals, which Nsey and Leopard were not. The usual symbol of political power, Leopard here is, as most often, the evil chief, afraid that a rumor of his misdoings will reach his superiors. Nsey is not looking for an immediate benefit; he is trying, through intimidation, both to take vengeance and to be recognized for what he truly is: the most intelligent of all. He will not take in Leopard's wives—what would he do with them? The storyteller eludes the difficulty by having these encumbering characters killed by their husband for having refused an absurd request. The only rational one is the last one, who prefers her terrible husband's death to her own. Other differences are perceptible in this transposition of a story of Hare. The roles are reversed; from deceived, the Trickster becomes once again the deceiver: Hare was tricked by Cock, but it would be unthinkable in the conventions of the tale for Nsey to be cheated by Leopard. On the other hand, Cock, in order to go to sleep, puts his head well under his wing. The storyteller could not attribute that ability to an antelope; for want of a better device, he has him bury himself, leaving only his head showing at the surface of the ground, his open eyes looking at the sky, "as if he had been caught in a trap." Translating the adventure of Cock and Hare in terms of Antelope and Leopard, the storyteller was perhaps reminded of the story told above (no. 26), in the first part of which the same Antelope was seen to bury himself in order to trip Leopard and lick up the wine thus spilled. Trying once more to satirize the evil chief and his abuse of power through the character of Leopard, the storyteller combined the two distinct stories. The message of the two versions (Tiv and Buma) corresponds with two different situations: the Tiv storyteller shows two equally rich rivals who are jealous of each other, while his Buma colleague is aware of the problems presented to his listeners by the very heavy burdens that political power imposes on its ministers.

The longer stories which show Spider's punishment along the same lines are broken into two parts. Spider, at an earlier time, deceives his partner; the latter will take his vengeance by inciting the former into an impossible imitation, which brings about his ruination. Our collection includes several Agni versions, the richest of which is the following:

No. 32. *Turtle and Spider* (Agni)

> The relationship between Turtle and Spider is one of false friendship. Turtle kills a pig, covers himself with its flesh and some onions, and orders his daughters to prepare a meal for his friend Spider. The latter finds the sauce delicious; Turtle shows precisely how he cuts into his own flesh to prepare it and suggests that Spider jump into the fire in order to get the same result.
>
> Back home, Spider follows the advice and jumps into the fire. Cruelly burned, he demands that Turtle be summoned and refuses to let himself be cut.
>
> Turtle then explains that he has got his revenge. During the famine which had raged some time before, Spider had made him cut his corn, which was still green.
>
> This is the origin of the bent arms of Spider.

The flashback to explain Turtle's attitude and his misleading advice is unusual in the stories, in which the tale generally follows a chronological order. If that order is restored, "Turtle and Spider" can be read as belonging in the familiar formula:

Movements	Turtle	Spider
1	D+	A+
2	A+	D+

Made a fool of at an earlier time, Turtle takes his revenge by calling upon the gluttony of Spider, whom he knows to be incapable of turning away from the prospect of a good meal. Spider's initial motive is hardly clear here. The trap being for the trap's sake, the laconic quality of the tale reveals only the perverse taste for disorder in Spider's motive. But the most surprising characteristic is the appearance of Turtle and his victory over Spider. Present chiefly in the stories of equatorial Africa, from the Congo to southern Cameroon, Turtle is found sporadically as the Trickster along the Atlantic coast up to Sierra Leone; Spider in the same role and the same region belongs chiefly to the Akan group and to the Hausa. The Agni, part of the Akan group, arrived in the area they occupy today only very recently. Would Turtle be the final evidence of a previous condition, the traces of which have been almost erased by the last comers? We observe that Spider, the oppressor (he deprives Turtle of food), is finally tricked—ridicule is the weapon of the weak. We observe as well the nutrition context: earlier Spider is involved with what is overly green (he misleads Turtle into cutting his corn too soon); then he is a victim of the overly cooked (Turtle has him try a sauce cooked from his own flesh), an antithesis found in other versions. The Agni tell the same story of Spider, in fact, with his partner being Goat or Hyena, whose ruse for once is successful.[20]

Neighbors of the Agni to the west, the Dan tell the story, giving Silkworm[21] the role of the victorious partner.

No. 35. *Spider and Silkworm* (Dan)

Spider and Silkworm dam a current and place some nets. Spider's net takes in some crabs, Silkworm's some catfish, which are the better catch. After resorting unsuccessfully to a talisman, Spider goes to the river one morning very early and reverses the contents of the nets, then goes back home to bed. Silkworm comes to wake him up; Spider pretends to be asleep, but Silkworm sees that his feet are covered with dust. They go to

empty their nets, the Silkworm finds only crabs in his. Spider
makes fun of him; Silkworm is aware that his friend has
betrayed him.

Silkworm chops up the crabs, prepares a dish from them,
and invites Spider: "Come taste the dish of my wife!" Spider,
after first refusing, accepts, finds the dish excellent, and tries to
imitate it. Back home, he beats his wife to death, chops her
up, but the dish thus obtained is not satisfactorily seasoned.
He calls Silkworm: "Come see the dish of my wife!" Silkworm's
wives make fun of Spider, and Silkworm explains: "The other
day those were the crabs you put in my net that I chopped up,
not my wife!"

A frequent artifice in the Trickster tales, a reversal (the exchange of
the contents of the nets) replaces the first deception of the story with
Turtle (the unripe corn). The second deception therefore is no longer
a reflection of the first. Silkworm simply resorts to the same artifice as
Turtle used to incite Spider to kill and eat his wife. The trap is in the
elliptical expression—"the dish of my wife"—that Spider, once again
blinded by his gluttony, takes in a literal sense.

A much longer Hausa text opposes Iguana and Spider along the
same lines.[22]

No. 36. *The iguana* (Hausa)

Spider steals Iguana's seeds and roasts and eats them. At the
harvest, he again finds means of stealing two baskets of grain
from his friend. Iguana decides to punish him.

Iguana has his wife cut him up in pieces and cook him with
rice that she brings to Spider. Spider finds the dish delicious
and swallows it all. Iguana, in Spider's stomach, demands his
grain back: "If you don't give it back, I am going to split you
open to get it out and you will die." Spider tries to cheat by
keeping part of the grain, but he must finally give it all back.

Spider wants vengeance. He asks his wife to cut him in pieces
and cook him. But, at the first cut, he gives up his plan and
only hides himself under the sauce. Spider's wife carries the
dish to Iguana. The latter is suspicious; he announces: "We
tailors, before eating, always prick our food with a needle."
Spider wishes to hear no more; he jumps out of the dish
and runs away.

The storyteller could have stopped after Iguana's victory; his text
then would no longer resemble the preceding ones. It is Spider who

recommences the action by trying, like the Sorcerer's Apprentice, to imitate the master without having the means to do so. He is conquered twice: his trick being cut short (he very quickly gives up having himself cut into pieces), he then runs away before Iguana's threat to prick him with a needle. The disproportion between his initial intention and this disgraceful escape adds a comic effect absent from the preceding texts. On the other hand, while Turtle, to avenge himself, pretended to be sliced up to prepare the sauce, Iguana was really cut up and cooked, and it is from Spider's stomach that he demands what is due him. Turtle resorted to misleading advice; Iguana, a master magician, acted through intimidation.

Two versions very close to the Hausa text have been observed, the first in the south from the Chad, with the same partners—Spider (Su) and Lizard (Bur), no. 37—and the other among the Mofu of the northern Cameroon, with the burrowing Squirrel playing the Trickster in the stories of this group, always with Lizard (no. 38).

Both close to and yet different from the Hausa text, a variant from northern Togo has as characters Margouillat, a relative of Lizard, and Hare in the role up to here played by Spider.

No. 39. *Untitled tale* (Mango)

    Challenged by Hare ("Hyena told me you were the most cunning of the wild animals"), Margouillat hides in an oily and spicy sauce that he had his wife prepare the day before and take cold with a dish of rice to Hare. "Your friend died last night; I bring him to you so you can eat him." Hare is pleased, eats the rice without a qualm, and is just taking delight in licking up Margouillat when the latter defecates in his mouth and runs away. Hare realizes that Margouillat is indeed the creature he pretends to be.

    Hare tries to avenge himself and resorts to what he thinks is the same procedure, but he howls with pain when his wife plunges him into the boiling sauce. Nevertheless, the wife follows her husband's instructions and carries the dish to Margouillat, who stabs Hare to make sure he is indeed dead. Margouillat and his children eat Hare; Margouillat gives the bones to Hare's wife, and she runs away.

The plot is the same as in the preceding story, but Margouillat does not really have himself cooked. His ruse is that of Turtle in the Agni version—both stake their deception on the gluttony of their dupe, an unusual gluttony in the case of Hare, and both tales, moreover, have

No. of story	Trickster duped	Partner	Initial fault of Trickster	Partner's ruse	Purpose of ruse	Conclusion
32 Agni	Spider	Turtle	Gluttony	T. pretends to be cooked	Revenge	S. refuses to be cut
33 Agni	Spider	Goat	Gluttony	Same as above	Revenge	S. dies
34 Agni	Spider	Hyena	Gluttony	Same as above	Revenge	S. howls in pain
35 Dan	Spider	Silkworm	Gluttony	Si. pretends to cook wife	Revenge	Sp. kills & cooks wife
36 Hausa	Spider	Lizard	Gluttony	L. is cooked	Revenge	S. runs away
37 Mbaï	Spider	Lizard	Pride	Same as above	Revenge	Same as above
38 Mofu	Squirrel	Lizard	Pride	Same as above	Revenge	Same as above
39 Togo	Hare	Margouillat	Pride	M. pretends to be cooked	Punishment	H. dies; his wife runs away

an element of derision, missing in the Agni version. On the other hand, Hare really dies, a different outcome from those of all the versions with Spider. The latter's escape at the end of the Hausa text is transferred to Hare's wife. The differences among the four reported versions are summed up in the table on page 84, which allows us to see a geographical distribution.

In the three Agni versions, as in the one observed among their neighbors, the Dan, Spider's initial fault is an irrepressible gluttony. Each time a different partner takes vengeance by pretending to jump into boiling water; his dupe imitates him and is burned (in the Dan version, Spider kills his wife in order to cook her). In the other texts, the partner possesses supernatural powers which bring him close to Gbaso in the Ngbaka tales: a reptile at ease on as well as under the ground, friend of water so why not of fire, he does not need to rely upon a ruse; the presumptuous creature who tries to imitate him gives up and runs away in terror (in the version taken from Togo, Hare is killed, and it is his wife who runs off).

All these stories emphasize again the "Bungling Host" theme we have already encountered: a Trickster who returns an invitation tries to get food by imitating his partner's method without ever actually understanding it—with the important detail here that the imitation is suggested to the Trickster by his model. The latter tries to avenge himself upon Spider, or teach a lesson to Hare or Squirrel, whose conceit goes beyond all limits. A last variant has been observed quite far from the preceding, all of which were gathered in West Africa. This one comes from Kenya.

No. 40. *Hare and Yoove* (Kamba)

The nocturnal bird Yoove[23] having declared himself wiser than Hare, the latter asks him where he gets his wisdom. "I cook it up," answers the former, inviting Hare for the next day.

At home, Yoove has his wife tear out a few of his feathers. "Tomorrow, when Hare comes, you will put these feathers in a pot of boiling water, and you will tell him you have cooked me." He hides himself near the fire. His wife obeys him. When the water is boiled away, Yoove comes out from his hiding place.

Surprised, Hare tries to imitate Yoove and asks his wife to cook him. He dies from it. Yoove arrives and asks to see him. Hare is cooked to the point where the flesh comes off his bones. "You are really a good cook," he says to the widow. "Come home with me; you will be my second wife."

Simpler than the preceding ones, the story admits only a single movement, in which Hare lets himself be enticed and taken in, not through gluttony like Spider but from his inexcusable credulity. We observe the motives of his partner, who, in ridding himself of a rival who could become troublesome, finds the means of increasing the number of his wives. It was the same as in the story mentioned above (no. 28), in which Cock, having induced Hare to cut off his head, pitied the lot of the widows and invited them to come live with him.[24]

To sum up, it seems that the tales of impossible imitation in which the Trickster, as opposed to his usual practice, allows himself to be trapped are divided into two groups. In the first, which is more specific in central and eastern Africa, a bird rival advises Hare to imitate him and finds in Hare's disappearance a means of enriching himself. The tales of the second group, with Spider, are more numerous in the center and the west of the continent. Succumbing to his gluttony, a characteristic he shares with Hyena but which is only rarely the case with Hare, Spider has himself cooked or cooks and eats his wife. His tormentor is a reptile, Lizard or Turtle, who thus takes his revenge for a previous trick in which he had been the victim of Spider's gluttony. When the story presents Hare as the main character, it is no longer a matter of vengeance or of juicy food: Hare acts against a master to whom he wishes to become an equal; his partner punishes him for excessive ambition.

As a curiosity, we shall cite a final story of inept imitation in D+ (the imitator falls into a trap), observed in Gabon, with Elephant and with Parrot in the role of Cock—though both characters are secondary ones in animal stories. Elephant usually represents blind force; he is indeed that in his role here:

No. 41. *The parrot and the elephant* (Mpongwe)
Awaiting a visit from Elephant, Parrot hides one leg under his wing. He pretends to have sent it "to watch over the children who are playing in the yard." Elephant, trying to prove to his friend that he is as clever, has his leg cut off and explains that he has sent it "to watch over the children in the forest." Parrot is not deceived. Elephant dies of his wound a few days later.

The plot remains the same, but the absence of a motive for the cruel deception by Parrot weakens the purpose of the storyteller, who concludes with a banality: "Before acting, think of the consequences of your actions."

The last formal category having the impossible imitation as outcome belongs to the group of mirror tales, in which two Tricksters confront each other, each striving to deceive the other.[25] As in the preceding examples, the storyteller tells of two successive "contests," the second being instigated by the first; it is also a lesson at the end of which, at least in the European version such as La Fontaine tells in "The Fox and the Stork," the two partners find each other to be equals and acknowledge the equal strength of the other. The text brings in two dimensions, vertical and horizontal, the equal importance of which it emphasizes: on the horizontal, Fox wins the first contest; but he has forgotten the second, which Stork wins easily. The Bantu tell of a similar lesson with Turtle and Monkey as protagonists.

No. 42. *The turtle and the monkey* (Mongo)
>   Monkey proposes a pact of friendship with Turtle. Every month, Monkey sends Turtle a present, but the latter doesn't give him anything. Angry, Monkey invites Turtle; he puts food on a table that Turtle cannot reach. In trying, Turtle is turned upside down in a spicy sauce.
>   In turn, Turtle invites Monkey but asks him to wash his hands before coming to the table: "I have made a vow never to eat with anyone who has dirty hands." Monkey cannot get his hands clean; he goes home ashamed and hungry.

This third impossible imitation formula implies something like an echo of the first. Though expressed less harshly here, the moral is still the same: no two creatures are alike; every condition has its limitations. Wiser than Spider, who gets burned and loses face in the attempt to imitate oily Caterpillar (no. 7), Turtle consoles himself for not being able to gambol in the trees by obliging Monkey to recognize his inferiority on another plane; the shame is all his.

With the same characters but without the initial motive (Turtle's stinginess which offends Monkey and pushes him to avenge himself), the fable is found in Gabon and southern Cameroon as well as in Rhodesia.[26]

Deceived previously, Stork placed a flavorful meal in the bottom of a vase "with a long neck and a small opening." Monkey opens the hostilities by putting the dish too high, whether on a table, in the loft, or on a high branch; in the only Fang version (no. 43), he has roasted bananas served in a deep basket that is too low. The working of the trap is not thereby changed. The differences are much more perceptible in what happens in the second deception. Turtle's vengeance is not directly inspired by Monkey's behavior, as it was with Stork, whose lesson was taught without spitefulness. Turtle insists that Monkey go wash his hands. (Remember that in Africa there is no tableware; those who eat together put their hands into the common dish.) In several versions, Turtle had taken care to burn the grass around his house, forcing his partner to show up with the palms of his hands blackened like the soles of his feet by the ashes (the storyteller thus indirectly recounts that Monkey walks on all fours).[27] In all versions, Turtle requires that Monkey touch the dish only with clean hands. The desire to humiliate the partner is emphasized when there are spectators, Turtle having taken care to invite other animals.[28] To a defeat resulting only from a physical weakness (he cannot climb trees), Turtle responds therefore with an attack that brings discredit upon the upbringing of his dupe; he throws Monkey out of the civilized world back into that of the savage. The deception of a brief moment is surpassed by a lasting insult. The two characters here conform to their usual image, Monkey playing the individual who remains unable to obey any of the rules necessary to life in society and who acts impulsively, guided only by malice. Turtle is, with Gazelle, one of the two positive Tricksters of the Bantu world; as in the story cited at the beginning (no. 2), his physical weakness is always insisted upon. His safety is in his multiple methods of escape: on the point of being captured or killed, he can take refuge by going into his shell as well as by burying himself in the ground.

One version observed in Zambia speaks of Monkeys in the plural; their partner is no longer Turtle but Hare, who cannot climb the tree in which the meal is served, and he too takes vengeance by burning the grass around his house and requiring the pot of beer that he offers not be touched with dirty hands; the monkeys go to wash but blacken themselves again as they return and so must give up. Hare and his family drink everything after their departure.[29]

Another version from Zambia replaces Monkey by Hare: the game is played by two Tricksters. Hare attacks first by inviting Turtle, whom he places on an elevated seat (through derision?) from which the latter cannot reach the dish, which one supposes is placed on the ground (this is the trap set by Stork for Fox). Turtle avenges himself by sending Hare to wash his feet (!), dirtied by the grass that he had taken pains to burn just around his house.[30]

In a word, Turtle always gets the better of it. The introduction of Hare in the role of one partner or the other would indicate that the story has been spread, perhaps across a cultural border.

The tale seems less known in western Africa. Nevertheless, I have found two intact versions in the forests of Guinea, in which Monkey invites Turtle but serves the rice at the top of a staircase (no. 51) or at the top of a mountain (no. 52) that Turtle cannot reach. A few days later Turtle invites Monkey but requests that he wash his hands. In spite of all his efforts, Monkey evidently cannot do so and Turtle empties the dish by himself.

Tauxier has noted a tale in Upper Volta with Wasp and Toad, in which the adventure is transposed.

No. 53. *The wasp and the toad* (Upper Volta)[31]
> Wasp and Toad are friends. Toad invites the former. Wasp arrives darting about. Toad says to him: "Stop and come eat." But Wasp cannot stop himself and Toad eats everything.
>
> Some time later, Wasp invites Toad. When he shows up, Wasp asks him to wash his dirty feet. But, each time he comes back from the water, Toad gets dirty again. Wasp and the other guests eat everything.

The storyteller has remembered the two oppositions: the first between an animal living in the trees (Wasp moves as easily as Monkey in the air as well as on the ground) and an amphibious animal, but the latter is no longer the Trickster, a role Hare has in this region. The storyteller also opposes, but reversing them, a physical weakness—Wasp's darting about replaces Turtle's inability to climb trees—and a dirtiness here attributed to Toad, whose feet (no longer the hands) remain soiled. (Turtle is never reproached for such a fault.) The different distribution of the elements confuses the game. What remains is a story of a double frustration; Wasp and Toad are not made to live together.

Here is the only example of the story with the last of the great African Tricksters, Spider, in the role usually taken by Turtle.

No. 54. *The monkey cannot change hands* (Krio)
> Spider, finding a pig caught in his trap, invites his friend Monkey to come eat it. But, when Monkey arrives, Spider reproaches him for his dirty hands and sends him several times in succession to wash them. When Monkey comes back for the last time, Spider and his family have eaten everything.
>
> Having trapped a chimpanzee, Monkey in turn invites Spider. However, before touching the dish, Monkey asks Spider to show his teeth, which he knows to be black and decayed, and requires that Spider go wash them. Meanwhile, Monkey, his

wife, and their children eat everything.

No more is there an opposition between high and low or the savage and the civilized world: Monkey's ruse is copied from that of Spider; both rely upon table manners. Occurring first, Spider's victory is nevertheless less clear than that of Turtle in the preceding versions. The text remains interesting because of this impoverishment, which is probably related to its origin: it was observed in Freetown among the Krio.[32]

I have gathered only one variant of "The Fox and the Stork" in West Africa with Hare. The story belongs to the Hare and Hyena cycle; it is surely a modern composition.

No. 55. *Why the hyena and the hare never agree* (Diola)
>   Hyena invites Hare to go with him to see his relatives. In Hyena's father's village, the people cook a pig in their honor. Hyena claims: "Hare is Moslem; I will eat everything."
>   On the way back, Hare proposes that they take a route through his own village: "My father is old; my mother is a good cook." Hyena accepts. Hare's father kills his biggest bull expressly for the young men. When the meal is ready, Hare announces: "Old father, I forgot to tell you that Hyena is a fervent Catholic. Today is Good Friday; he can neither eat nor drink."
>   Since then, Hyena and Hare have never missed an occasion to quarrel.

Once more, the story is a mirror tale and revolves again around table manners. But the two oppositions on which the fable of Monkey and Turtle rests (high/low, good education/ignorance of good manners) have disappeared; what remains is only an anecdote very close in form to "The Fox and the Stork," which makes fun of affected manners and the snobbery of the recently converted by showing them back to back.

Finally, always along these lines, the fable can exist without a ruse, with the same moral of a friendship broken through incompatibility of temperament: both partners, here a partridge and a dog, are too different to be friends. Without the detail of the double trap, the zest has disappeared and the anecdote is flat.

No. 56. *The partridge and the dog* (Angass)
>   Partridge and Dog are cultivating their fields together.
>   On his field, Partridge prepares his grain and throws it on the ground.

Dog mixes up a gruel and turns it out on a flat stone.

The friendship between them is broken because neither can respect the table manners of the other.

Our last story is much longer. Observed among the Birom of northern Nigeria, it includes two examples of impossible imitation. The principal character is Hare, who knows alternative success and failure in his relationships first with Leopard, whom he ends up killing, next with Turtle, and the outcome is then negative.

No. 57. *Story of the crested crane, the hare, and the turtle* (Birom)

1. Hare and Crane see some honey at the top of a tree; they climb up the tree.
2. Leopard arrives; he demands the honey.
3. Hare and Crane throw him a little of it, then direct stinging bees onto him.
4. Leopard climbs up the tree.
5. Hare catches hold of Crane's crest and they fly away. Hare goes into hiding; Crane disappears into the air.
6. The next day, Hare calls Turtle and proposes that they go hunt for honey.
7. Leopard arrives; he demands the honey.
8. Hare and Turtle hurl the bees at Leopard.
9. Leopard climbs the tree.
10. Hare tells Turtle to hang onto the hair of his head: "We are going to fly away." But they fall to the foot of the tree. Turtle takes refuge in a hole; Leopard begins to dig him out.
11. Hare pretends to help Leopard; he suggests that he cover the hole with stones and come back the next day.
12. After Leopard leaves, Hare goes to look for a leather thong and some red ocher. He gives them to Turtle, to whom he explains: "I will pass some grass in to you; you coat it with the ocher, and I shall tell Leopard that I have brought out blood and that he should stick his tail in there to bring you out. You will tie the thong to his tail." On the first try, Hare beats Leopard with a flail, but the thong breaks and Leopard rushes in pursuit of Hare, who takes refuge in a termite hill.
13. Hare, however, persuades Leopard that he is not guilty, that another hare had done it.
14. On the second try, with a stronger thong, Hare beats Leopard to death.

15. Hare says to Turtle: "Come out. Tomorrow we will cut him up in pieces." In fact, he is planning to come at night to carry off the body. Mistrustful, Turtle comes back to stand the dead beast up by piling stones around him. When Hare and his wife see Leopard standing up, they run away terrified. In the morning, Turtle and Hare come with their wives to cut up the body. Turtle is aware that Hare came at night but ran away.

16. Hare says to Turtle: "You stand watch over the meat. I will carry the pieces off with the wives." But Hare carries off all the meat to his own house. Turtle finds only Leopard's head hung over his door.

17. Turtle asks his wife to roast him and season him with sesame seeds. She carries the dish to Hare, telling him: "Here is Leopard's head; you must swallow it without chewing; eat it up all by yourself."

18. In Hare's stomach, Turtle reproaches him and threatens to devour his entrails if Hare does not take all the meat to Turtle's house. Hare does so.

19. Hare says to his wife: "Roast me and season me with sesame seeds like Turtle, but leave me out in the open."

20. Turtle places the meat in a calabash and fills it with smoke. Hare coughs. Turtle calls his dogs. Hare jumps to the ground and runs away.

21. The sesame seeds fall to the ground, and the dogs lick them up. Hare is saved, but he has lost the meat of Leopard.

The story is divided into three successive "games" which can be transcribed from Hare's point of view—Do, A+, and, finally, according to the formula of the Trickster tricked:

Hare	Turtle
A+	D+
D+	A+

In the first game (movements 1 to 10), Hare tries an impossible imitation without being deceived (he forgets that he is not a bird, that he does not have Crane's crest on his head, and finally that he cannot fly). It is a failure, but Hare gets out of it with Turtle, for both are necessary to what follows. Besides, a victory of Leopard, always a negative deceiver, would go against the rules of the tale.

The second game goes from movements 11 to 14. It is no longer played in the air but on the surface of and even under the ground (Turtle buries himself in a hole, to dislodge him from which Hare pretends to help Leopard; Hare himself, pursued by Leopard, takes refuge in a termite hill). After a first unfortunate attempt, Hare's plan works and he beats Leopard to death. The partners are Leopard and Hare, Turtle having only a secondary role.

With Leopard eliminated, the third game sets the two cronies— Turtle and Hare—at odds. After his nocturnal attempt at stealing has been foiled, Hare nonetheless succeeds in deceiving Turtle's vigilance and stealing his part of Leopard's carcass from him. Having decided not to let him, Turtle resorts to the same method that Iguana used in the Hausa story (no. 36): having himself swallowed by Hare, he demands and obtains restitution of his plunder. Like his Hausa colleague, the Birom storyteller follows that with an unfortunate attempt at imitation: Hare in turn tries to get Turtle to swallow him— mutual ingestion is, with successive metamorphoses, a constant feature in duels between magicians. But Hare is only a sorcerer's apprentice; he does not dare have himself cooked: "leave me out in the open," he orders his wife. Turtle discovers the ruse easily; he smokes out Hare, who coughs and runs away. (In the Hausa version, Spider preferred flight to being stabbed with the needle that Iguana, having become a tailor for the occasion, threatened him with.) The conclusion leaves the two Tricksters alive. Hare saves himself, but the true victor is Turtle, who, having escaped from two traps, will keep all the meat of their common enemy for himself and his family.

The relation of this last game with "The Iguana" is evident: the only important difference is in the choice of characters, Iguana and Spider of the Hausa version here becoming Turtle and Hare. Let us recall that the Trickster in Hausa stories is played equally by Spider, Hare, or Jackal (the latter has the role in the Sahara and up to Kabylie). Great travelers, the Hausa spread these types of more or less universal stories everywhere they went, from the Mediterranan to central Africa and from Lake Tchad to the Atlantic coast. Different at each stopping place, their audience retained part, if not the whole, of the alternating success and failure, changing the characters according to their particular code. In an Agni version of the same theme given above (no. 32), Turtle, injured by Spider, catches him in a trap by arousing his gluttony. We have thought it possible that in this we find a vestige of the champion of the former inhabitants, facing the more recent comers, whom one makes fun of only prudently and indirectly. In the

Birom story, Hare having deprived him of his share, Turtle demands restitution of the same. The comparison gives cause for reflection: in the Birom tales, would Turtle in respect to Hare coming from the savanna occupy a place comparable to that which the Agni seem to identify with Spider?

Two other texts, one from Chad, the other from northern Cameroon, show enough points in common with the Birom stories so that one can see in them all variations of the same theme. The note of initiation is particularly perceptible in the Cameroon version. The three texts involve the quest for honey, a supreme delicacy, in which the impossible imitation attempted by the Trickster comes to no good. In the three cases, an elder, winged creature invites the Trickster to gorge himself with honey on a prohibited tree. The owner of the tree surprises them; the elder flies away, carrying with him the novice holding on to his sides. Another time, Hare or Spider, having tasted the honey, wants to repeat the experience, imitating his elder without reflecting that he does not have the means to do so. He takes along with him a friend whom he tries to carry up into the air when the owner happens by; both fall on the ground and bruise themselves.

Characters	Birom (no. 57)	North Cameroon (no. 58)	Chad (no. 59)
Inept Trickster	Hare	Squirrel	Spider
Initiating elder	Crested Crane	Crested Crane	Wasp
Owner of tree	Leopard	Panther	Elephant
Unlucky friend	Turtle	Turtle	Toad

What follows differs, but some resemblances remain perceptible. In the Mofu tale (no. 58, "Story of the Crested Crane and the Squirrel"), Panther having taken Turtle in his mouth, the latter bites him on the tongue and makes him carry him near the sea; he cuts into Panther's tongue again before jumping into the water. For his part, Squirrel goes to the home of his uncle Crested Crane, who makes fun of him before restoring to him an eye and a foot lost in the adventure: "I told you not to carry anyone away and you disobeyed." The sequence sees the victory of Turtle (in the Birom tale, the final trick comes as well from Turtle triumphing over Hare, himself the conqueror of Leopard) but not the ruse of the presumptuous Trickster, whose adventure forcefully recalls the mistakes of To among the Ngbaka and of Ture among the Zande.

In the Mbaï-Mossala version observed by P. Fortier, of the two thieves who fall to the ground, Toad hides and disappears from the story. Spider, locked up by Elephant in a stable, calls for help from his uncle Wasp, who digs a tunnel through which Spider escapes, stealing Elephant's goats. Thus, there is a successful ruse, but one in which the assistance of the elder (the master) is indispensable. As for Toad—substitute for Turtle, whom the stories of this region no longer seem to know as a Trickster—he plays here only an insigificant role.

We shall linger still a while over the Birom story, the three parts of which, remarkably balanced, give a last, faintly different image of the Trickster. In the first part, Hare, the inept imitator, tries to overthrow the established order; he is immediately punished and gets out of the fix, one can believe, only because his adversary is Leopard, whose defeat the whole audience is expecting. It comes in the course of the middle part, which in fact sees Hare do Leopard in. It is the victory of the weak over the strong, the triumph of the lone individual over power and social pressures. It is a classic scene, the model of which literature will use indefinitely, always with the same success. But the story retains a sense of moderation; realistically, its third part reminding him that he is not definitely victorious, Hare himself finds his master in Turtle, who is not all outward show but who "knows the secrets." Acquired through, one supposes, long experience, this knowledge makes Turtle the model finally set forth for the audience's consideration.

What conclusions can be drawn from such a quick survey? First, witnessed by the great differences in their behavior, the presence of not one but several African Tricksters: if all have deception and dishonesty in common, each nonetheless offers a different physiognomy according to the context from which he springs. The little tale of the "Bungling Host" is in this regard very illuminating; without being able to affirm that it does not exist, I have not found an example of it with Hare in West Africa. The story is assuredly very old; its present distribution ascertains an evolution in the character in the course of which Spider, who along with Hare is the most frequent embodiment of it, would perhaps be the least diminished through the ages. The most fascinating of all the African Tricksters, Spider adds to his qualities of cunning and wily intelligence some serious faults, notably laziness, insatiable gluttony, presumptuousness, and at least an excessive optimism which the tales presented here well illustrate. Along with the brilliant successes in which he shows the weaknesses of the powerful, Spider's great faults often lead him into defeat. In comparison to so rich a character in whom we can, according to our own tastes, recognize ourselves (intelligent, cunning) or see the image of a neighbor (stupid, gluttonous), his homologue from Senegal or Mali— Hare, who almost always wins each match and loses face only in an exceptional fashion—seems simplified and reduced to two dimensions. The frequent presence of Hyena at Hare's side emphasizes the success the latter has in his own methods of action. If one may not set up Hare and Hyena beside the great figures of Greek mythology, Prometheus and Epimetheus, there is nevertheless an echo of a relationship of that order which their association calls forth. Anticipating those who can temporize, flatter, be patient, Hare succeeds where Hyena acts without thinking, listens only to his gluttony, and is condemned beforehand— he may momentarily carry it off but his victory is ever only temporary; it is known from the beginning that he will end up the loser. Whether the action opposes Hare and Hyena (mirror tales) or submits them to the same experiences (parallel tales), the accent is always on the positive aspects of the former and the negative aspects of the latter. The same stories are found with Spider, but he can equally assume either role; whether it be the "Treasure Tree" or a variant of the "Two Girls," Spider is the winner or the loser depending on the partner assigned to him. In an action of the "Open Sesame" type, in which Hare has the role of the hero who knows enough to stop and get out in time, Hyena the role of the bungler who delays and is taken prisoner, Spider will be on the winning side when his companion is Hyena or Leopard, the image of the predatory chief. But, if he is paralleled with the orphan, the creature in this world most worthy of compassion, the gluttonous, impulsive aspect of Spider will carry him away and he will be thrown to the negative side.[33] He will also lose when the same "Open Sesame" tale—or that of the "Magical Objects," calabash and whip—shows him with his own son.[34] The reverse of the usual stories in which the disastrous consequences of a lack of respect toward parents are insisted upon, those of Spider make him a bad father who too often neglects his family and must be called to order: his wife bullies him; even his children disobey him and often have the last word. This realistic picture proves that the Africans know what to believe about the differences in family relationships between the proposed model and daily life.[35]

Even when Hyena does not appear at Hare's side, it happens that Spider fails where Hare succeeds. In the "Sorcerer's Apprentice,"

Spider is the inept apprentice initiating disasters, since they cause Africans to lose a previous superiority, the advantage of which will be turned against them because of his error.[36] On the same theme, the Bambara Hare plays the role of the good pupil, amenable to the lessons of the master, compared to the poorly brought up Hyena, always coarse, greedy, stupid, and ridiculous.[37] Everything takes place as if an original figure, to whom Spider even with his contradictions remains very close, was separated in two—Hare and Hyena being finally only the two faces of the same character. For all that, Hare is not a model one must copy blindly. An expert in smooth talking, a shameless flatterer whose words lull and seduce, he is to be mistrusted. But how can one resist the pleasure of seeing him, weak and defenseless, make a fool of all the others?

The Tricksters' ends no less than their means are not identical. Hare succumbs to the advances of Cock, who suggests to him the means of increasing his wealth and social importance in watching over his wives better.[38] Spider is more simply endowed with the same insatiable gluttony as Hyena. He perishes, the victim of vengeance, while Cock, in trapping Hare, finds a direct profit in its outcome: insincerely generous, he will take in his dupe's widows.

A map showing the distribution of the Tricksters would pose a certain number of problems instead of solving them. How can one explain otherwise than through history and former contacts the presence of Turtle on the Atlantic coast up to Sierra Leone (immigrants from Nigeria?) and to Guinea? Or his still observable traces among the Mossi, or his survival among the Agni, where he resists Spider just as he gets the better of Hare among the Birom?[39]

The diverse ancestry of the Krio would explain the appearance in their tales of the three great African Tricksters; Hare, Spider, and Turtle, who usually exist exclusive of one another, resort in them to similar procedures, though the results of them are distinctly different: Hare wins in everything, Spider is betrayed through his gluttony, and Turtle survives in tales other than those told here in which the transfer of his role to Spider brings modifications suitable to the nature assigned to the latter. No longer an opposition between high and low, without provocation Spider begins the action by inviting Monkey, immediately to insult him by sending him to wash his hands. The other retorts by reproaching Spider for his rotten teeth, which can be taken as an allusion to his insatiable gluttony.

A better knowledge of the purposes and methods of these Tricksters —the witnesses to and the spokesmen for the cultures from which they come—would require great patience. First, a collection, if possible in the original language, of as large a number as possible of these stories which come from a specific society in which deception occurs will make clear the principal features of the character; no less important, the comments and thoughts of authorities on his successes as well as on his failures will illuminate the ideology and the norms of the official ethic, at the same time illuminating the tolerable variations in their observance.

The literature finds here its justifications: its themes are universal, and the picture would not stand out without a comparison of, if not the same story, at least a few of its variations with the sometimes far distant sources. The storyteller—the artist—has at his command a scheme upon which he elaborates: drawing his inspiration very generally from the types of motifs put forth by A. Dundes—shortcoming/shortcoming made up for, prohibition/prohibition violated, impossible obstacle/deception which gets around it[40]—he will transpose and alter characters and actions. He will also be able to pass from one type of story to another or to connect end to end two stories elsewhere distinct, but he will never proceed in an entirely arbitrary manner. Without knowing it, he obeys implicit conventions which his audience would recall to his mind if he had need of it.

Translated by Judith H. McDowell

NOTES

1. Without the Enenga text, we shall suppose that Gazelle is here taking the place of the mouse-colored antelope or "dwarf sylvacapra" antelope, who plays the Trickster role in all of central Africa (cf. n. 18).

The Hausa tell the same adventure, attributing it to Spider; led to an elephant hunt by a giant, he then tries to imitate him and he and his wife are trampled to death (Skinner, N., *Hausa Tales and Traditions*. London, 1969, "Butorami," pp. 15–16).

2. Paulme, D., "Typologie des contes africains du Décepteur," *Cahiers d'études africaines* 60 (1976): 569–600. Let us recall that the whole sequence of a Trickster tale can be coded according to one of the following categories:

A+: deception of the Trickster which succeeds
A—: deception of the partner which fails
D+: deception of the partner which succeeds
D—: deception of the Trickster which fails
Ao: success without deception
Do: failure without deception

3. Our interpretation seems to us reconcilable with that of Lévi-Strauss,

based on the misfortunes of the American Trickster: "The misfortunes of the bungling host [the imitator] constitute symmetrical propositions reversing the cycle of the acts of the Demiurge. The latter has changed animate or inanimate creatures from what they were into what henceforth they will be. On the other hand, the Trickster, the bungling host to a whole series of creatures, is obstinately set upon imitating them as they once were in mythical times but never shall be again. He thus tries to make generalizations from other natures and to perpetuate abnormal behavior or manners into the present, and consequently he acts *as if* privileges, exceptions, or anomalies could be the rule, opposite from the Demiurge whose role is to put an end to peculiarities and to promulgate universal rules applicable to each species and each category" (Lévi-Strauss, C., *L'Homme nu.* Paris, 1971, p. 343).

4. Tauxier, L., *Religion, moeurs et coutumes des Agni de la Côte d'Ivoire (Indénié et Sanvi).* Paris, 1932, p. 234.

5. Guilhem, M., *Contes et fableaux de la savane.* Paris, 1962, vol. 2, p. 7.

6. Thompson, S., *Motif-Index of Folk Literature.* Helsinki, 1932–1937.

7. A variant with Rat in the role of Caterpillar has Rat offering his back to his wife, so that she can pound the hot yam on it. Spider wants to do the same, but at the last moment he cries out, "You are going to burn me," and runs away into the forest. The guests remain with empty bellies. As well as the physical impossibility, the storyteller contrasts the excessive delicacy of Spider with the endurance of his model (story no. 8).

8. To fully appreciate this anecdote, it is necessary to know the exact circumstances in which it was told.

9. Cf. Dundes, A., "The Making and Breaking of Friendship As a Structural Frame in African Folklore," in Maranda, P. and E. K., eds., *Structural Analysis of Oral Tradition.* Philadelphia, 1971, pp. 171–188.

10. Cf. story no. 13.

11. Cf. story no. 14. The same tale exists among the Agni, with Spider and Elephant in the role of Gbaso (story no. 15).

12. Evans-Pritchard, E. E., *The Zande Trickster.* Oxford, 1967.

13. Cf. Street, Brian V., "The Trickster Theme: Winnebago and Azande," in Singer, A., and Street, Brian V., eds., *Zande Themes.* Oxford, 1972.

14. On the story of the "Magical Objects," cf. Calame-Griaule, G., and V. Görög-Karady, "La calebasse et le fouet: Le thème des 'Objets magiques' en Afrique occidentale," *Cahiers d'études africaines* 45 (1972): 12–75.

15. Unpublished tale (no. 18) collected by Goulard and Ferrer. An echo of To's misfortunes is also perceptible in a Gabon tale which shows two characters, both rich and powerful, one living on the seashore, the other deep in the woods. R'Agnambié from the ocean tries to imitate the behavior of R'Agnambié from the forest, arguing: "Are we not the same age?" But, not having the secret of his namesake, he brings on a catastrophe and kills his children. In conclusion, "each has different gifts, and no one is supreme in all spheres" (story no. 19).

16. On the dual image of the woman, cf. Paulme, D., *La mère dévorante: Essai sur la morphologie des contes africains*. Paris, 1976.

17. *Kakuluku, mbuluku, mboloko*— a dwarf sylvacapra antelope (the word comes from the Portuguese *burrico*). Crafty but not really harmful or dishonest, this little animal finds safety in running away. His usual antagonist in the tales is Leopard, the symbol of the chief (cf. Hulstaert, R. P. G., *Fables mongo*. Brussels, 1970).

18. Cf. stories no. 29 and 30.

19. The Zande storyteller tries to explain the enmity between the two species: Kite has cut off his leg in order to imitate Hen ("I give my leg to my children when they leave to go hunting; then they bring back much game"); undeceived, on the point of dying, Kite orders his children never again to spare hens or chickens (Evans Pritchard, E. E., "Some Zande Animal Tales from the Gore Collection," *Man* 65 [May–June 1965]: 70).

20. Stories no. 33 and 34. Hyena appears only rarely in Agni tales; the animal is not even known except by hearsay. J. P. Eschlimann's informants explain the unusual victory of Hyena by the late hour in which the story was told, the storyteller taking care to balance the defeats suffered by the same character in the course of the evening. Always, the presence in other regions of the same tale of Spider tricking his partner through gluttony, then incited to an impossible imitation by a partner who capitalizes on that same gluttony, would cause one to see here in Hyena not the usual unfortunate partner of Hare but a substitute for Lizard in the other versions.

21. Not having the text in the original tongue, we have not been able to verify whether the character is Worm or Caterpillar. "Silkworm" could be the very free translation of an informant who had been to school.

22. "Iguana" is here an erroneous translation: the iguana (a fleshy crest runs the length of his back) is found only in tropical America. It shows up in the tale of the great brown lizard which lives at the edge of pools and feeds on insects.

23. Yoove, the nocturnal bird of the family Caprimulgidae, who hides during the day. We have put aside one version from southern Nigeria which shows Oyot, the bush-rat (would that be the burrowing squirrel of the Mofu version, no. 38, often called "palm-squirrel" by Europeans?), and Bat (who reminds one of Yoove because of his nocturnal habits). Jealous of Rat, Bat pretends to have himself cooked. Rat tries to imitate him and dies because of it. But the characters are less typical and the victory of Bat is dubious: the king, learning of Rat's death and suspecting foul play, looks for Bat, who prefers exile and since that time no longer dares to go out during the day (Dayrell, E., *Folk Stories from Southern Nigeria, West Africa*. London, 1910, "Why Bat Flies at Night," pp. 36–37).

24. We have noted the existence of a Kamba version of story no. 28; in this version (no. 30), the animal that Cock persuades to cut off his head

is not Hare but Hyena, whose tricks fail most often; after the death of Hyena, Cock marries his widow.

25. Cf. Paulme, D., "Morphologie du conte africain," *Cahiers d'études africaines* 45 (1972): 150 passim; also "Typologie des contes africains du Décepteur," *La mère dévorante*, pp. 584 passim.

26. Stories no. 43 to 48.

27. Stories no. 47 to 50.

28. Story no. 45.

29. Story no. 50.

30. Story no. 49.

31. Tauxier translates as "Wasp" in the title, as "Fly" in the text. There is no text in the native language. At any rate, the character in question is an insect.

32. The Krio ancestors come from very distant places; the people regrouped at the time of the abolition of slavery in a spot which received the symbolic name of Freetown. The blacks coming back from Europe or America were joined there by some unfortunate people on board slave ships, which were going to transport them across the Atlantic. Many of these survivors were originally from the gulf of Guinea; some were from the Congo. The same as their language, the literature of the Krio is marked by their multiple origins, in which the Yoruba element seems to have been important.

33. Cf. Holas, B., "Echantillons de folklore kono," *Etudes guinéennes* 9 (1952) ("L'Orphelin, la corne, l'araignée, et le fouet," pp. 71–72), and Mengrelis, T., "Contes de la forêt," *Etudes guinéennes* 5 (1950) ("L'Araignée et l'orphelin," pp. 24–25).

34. Cf. Rattray, R. S., *Akan Ashanti Folktales*. Oxford, 1930, pp. 63–67.

35. "A narcissistic creature, sacrificing his family duties to the satisfaction of his instincts and his insatiable gluttony, but sometimes carrying this attitude to the point of a courageous rejection of norms and of social hierarchies, Spider presents an image of humanity in which the audience of the tales well recognize the weaknesses and the contradictions of their own nature, all the while giving them, through the childish and unsociable nature of his behavior, the reassuring impression of themselves having passed this stage and having reconciled their own ambivalent emotions through the discipline of life in society. It is probably thus that the immense popularity of this character must be explained" (Calame-Griaule, G., and V. Görög-Karady, "La calebasse et le fouet," p. 52).

36. Cf. story no. 22.

37. Cf. story no. 24.

38. Cf. story no. 28.

39. Cf. story no. 57.

40. Dundes, A., *The Morphology of North American Indian Folktales.* Helsinki, 1964.

STORIES CITED

1. Walker, A. R., *Contes gabonais*. Paris, 1967, pp. 152–153.
2. Hulstaert, R. P. G., *Fables mongo*. Brussels, 1970, pp. 328–331.
3. Finnegan, R., *Limba Stories and Story-telling*. Oxford, 1967, pp. 296–297.
4. Noss, P. A., "Wanto: The Hero of Gbaya Tradition." *Journal of the Folklore Institute* 8: 12–14.
5. Tauxier, L., *Nègres Gouro et Gagou*. Paris, 1924, p. 280.
6. Fortier, J., *Contes ngambaye*. Fort-Lamy, 1972, ronéotée, pp. 224–229.
7. Unedited story, collected in 1958. A close example figures in Migeod, F. W., *The Mende Language*, pp. 220–222; another in Holas, B., "Echantillons du folklore kono," *Etudes guinéennes* 9 (1952): 68–69.
8. Holas, B., "Echantillons du folklore kono," p. 70.
9. Fortier, J., *Contes ngambaye*, pp. 163–169.
10. Rodegem, J., *Anthologie rundi*. Paris, 1973, pp. 298–301.
11. Thomas, J., *Contes, proverbes, devinettes ou énigmes, chants, et prières ngbaka ma'bo* . . . Paris, 1970, pp. 129–133.
12. Thomas, J., ibid., pp. 134–139.
13. Thomas, J., ibid., pp. 140–147.
14. Thomas, J., ibid., pp. 154–165.
15. Ano Nguessan, M., *La femme dans le conte agni*. Paris, 1974, thèse de 3ᵉ cycle, ronéotée, pp. 92–94.
16. Thomas, J., *Contes ngbaka ma'bo*, pp. 166–185.
17. Evans-Pritchard, E. E., *The Zande Trickster*. Oxford, 1967, pp. 139–140.
18. Goulard, J., and Ferrer, J., unedited Massa story.
19. Walker, A. R., *Contes gabonais*, pp. 286–289.
20. Ano Nguessan, M., *La femme dans le conte agni*, pp. 167–172.
21. Ano Nguessan, M., ibid., pp. 130–133.
22. Rattray, R. S., *Akan Ashanti Folktales*. Oxford, 1930, p. 43.
23. Fuja, A., *Fourteen Hundred Cowries*. London-Ibadan, 1962, pp. 7–9.
24. Richeux-Palier, B., unedited story.
25. Evans-Pritchard, E. E., *Zande Trickster*, pp. 137–139.
26. Holladay, V., *Bantu Tales*. Ed. L. Crane. New York, 1970, pp. 63–65.
27. Hochegger, H., unedited story.
28. Bergsma, H. and R., *Tales Tiv Tell*. Ibadan, 1969, pp. 42–44.
29. Junod, H., *Moeurs et coutumes des Bantou*. Paris, 1937, vol. 2, p. 205.
30. Lindblom, G., *Kamba Tales of Animals*. Uppsala, 1930, pp. 11–13. The same story occurs among the Digo with Goat as the dupe (Dammann, E., "Digo Märchen," *Zeitschrift für Eingeborenen Sprachen* 26 [1938]: 228) and among the Namwanga (Busse, J., "Inamwanga Texte," *Zeitschrift für Eingeborenen Sprachen* 27 [1937]: 254).

31. Hochegger, H., *Le soleil ne se lève plus*. Bandundu, 1975, narrative 0106, ronéotée.

32. Ano Nguessan, M., *La femme dans le conte agni*, pp. 162–164.

33. Fernor, C., "Contes de la Côte d'Ivoire." *Revue des traditions populaires* 27 (1912): 381–382.

34. Eschlimann, J. P., *Araignée chez les Agni Bona*. Paris, 1975, thèse de 3e cycle, ronéotée, story 32.

35. Zemp, H., *La littérature orale des Dan*. Paris, 1963, pp. 91–92.

36. Skinner, N., *Hausa Tales and Traditions*. London, 1969, pp. 10–11.

37. Fortier, J., *Le mythe et les contes de Sou en pays mbaï-mossala*. Paris, 1967, pp. 215–219.

38. Unedited story, noted among the Mofu-Gudur by L. Barreteau.

39. Le Boul et Verdier, P., "Le personnage dans le conte togolais." *Bull. de l'enseignement supérieur au Bénin* 5 (March–April 1968): 18–19.

40. Mbiti, J. B., *Akamba Stories*. Oxford, 1966, pp. 107–109.

41. Walker, A. R., *Contes gabonais*, pp. 314–315.

42. Hulstaert, R. P. G., *Fables mongo*, pp. 362–367.

43. Walker, A. R., *Contes gabonais*, pp. 169–170.

44. Tardy, L., "Fables, devinettes, et proverbes fang." *Anthropos* 28 (1935): 292.

45. Nassau, R. H., *Where Animals Talk: West African Folk-lore Tales*. Boston, 1912, pp. 112–113.

46. Krug, A., "Bulu Tales from Kamerun, West Africa." *Journal of American Folklore* 25: 106 passim.

47. Posselt, F. W. T., "Mashona Folklore." *Nada* 5 (1927).

48. Rattray, R. S., *Some Folklore Stories and Songs in Chinyanja*. London, 1907, pp. 145 passim.

49. Dewar, E. H., *Chinamwanga Stories*. Livingstone, 1900, p. 47.

50. Worthington, E., *The Little Wise One*. London, 1930, pp. 25 passim.

51. Mengrelis, T., "Contes de la forêt." *Etudes guinéennes* 5 (1950): 48–49.

52. Holas, B., "Echantillons du folklore kono," p. 57.

53. Tauxier, L., *Le Noir du Yatenga*. Paris, 1917, pp. 458 passim.

54. Short, M., *Littérature orale africaine: Les contes krio*. Paris, 1975, thèse pour le doctorat de 3e cycle, ronéotée.

55. Thomas, L. V., "Nouvel exemple d'oralité africaine: Récits narangdji-ragong, diola-karaban, et dyiwat (Basse Casamance)." *Bull. IFAN*, series B, no. 32 (January 1970): 273–274.

56. Foulkes, H. D., *Angass Manual* . . . London, 1915, pp. 103 passim.

57. Bouquiaux, L., *Textes birom (Nigeria septentrional)*. Paris, 1970, pp. 161–191.

58. "Histoire de la grue couronnée et de l'écureuil," unedited story, noted among the Mofu-Gudur by L. Barreteau.

59. Fortier, J., *Le mythe et les contes de Sou*, pp. 191–195.

Parental Preference and Racial Inequality: An Ideological Theme in African Oral Literature

VERONIKA GÖRÖG-KARADY

In a recent work,[1] I undertook the analysis of a representative body of African oral texts dealing with the interethnic relationships created by the colonial system. The main theme of that study was an inquiry into the encounter between two radically different social experiences: how do traditional, archaic societies manage to integrate the irruption of the dramatic historical experience of colonial domination into what they say about themselves (in their oral literature)? Analysis of a body of some 290 titles quickly established that the principal problems brought forward in these texts concern the origin of inequalities. The mythical foundation of domination explains it, makes it in a way acceptable to the mind, even serves to legitimate it in African eyes. Consequently, it is understandable that the typical genre involved is the genetic myth or tale describing the origin of racial groups and of social stratification. But, among the African genetic representations, only certain ones are useful for resolution of the mytho-logical problem of the origin of inequalities. It is possible to distinguish three types among the narrative supports of this preeminently ideological problem. The first type has for paradigm a primordial accident (generally ecological); the second makes use of the arbitrary decision of the mythical ancestor (God, ancestral father); and the third interposes an error (in a test), a misdeed, or a violation of moral rules, usually imputed to the African ancestor. Although the narrative models preferentially carry certain messages rather than others (the accidental and the arbitrary do not imply human responsibility, while failure in a test does, for example), in practice they turn out to be extremely malleable and lend themselves to multiple ideological uses. Thus, if one methodically brings together the root-themes, one witnesses sometimes unexpected transformations of the narrative structures, transformations seemingly induced by the needs of the proposed message. On the other hand, the manifest content of many tales frequently bends beneath the weight of the structural inertia of the initial theme.

Here I propose to analyze these modalities of transformation in one of the most singular root-themes of my body of texts, one situated at the point linking the texts that invoke the ancestors' mythical responsibility and those that exclude it. It is the obvious example of a narrative model, ideologically "neutral" in its simplest form, that can be exploited in various ways as a function of the developments and actualizations given it by the African imagination. Among the outstanding texts of this type, three subcategories can be clearly distinguished, differing both in narrative structure and in ideological content. The first type introduces the theme, which seems to be authentically African, of cross-sexual association between parents and children; the second relates the story of the children of Eve; and the third (similar to the first) comprises the African versions of the Biblical story of the sons of Isaac (Jacob and Esau). It will then be possible to compare the modalities of the three related narrative structures, which would be identical if the inertia of the potentialities included in the three original models did not impose slightly different solutions to the same mythological problem.

1. Association between the Father and the White Child

The four stories in the first subcategory show great unity. The texts come from the four corners of Africa and were recorded as early as 1906 and as late as 1969—facts which lend some verisimilitude to the hypothesis that they are transformations of an ancient and unique thematic structure.

A Shilluk tale seems to offer the most complete range of potentialities inherent in the root-theme. The first humans, born of God the father and a woman (here, a gourd), are racially divided into black and white. This division is thus an original given and not, as in the second group of texts, the result of a divine action.

TEXT NO. 1[2]

The cow is our grandmother, she bore a gourd. Our father is God. We were two of us born by God (a black one and a white one). The black one was beloved by his mother, but the white one was hated. When God came, she showed him the white one,

> but the black one she hid. God asked, "Why do you hide him?"
> She said, "For nothing." Then God said, "Well, do but hide
> him, I like the white one. The black people shall be ruled by
> the white people." On that she brought the black one out too.
> God asked, "Why do you bring him out?" She said: "Oh, I just
> brought him out (without any special reason)."
>
>   To the white one were given the book, and the gun, and
> the sword, and all kinds of goods, he is loved by God. So
> now the black people are governed by the white.

The primitive parents intervene only in the structure of relations linking the black child to the mother and the white child to the father. The preferential choices being clearly established (the mother loves the black and detests the white; the father loves the white without detesting the black), let us look at the episode of the mother hiding her protégé. To hide is to protect, and, here, hiding one but not the other is at the same time a way of distinguishing the hidden one by keeping him close to oneself, reserving him for oneself, or, in a more general way, associating him with oneself.[3] Let us examine separately these two possible semantic elaborations of the act of "hiding." To protect from whom or from what? Who represents a danger? There is no other actor but God, the supreme being, who is in any case superior to the mother in two ways in these collective productions: as God, who creates as he engenders, and as male. He can constitute a threat only by virtue of these two qualities, since he has no others. It is hard to see how his divinity could dictate his preferences and threaten one of the children, since there is no indication in the texts, here or elsewhere, of any challenge to his authority. His union with the mother excludes such an interpretation. But precisely because of this union his maleness quite naturally opposes him to the representative of the feminine, maternal principle. The danger comes from the structure of the relations between the sexes, opposed and complementary at the same time—opposed as structural limits of the world and complementary in order to insure the dynamism of the world, that is, to produce descendants. If there is a danger, it is because *the world cannot be conceived except in an ordered fashion.* Now the most economical way of ordering the world is by means of binary oppositions, of which the bisexual organization of humanity is a perfect model. Thus one of the constants of archaic logic can be seen at work in this brief text: the original conflict derives from binary order, which is the simplest way to structure chaos and which requires that the first couple's offspring be divided into two opposing moieties. Of course, this is a question not of an inherently necessary structure, but of one possible model. But, once this model has been adopted, it entails consequences expressed here by the *cross-association* between parents and children.

The nature of this "association" must be one of two sorts in such a binary system: positive (love, preference, etc.) or negative (hate, rejection, hostility, etc.), either true association or dissociation. Given this elementary system, a narrative structure appears which acts as a veritable code of meanings, producing multiple modalities of realization or actualization such as one finds in the available texts. It will be seen that some of their peculiarities (thematic contradictions, gaps) can be understood only in light of this model, to which, consequently, a sort of logical primacy can be attributed.

Two aspects must be distinguished in the cross-association itself: first, the "structural" (i.e., lacking affective or social motivation) character of the hostility manifested by one parent for the child associated with the other. This aspect is clearly marked in our text. ("God asked, 'Why do you hide him?' She said, 'For nothing.'")

The father's "structural" hostility threatens the black child only as long as the fate of the descendants is not settled—that is, as long as the order of the world, valid for the children, is not established. It is established as soon as the father decrees their inequality, transforming the binary sexual order—which affects the children only through their association with one of the parents, indirectly—into a binary social order—which directly affects the children and their descendants. The mother no longer needs to maintain the symbolic expression of her association with the black child, since this association is institutionalized for the future in the social order. The fundamental disequilibrium between the sexes (powerful father and weak mother), basis of the primary order, is definitively changed into another type of disequilibrium (powerful whites and weak blacks), basis of the secondary order, which is the inegalitarian social regime.

In this African milieu, at once patriarchal and warlike in social structure and values, the association of the racial ancestor with the feminine principle carries a specific ideological burden.[4] We must remember that the social image of the woman in the most prevalent African productions includes not only weakness but also an aggregate of negative or ambivalent and often malignant ethical qualities. Here, in "hiding" the black child, but still more in the other stories of this thematic group (as in nos. 2, 3, and 4), the woman clearly appears

as the evil element, one of the two agents who starves her child or
exposes him to danger with intent to kill. By this logic, blacks are
predestined to a history of being dominated, inferior to whites in
intelligence, military force, and well-being, marked by their association
with the principle of negativity.

TEXT NO. 2[5]

Once upon a time the god of all the earth had a wife who
bore him twin-children—a male and a female. The male was
black and the female white. The mother was very disgusted
with them as she felt herself very humiliated by their birth;
but the god who knew all things told her not to be angry, as
she had already born them and it would be wicked to kill them.
The female child having grown up went to live in some other
country as she was not loved by her mother. During her lonely
journey to that other country she picked up a book which she
saw dropped from the sky. When she reached her destination
she settled down there and acquired the knowledge that was
in the book. She married a young man of that country and had
sons and daughters, who resembled herself. Her children
became multiplied, and when they were strong, they drove
away the black inhabitants of that country by means of the
knowledge of the arts of war they had acquired from the book.
Thus was created the white race who became very numerous
and more learned in everything than the black race, because
their black ancestor was more loved by their mother, the
wife of the god of all the earth.

The Calabar myth at first seems to show no evidence of the double
system of preferences established in the preceding Shilluk tale. The
text does not speak, in the beginning, of any affection of the mother
for the black child—who in fact is not even mentioned in the story
except when the twins' birth is announced. The emphasis is on the
aversion she feels for *both children*, to the point of thinking about
destroying them.[6] Thus, in the first part of the text there is a manifest
dissociation between the mother and *both* children, but also a
dissociation, although less strong, between the father and the children.
All he does is keep them alive. Up to this point, from all appearances,
our "generative structure" is unsupported by this myth, the more so
in that not only do its principal elements seem to be lacking, but the

text also presents a new element which seems totally beside the point. This is the humiliation felt by the mother (a theme that will be found again, transformed into shame at the *large number* of children, in text no. 5). One could search in vain for an explanation of this theme in the African mythical universe, where fecundity is consistently valued.

But this theme, aberrant according to a sociological interpretation (provided the mother does not detest her children by virtue of their being twins, and it will be seen that this is not the case), acquires an obvious meaning if it is seen as an altered modality of the narrative structure set out above. If there are two opposed systems of preferences concerning offspring, for the mother, only the birth of the child (or children) who is (are) associated with her constitutes a gain and has positive value. The coming of the other child (or children) can be qualified only negatively, as expressed by the mother's "humiliation" or "shame." Even if this interpretation seems to be contradicted by a literal reading of the text, it will be amply confirmed by the remainder of the story. The second episode in effect turns the situation upside down and reestablishes it to some extent in conformity with the "structure," restoring and enriching its basic elements, which had been amputated, as it were. One of the children, the daughter, leaves, once she has grown up, fleeing from maternal hatred. She receives the book (i.e., knowledge) from the sky and settles down far from her birthplace to marry an unknown husband and give birth to numerous offspring who resemble her (i.e., who are white). There is thus dissociation between the mother and *only one* of the children by spatial removal (exile)—a symbolic dissociation of the most explicit sort, removal forced by rejection, the exact opposite of the state of being "hidden." At the same time, there is an explicit association with the father, strongly expressed by the gift of the book (sky = God-father; book and knowledge = paternal endowment). It is true that nothing is said as yet of the black child, but deductive reason and the text itself, later on, implicitly fill the gap: if one child is forced to go away, it is assumed that the other remains near the mother and therefore is associated with her. If one is endowed by the father, it can be assumed that the other is not. So the system of cross-association between mother and black child, father and white child turns out to be established as clearly here as in the preceding myth, even if it is not explicit in the text. But this myth also enriches the primitive model by the addition of an *Oedipal motivation* for the preferences: the black child associated with the mother is the boy. The white child associated with the father is the girl. With the Oedipal element, we come to what is probably one of the most complete expressions of the potentialities of the theme's generative structure.

The tale's third episode adds nothing essential to the elements already described, but it confirms the interpretation that has been given to them. Strong by virtue of their divine endowment, the white children "drive away" the blacks (who, in turn, must have multiplied). Whites driving blacks away—this is the historical means of expression of the "structural" hostility between associates of the father and associates of the mother.

The text finally says what has been deduced by logical analysis: the preeminence of whites is due to the fact that the black ancestor "was more loved by [his] mother." The ideological reasoning, therefore, remains identical to that of the preceding story: superiority goes to the *father's* associate.

TEXT NO. 3[7]

The white man and the black man had the same father and the same mother. Our grandmother, our mother[8] gave birth to us.[9]

She gave birth to the white man; because that brings bad luck she went and threw him into the river.[10] Nommo took him and brought him up and taught them[11] the science of all things.[12]

He told them to go outside and look around.

As he had given them science, because they went out with this science, today they are more, that is, they have superiority, it's because of that.

The Dogo—except that his family never comes to an end— the Dogo has never had strength,[13] that is, authority, power— so they say.

The Dogo version of the story (text no. 3) is rather poor in new elements, but it is here that the "dissociation of the mother and the white child" is realized with the greatest consequences. The mother not only rejects the child but literally throws him into the river in order to kill him. The role of God the father is transformed into that of an aquatic divinity who does not beget the child but simply protects him, endowing him later on with the attributes of superiority. It can be seen, then, that here again we are far from the realization of all four of the relations found in the story taken as a model of generative structure (text no. 1). It is sufficient and important to realize certain ones (here, the association of the divinity and the white child, the association of the mother with the black child, and her dissociation from the white child—or three relations out of four) for the original structure to be maintained intact. *It is not even necessary for the agent opposed to the mother to be the father.*[14] What is necessary is that he be capable of being assimilated to the father by virtue of the functional role he assumes in the events. One side of the coin illuminates the other even if the latter remains in the shade. Thus it is possible to find an important thematic prolongation that the text contains without expressing it in so many words. One notices the little phrase which comprises the specific motivation given for the mother's rejection of the white child: "that brings bad luck" (i.e., the birth of a white child—albino?—is a bad sign). This apparently insignificant element can certainly be read in several ways.

It provides, in the first place, a cultural justification for the behavior of the mother, who, rather than being an unworthy woman, is simply following the dictates of her faith. It is also a crafty literary device, anticipating the story's moral: "whites cannot be trusted." Finally, and essentially for our purposes, it provides proof of the racial nature of the ancestors: the mother is black, since she adopts the attitude of blacks vis-à-vis her white offspring; otherwise she would not find it shocking to give birth to a white child! If the mother rejects the white child *because he is white*, the protecting god must also take him in for the same reason, that is, *he in turn must be associated with the color white.*[15]

If the dissociation is expressed in a racial code, the association should be expressed in the same code, hence the opposing skin colors of the two antagonistic and complementary agents of the story. Thus an important adjunct is added to our basic schema. It includes the explanation, in *racial* terms, of the cross-preferences, which, it will be remembered, were justified in the first tale only by structural reasons, dependent on the nature of the (sexual) relations of the original couple. *Racial opposition can be seen to constitute an elaboration of the generative theme of "structural hostility,"* on the same grounds, we must insist, as the Oedipal type of opposition (in text no. 2). But this racial element is ideologically superior to the Oedipal theme because it results in the *identification* of the whites, in the masculine line, with a divinity, while the Oedipal schema puts a feminine ancestor between God the father and the white descendants.

TEXT NO. 4[16]

Long ago, when they were created, the young Turk, Abyssinian,
Darfurien, and Shilluk were the sons of God. God came. He
called to the boys' mother, who was named Rao [the Arabic
Eve], to have the boys brought to him. But Rao, the mother
of the boys, brought only three; the fourth, the Shilluk, she hid.
Then Jwok [God] said, "Is that all?" She replied, "Yes."
Then God went away. Later he came back, and he found four
boys. Then he called Rao, the mother, and asked her, "Didn't
you tell me there were three? Where does this one come from,
then?" Rao said, "What can I do, how can one hide a man
from the one who begot him?" And God went away and
remained at home a long time. Later, one morning he came
back and said, "Why is this boy so thin—this one, the Turk?"
The Turk said, "I don't eat." He was given very little to eat.
The Shilluk eats all he wants, the Darfurien eats all he wants,
and so does the Abyssinian. Then God went away. And he came
back again and said, "Come with me." And the Shilluk didn't
want to and the Abyssinian didn't want to and the one from
Darfur didn't want to. Then God kissed the Turk on the mouth
and said to him, "You aren't afraid of me, you are my son."
And he cursed the others.

The second Shilluk myth (text no. 4) presents a fairly plain variation
on the central theme, enriched by a few minor elements. The original
couple has four children. The white child (the Turk) is starved by
the mother, who "hides" only the Shilluk. All show "fear" of God
the father, except the white child. The multiplication of the offspring,
who are the stakes in the parental rivalry, does not introduce any
modification in the primitive schema. For the structure to recover its
equilibrium, it is sufficient to distinguish two parties, associated with
the mother and the father respectively. This distinction can be made
either by dividing the children into two groups (as in text no. 5), or
by singularizing the children with opposing functions (opposed
because of their association with a single parent), or by reserving an
intermediate or neutral role to the other children, as here. It is through
this last structural solution that the Shilluk is associated with and the
Turk dissociated from the mother. To refuse food to a child is a radical
way of expressing rejection, the direct equivalent of the wish to kill
in the preceding story. If the two other children are not positively
distinguished by the mother—reflecting a strictly ethnocentric Shilluk

mythic production—they nevertheless are doubly attached to her or, what amounts to the same thing, detached from the father. They receive food from the mother, and they are afraid of the father. In its very simplicity, this symmetrical expression of cross-preferences presents a perfect homology of meaning. In the end, the three African children are associated with the mother, and God the father includes them all in the same curse.

2. *The Ashamed Mother*

TEXT NO. 5[17]

> . . . Eve gave birth to everybody, and all were white at first. She could not cease child-bearing, and at last she became ashamed of the number of her offspring, especially as she had used up all the water in the world in washing them. Others kept arriving, however, and, as they could not be washed, they remained black, so she condemned them to serve their white brothers, making them all the more conscious of their inferiority by not letting them appear more often than she could help. "It is because of this that blacks always run away from whites to-day."

The Hausa myth (text no. 5), representing the second subcategory, offers the example of a text that is very probably syncretic. Its schema is also found in many places in Europe. Aarne and Thompson summarize it under the title "The Different Children of Eve."[18]

Let us examine the principal ways in which the Hausa text departs thematically from the European schema:

1. The text clearly suggests that Eve is ashamed only of *some* of her children,[19] those who will later be the blacks, or children who are somehow superfluous.

2. The role of God the father, distributor of benedictions, is passed over in silence. In fact, this role is taken over by Eve, at once mother, begetter, and judge carrying out the condemnation of the black children.

3. The original theme is enriched by the justification—"ecological" in type—of the fate reserved for the blacks: they are rejected because they have remained unclean as a result of the exhaustion of earthly supplies of water.[20]

4. Finally, the text explains the fear the blacks would feel for the

whites by Eve's refusal to let them appear, dirty as they were (in front of the others?).

It will be seen that the inertia of the imported schema encountered a similar inertia in the African theme, giving rise to this curious modality halfway between the two. Obviously, what interests us in this transformation is the way it modifies the ideological illumination of the origins of racial inequality.

It will be noticed immediately that the European schema seems closer to the African modalities discussed so far than does this Hausa story, which nevertheless derives directly from them (as shown by the elements of detail that have been pointed out: shame felt because of the numerous births, dissimulation of the undesired children). What needs explanation is the relative originality of the story with respect to the two structural models. The models are opposed essentially by the semantic elaboration of the act of "hiding certain children." In the African model analyzed above, "hiding" clearly equaled the mother's association with the "hidden" children. In the European model, Eve seems to hide those whom she *does not want to see blessed* (endowed) by God, which means dissociation between the mother and her children.

Thus both models include the four preferential relations (at least in potentiality), but by means of an inversed semantic elaboration, which perhaps allows us to grasp an aspect of the differences in African and European gestic expression. This affirmation must be qualified, however: it may also be possible to interpret the dissimulation of the children in the European model as an act of protection, as in the African model—in this case there is obviously no question of different semantic systems. In any case, the great novelty of this Hausa tale is the union of the two relational functions, which are assumed by different agents in the African and European models. This transformation entails a series of other thematic transformations of functional elements which derive nevertheless from the previously cited models:

1. The father's absence has little effect, since the common origin of the children is expressed just as well (if not better) without a father as with a father.

2. If, with two antagonistic agents, the act of "hiding certain children" could mean protecting them against one of the agents, with a single agent the relational system must necessarily be simplified, and the four implied (potential) relationships must be reduced to two (actual) relationships. There results an inevitable transformation of the meaning of "dissimulation": if there is no longer anyone *from*

whom certain children must be hidden, then "to hide" (i.e., to protect) no longer has an object. Thus the inversion of the structural meaning of "hiding," from association to dissociation, becomes comprehensible —no matter how one interprets the theme of dissimulation in the European model!

3. But with a single agent the real meaning of the mother's humiliation (because of her too numerous offspring) also becomes clear. Eve is ashamed only of the undesired children, who are, as is literally stated in the text, supernumerary: "She could not cease child-bearing, and at last she became ashamed of the number of her offspring, especially as she had used up all the water in the world in washing them. Others kept arriving . . . " These other, superfluous children are the only ones who are rejected.

4. It follows that the children are not distinguished *from the beginning* by (different) skin color(s), as was naturally the case in the two-agent model, in which skin color was the basis for the preferential associations. Although the Hausa storyteller's *text* seems to contradict this affirmation, closer examination reveals that it contains a countersense or at least an ambiguous expression. The text says of Eve's children that "all were white at first,"[21] but it adds further on that the late arrivals, who could not be washed, *"remained black"* (italics added). In other words, all the children must really have been black in the first place and thus capable of being whitened by washing . . . What is noteworthy here is that the textual ambiguity *proceeds* from the confusion of two functions (two agents) in one, since this makes the initial differentiation of colors superfluous, given the absence of any preferential relations that this initial differentiation could control.

5. But, if there is no initial racial differentiation, and—what is more important—if there is no initial preferential relation between the children and one parent—in other words, if the historical inequality of racial groups is not inscribed in the structure of original preferential relations—then it is indisputably necessary for the myth to introduce a supplementary justification for inequality. This function is fulfilled by the "dirtiness" of the supernumerary children, by virtue of the association of this "dirtiness"[22] with shameful negative qualities that condemn these children to become the servants of their well-washed brothers. (It may not be out of place to invoke the birthright of the whites, as the elders, as another implicit justification of their superiority, although the text makes no allusion to this.)

The theme "black equals dirty" seems therefore to spring directly from the structural transformation undergone by this root-theme as a result of the contraction of two characters into one. One can question the reason for its presence here, since, as has been seen, most of the models do not admit it.

It seems that this important transformation depends directly on ideological considerations. There is no other reason for it, especially in this heavily Islamized milieu (the tale is even told as a Biblical story!), in which it must have been with some gritting of the teeth that the storyteller acceded to the elimination (by pure and simple legerdemain) of the role of God the father . . .

In fact, the model with two agents represents a vision of total predestination of blacks to a mediocre condition. It establishes a quasinatural difference between the two racial groups, an original difference in any case, barely attenuated by their common origin. Moreover, blacks appear there as being rejected by the Creator (the father) and associated with the mother, that is, with woman. It is understandable that it was difficult for this version to be accepted by a public imbued with the cult of the divine father. The model with one character upsets this fatalistic conception of origins in a remarkable way. It strongly reaffirms the original equality of the races (even suggesting, if our analysis is correct, that the elders were *first* black, before being washed, a fact which does not prevent the *blacks turned white* from being perceived as elders . . .). It reduces to nothing the primitive association with the feminine (weak or ambiguous) principle and refusal of God. Finally, it attributes the differentiation to a pure ecological accident, capable of explaining an inequality of fact without establishing, much less justifying, an inequality of right.

3. *African Versions of the Story of Jacob and Esau*

The story of Jacob and Esau (Genesis, chapters 25 and 27) has offered Africans a complete development of the model that has just been examined. In this account of the elevation of one descendant and the fall of the other, it was necessary only to identify the African with the dispossessed brother (Esau) and the European with the chosen one (Jacob) to obtain a perfect mythic equivalent of the first model. The significant thematic deviations are few and remain in all cases within the narrow circle of potentialities that have been distinguished.

The differences presented by the Biblical story are three in number:
   1. The *initial* preferential relations are differently arranged. It is Esau (the black) who appears as the father's associate and to whom

the paternal inheritance is destined; Jacob (the white) is initially the mother's associate, in consequence.

2. The paternal endowment is not carried out in conformity with the initial preferential relations.

3. The relations are reversed through a trick by the mother and her associate, the white.

All the structural elements are in place. The beginning is similar (except for the inversion of roles) and the ending identical to those of the previously examined stories. Only the intervening events differ. It is here that the specific thematic addition of the Biblical account can be seen: it has mother and son share the responsibility for the fatal denouement. The differentiation of the condition of men is brought back, at least partially, to an error, a misdeed (or a comparable act) of the first humans (or of those who can be assimilated to them).

The responsibility taken on by the ancestors constitutes an element which obviously modifies the ideological illumination of the reported events.

TEXT NO. 6[23]

There were a man and a woman who had no children. Late in their life, the woman became pregnant with twins, one black and one white. The black was the first and the white came afterward. At the moment of giving birth, the woman felt that the children were not coming out of her womb. She saw that the white child had caught the black one's foot and was holding him back to keep him from coming out first from his mother's womb. She said, "Never has such an extraordinary thing been seen." She called Nzapa. Nzapa was displeased and said, "What is this child who is already getting into disputes in his mother's womb?" He made them come out in order, the black child first and the white one second. From that time the black, who was the elder, gave orders to the second. The black son was always hunting in the bush; the white one always stayed in the village and was intelligent. The father loved the first son and wanted to give him the power to command, but the mother loved the second and wanted him to command. The father became old and blind. One day he called his elder son and told him to prepare him a dish; he would bless him then and give him his authority. The black son went into the bush to hunt and kill an animal. The white one stayed in the village.

He killed a sheep, cooked it, and presented it to his father
before the elder son returned. The father, hearing him, said,
"This is not my elder son." The younger son replied, "Yes, yes,
I am your elder son; touch my clothing." The father touched
his clothing and was not convinced. He tasted it with his mouth
and said again, "You are not my elder son." But finally he
blessed him and gave him the power to command. Since then
it is the whites who command.

The Nzakara tale (text no. 6) closely follows the Biblical story.
There are preferential relations between the father and the black son
and between the mother and the white son and a relation of rivalry
and opposition between the children. The text emphasizes the
extraordinary birth episode, which symbolically anticipates the
antagonism of the twin brothers and provides a motive for the father's
preference for his elder son and his antipathy for the younger son.
The Biblical story speaks only of Jacob's holding Esau's heel. The
development of this episode is ideologically interesting for two reasons:

    1. It emphasizes once more the aggressiveness of the white ancestor
—a literal *arriviste*.

    2. It anticipates his talkative and quarrelsome character, which is
the larger significance of the "intelligence" with which he will later
be qualified. Now it is in this sense that the Nzakara text elaborates
the indications of Genesis concerning the opposition of the two sons.
Genesis expresses the opposition in terms of relative proximity in
connection with activities concerning nature (Esau was a "cunning
hunter") and "culture" (Jacob was a "plain man, dwelling in tents"
[Gen. 25:27]). For the Nzakara, the opposition is expressed more
distinctly, and there is a reference to the white's "intelligence." But,
by virtue of the meaning of the birth episode, this "intelligence"
immediately takes on a negative, or at least an ambiguous, value, since
even in the mother's womb it is used for purposes contrary to the social
ethic, in order to obtain the birthright . . . The semantic illumination
of "intelligence" is ominous, therefore. And this fact, apparently minor
and little exploited in the story, takes on more importance when it is
compared with the other potentialities of the Biblical version.

    Three omissions seem remarkable in this connection:

    1. The preparations for the birth of the twins, when God announces
to the mother the inequality of the people who will issue from her
offspring. (Gen. 25:23—"And the Lord said unto her, Two nations
are in thy womb, and two manner of people shall be separated from

thy bowels; and the one people shall be stronger than the other people; and the elder shall serve the younger.") This announcement motivates the maternal preference for the younger son, which materializes in the episode of the fatal test to serve the cause of Jacob, the deceiver.

2. The equally premonitory episode of the (forced) sale of the birthright (Gen. 25:29–34).

3. The mother's participation in the final intrigue.

The emphasis on the white's "intelligence," dubious if not malignant in nature, is unimportant in itself, but it stands out in the structure of the Nzakara tale because of the absence of other motivations for the trick of the denouement. However, as a result of these omissions, the perfectly constructed Biblical story loses, in the Nzakara version, its most solid functional narrative pillars. What reason other than purely ideological considerations could have led the African storyteller to forego the use of the best resources of his raw material? Let us pause for a moment and examine these omissions to see in what direction they bend the "ideological line" of the Biblical model.

God's announcement to Rebecca about the fate destined for her twins' descendants gives a prearranged, inevitable character to subsequent events and, more important, presents them in advance as if they were the result of a divine decision. Thus Esau's ensuing fall has an air of predestination about it. His social inferiority no longer seems to be the consequence of a culpable machination of which he is the victim; instead, it appears as the inevitable result of a divine prejudice all the more derogatory in its disregard for the customary law regarding the birthright. Esau's sale of his birthright obviously constitutes a justification for his fall. The sale shows him to be not only weak but also unworthy of his presumptive prerogatives. ("Thus Esau despised his birthright" [Gen. 25:34].) Finally, in the Biblical story, the action of Rebecca, the mother, is decisive in the denouement. She is the one, in fact, who organizes the fraud from beginning to end and, to some extent, the one who carries it out. Jacob only follows her instructions. Thus the responsibility formally falls on the mother, although in reality she is in a way "covered" by Jehovah himself. In any case, the functional equivalent of the white is charged with only a minimal part of the responsibility for what happens. In other words, the Nzakara storyteller's omissions converge to systematically eliminate all ideologically significant elements of the original model that would tend to put the black in a bad position and acquit the white. Here, any predestination is passed over in silence, nothing tarnishes the innocence and naïveté of the black, and the white deceives his father on his own initiative, without instigation. If there is any predestination in the African account, it is in the black's favor. It is the father himself who causes the black to come out first from his mother's womb, and the storyteller takes pains to specify (in an addition to the Biblical story) that "from that time the black, who was the elder, gave orders to the second." Only trickery and fraud, his "intelligence," allowed the white to reverse the situation in his own favor. But this new presentation of the events comprises a profound reinterpretation of the story's ideological content. The white, having been rejected by the father from the beginning, can dominate only through an *illicit* stratagem, and his superiority is *fundamentally illegitimate*.[24] This story, therefore, effects a radical inversion of the conception of the origins of inequality with regard to the texts previously analyzed. In this respect, it forms one of the boundaries of the field of ideological attitudes that have marked our body of stories. It is indeed exceptional for these texts to include such a sharp judgment of the whites.

TEXT NO. 7[25]

I am Suriba Nevertire, of Bumban here. I am going to tell you a story about the Europeans and us, we the Limba. We are full brothers. A reason made us different, them to become white people, us to become black people.

Well, at that time, a man bore two children. Well, these two children, one had a white body, the other he bore with a black body. These people, Kanu made them, these two people he bore them in the light.[26] They lived there both of them in the world. They [the parents] had the two children. One was white, one black. But they were full brothers, one mother, one father.

But this child—his mother she loved the European, the white one. That pleased her. Now the black one—his father loved the black one.

Well, one day, he [the father] said, "Let us leave the earth," he and his wife. "Let us see what the children will do in the light. But one day I will tell you, we will see what the children are doing in the light, if they are hearing what we told them." That was their father.

He made a book. He wrote everything,[27] how to make a ship, aeroplane, money,[28] how to make everything. He wrote it in the book, to help the one he loved. He too, he took and made a hoe, he made a cutlass, he looked for millet, he made groundnuts, he made pepper, he made a garden, oranges, everything. He put them down, he gathered them into a pile. He took the hoe, he took the cutlass, he put them there.

If you see unfairness in bearing children, it is not today it begins. One man with two children—he likes to show unfairness to one.

At that time, well, the man said, "We will hide now, I with you, to see what the children will do."[29] Then the wife said, "What will we leave for the children?" He said, "No, I have got my plan." He was the one who married the woman, he the man. Behold, he was wanting to act unfairly. He was going to take the book to give it to the black one, he the father. He wanted to give the book to the black one. The mother wanted to give it to the European, the white one, to give him the book. She said, "What will we do?" . . .[30] He said, "We will bring what we are leaving for the children."

Now their father could not see well. He could not see the children clearly. He said, "Child, you, when you go to hunt, do not go very far." He just turned round, he caught a sheep, he killed it. He [the white one] came, he said, "Father, I have brought meat. I went to hunt for it." Well, that pleased his father. Because he could not see well, he thought he was lifting down the hoe to give the white one. Behold it was the book he took. "Take the book for me." The wife took the book. He said, "Give it to the child, the one who brought the meat." He was given it.[31] He was not afraid to peep at it. He started reading it. He started seeing the things, how to make an aeroplane, how to make everything, how to make a ship, he saw it in the book.

The black one came. He said, "Father, greetings. What have you kept for me?[32] I have killed a bird. It is what I have brought." He said, "Ah, my child, you are left as a foolish man.[33] Well, take this hoe. Here is a basket, rice is in it. Millet is in it. Groundnuts are in it. Everything that you use when you go to work is there. But you are likely always to be left behind. He is more than you. Everything, if you want to get it, you have to ask your companion, the white one."

You see us, the black people, we are left in suffering. The unfairness of our birth makes us remain in suffering. That is why they want to send us to learn the writing of the Europeans. But our mother did not agree, she did not love us. She loved the white people. She gave him the book. There they saw how to make everything in happiness [without suffering]. They were able to do that and to surpass us the black people. . . .

If you see the Europeans, everything they are doing, they have to put a black man there. He is a clerk; he sits in the store, he does everything. This is the way. Yesterday we were full brothers with them. We come from one descent, the same mother, the same father, but the unfairness of our birth, that is why we are different. We will not know what you know unless we learn from you. We are brothers of the same parents, that is why you learn from books, to teach us black people so that we may know. Why we are alike—we are full brothers.

I tell you the story, I Suriba Nevertire at Bumban here.

The Limba text (no. 7) constitutes a rather free variation on the story of Isaac's sons. The story resembles, in tenor and tone, a contemporary anecdote completely lacking the preceding myth's sobriety of expression, density, and precision. The preferential relations are firmly defined at the outset, but they are in no way motivated. There is no reference to any consultation of God before the births or to the conditions of birth, notably primogeniture, or to the personality differences in the two children, all episodes which functioned, in Genesis and in the Nzakara myth, to account for and justify the preferential relations.

The father's resolve to grant the rich heritage to the black son alone, pivot of the whole story, on which the teller insists and to which he returns several times, thus appears to be an arbitrary, unjust decision. The injustice of this paternal intention is vigorously elucidated. His authority is absolute; he does not consult his wife, does not even inform her of his project. Consequently, new light is thrown on the story's meaning by the fact that his stratagem, conceived in bad faith, fails and turns to the black ancestor's disadvantage.

In another connection, this thematic restructuring of the model entails significant modifications in the final episode, which is described in a rather curious way. Several elements of the model are telescoped there and lose their function or, more than that, appear in contradiction to other elements. The father, deceived, appears to be first and foremost a deceiver. He wants to maintain the egalitarian pretenses of the trial by hunting, but he warns his favorite not to go too far away, so that he can come back quickly. The white son profits from this (fraudulent) counsel rather than the black, for whom it was intended. This immediately diminishes the white's responsibility for the course of events, since all he has done is thwart the father's plot.

The mother's culpability is also greatly weakened in this text, if it is there at all: the crucial episode is described in a contradictory way. While the commentary on the episode does affirm the mother's participation in the black's downfall, the relation of the events is muddled. The storyteller seems to hesitate between a version that incriminates the father's "poor eyesight" and a version that imputes to the mother the responsibility for the unequal endowment of the children at the black's expense.

One might think that these hesitations result from the structural transformations made by the storyteller in the Biblical model. If he started out by suppressing all elements that might compromise the mother and her ally, while keeping the primitive thematic framework, he must have had trouble maintaining the same orientation in the account of the trial and the endowment.

Here the transposition of culpability from the mother to the father contrasts so strongly with the Biblical version that the text cannot help reflecting, in its confusing and contradictory aspects, a profound "thematic" tension between two biases, which are also ideological choices. If, in the final analysis, the father is exclusively charged with total responsibility for the bad fortune of the black descendants, it is because the text's message is linked with a genetic explanation of inequality by divine discretion.

Here conjugal rivalry figures only as a nonfunctional accessory to the story; it is far from supporting the whole narrative, as in the previously analyzed texts. The differentiation of conditions is traced back to the father's will, diverted from his original intention by chance (or the mother's intervention?). We are in the presence of a tolerably fatalistic presentation of events, which makes comprehensible the narrator's insistence, illogical in itself, on the black's "unfair birth."

The other two syncretic tales, one Ekoi and one Fang, are inspired only distantly by the story of Isaac's sons. Their interest lies in their prolongations of the Biblical text, always moving in the direction of simplification of the primitive narrative structure.

TEXT NO. 8[34]

In the beginning of things, Obassi had only one wife. These

two were the first of all people. Before them neither man nor woman had ever been.

In course of time the woman bore four children to her husband. Two were white and two black.

One day, when the children were yet young, the father called the two boys, and sent them out hunting, while the mother told both girls to go and fish.

Now when the white girl had been for a little time down by the river she saw a bird catching fish, and noticed that it had already thrown down several on the bank. These she took and ran quickly home to give them to her mother, but the black girl still went on slowly fishing with her nets in the river.

Meantime the white boy thought, "Why should I trouble to go hunting?" So he took his mother's goat and skinned it. Then he brought it to his father and said, "Here is an antelope which I have just killed in the bush."

When the black girl returned with the fish that she had caught, her mother said, "The white girl has brought me all that I want, and to her I have given the recompense which I promised to both of you."

After a time the black boy came back with a fine antelope (*Nsun*) which he had killed, but, when he laid it down before his father, the latter said:

"I have already accepted enough fresh meat from my white son, and to him have I given the hunter's reward."

In course of time the children grew up and thought of marriage. When this had taken place Obassi sent the black son and daughter into the bush, to live afar off, but the white children he kept with him always.

[Later the white son and daughter plead with their father to let them go and visit the black children. Obassi agrees reluctantly, after three unsuccessful requests. He shows them how to make a canoe out of wood and gives them guns, since their black brother may think that they come as enemies.]

At first, the Ekoi tale seems to present an enriched version of its model. It insists on the fact that the parents are the first people living on earth (which has not been implied in the other variants) and, especially, the two male ancestors are matched by two daughters, of different races, like their brothers. There are thus two potential couples, one black and one white, a situation which could make the preferential relations between parents and children more complex than in the other thematic variants. But it turns out that, rather than complicating things, this new structural arrangement simplifies these possible relations to such an extreme that it almost eliminates their substance.

As a matter of fact, all the antecedents of the final trial have been omitted here—all the elements that show and justify the preferential relations (birth, consultation of God, primogeniture, sale of the birthright, personality differences between the functional equivalents of black and white). Nothing is left but the parents' practical manifestation of preference for the children who prevail in the trial, that is, the white son and daughter. Since there are no cross-relations, the two parental roles constitute a useless repetition. The same relation could have been expressed with a single parent. The maternal role in particular and the redoubled children's roles as well no longer have any narrative function. They are entirely redundant. Rather than enriching, they visibly impoverish the story and its lesson. Indeed, hardly anything remains of the primitive intrigue except the trial, to which a supplementary episode is annexed. But the structure of the trial itself shows simplifications that reduce the significance of its message. In the first place, the trial itself is no longer crucial with regard to human fate. It is reduced to a simple domestic incident, hence the excessive minimization of the stakes. The differentiation of the destinies of the white and black children occurs considerably later, apparently without any connection with the trial. The latter is redoubled like the roles of the agents. The white son and daughter make use of somewhat fraudulent craftiness to accomplish the assigned task (hunting and fishing) before the blacks, who do not try to avoid the difficulties of the task. The opposition is set up in terms of slowness and speed (with connotations as to the characters' mental faculties). The whites, coming in first, carry off undefined rewards. The minimization of the stakes prevents the trial from leading directly to inequality. As a matter of fact, the story also minimizes the extent of the subsequent differentiation, since it consists only of the (forced) removal of the blacks. Even if this removal looks like exile, it still constitutes a minor degree of social distancing: spatial segregation appears as the functional substitute for inequality.

The added episode is interesting in several respects. It is one of the rare examples of a *non*ethnocentric vision of space in African folklore. The blacks are the ones who go into exile; therefore the territory of the whites is identified as the place in which the original events occur. This fact has two complementary implications:

1. The territory of the Africans is a land of exile and consequently disparaged, being contrasted with the country of the whites in terms of distance from God.

2. The final episode also presents a mythic version of colonization, when the whites come in search of the related but separated offspring. It is possible that this part of the story shows the effect of the teaching of missionaries, who could very well have explained their arrival, in such a way. It will be remarked that the essential obstacle to the reunion of the separated human branches, like the cause of the separation, comes from the same primitive character, at once paternal and divine (?). The mischief comes from the father's barely motivated arbitrary decision, but the human characters are ready to undo it. Thus the story's ideology, basically similar to the message of the Limba tale, is modified in the direction of the Christian ideal.

TEXT NO. 9[35]

Nzame, having gathered all his children together, told them, "One of my children is named Ekouagha, the other Ndan'gho." Nzame said, "Ekouagha, you who are the elder, go to your brother-in-law's place and get a white goat (or a red goat); bring it here; I will give you the talisman of riches." Then he asked for Ndan'gho to be called. Nzame said, "You too, go get a goat at your brother-in-law's place." Ekouagha said to himself, "First I will check the traps and then I will go to my brother-in-law's." The younger brother, Ndan'gho, carried out his father's orders: he took his spear, went to his brother-in-law's place, and came back with a white goat; he returned to his father, who was blind. The father asked, "Who is making this noise? Who is coming in?" The son replied, "It is I, Ndan'gho, I am returning from where I have been." The father repeated his question, adding, "Ndan'gho, do you return with the commission accomplished?" The son replied, "Yes, I have returned with what you asked for." The father said, "Go, get a big pot, grate some *odika*, get some salt and pimento and some onions." The son came back bringing all that.

The father went on: "Bring the goat with the knife to bleed it, skin it, cut it up, put it in the pot, and place it on the hearth; add water and *odika*; add salt, onion, pimento; cook it in the pot." He (the father) took a spoon and fed the child.

He said, "Riches! authority! knowledge!" He added, "All these things are in you!" He also said, "You will beget white children." The son who had gone out first came back in his turn. The father said, "Who is opening the door?" He replied, "It is I, Ekouagha." The father cried out, "Alas! My other son took all the fortune; where were you? Since you are here, take the pot your brother left; you also cut your goat's throat and cut it up in the pot." When it was cooked, the father took a spoon and fed him some of the talisman. Then he said, "There are no more riches for you, and your brother took all the riches. As for you, you will get by as you can; you will beget black men. You will be miserable; your children will become slaves."

The Fang myth (text no. 9) plunges us back into the solemn atmosphere of primeval times. The text is precise and well constructed. It follows the Biblical model closely but dismisses a good many of its elements, notably, here again, all motivation for the father's selective preferences—except primogeniture—and also the entire maternal role. With the father having to carry out the realization of the relations on his own, and without any supporting motivation, it is understandable that the relation linking him with the functional substitute for the white is expressed only weakly and indirectly.

This relation is nevertheless indicated, in spite of appearances, by three narrative elements:

1. When he sets up the test, the father speaks first to his favorite—no doubt to give him a head start.

2. He promises him the supreme reward ("the talisman of riches"), implying that it is reserved for him.

3. At the outcome of the test, he hesitates to endow the other son, who has won the contest, asking him twice if the task has been properly executed.

Here again a single character suffices to maintain the primitive model. But, if the mother is missing, the intrigue has to be reconstructed. It has been seen that the child dissociated from the father can undertake the trial alone, to all intents and purposes, even if the maternal figure is present in the story (cf. text no. 1). The mother can also be replaced by a substitute, as in the Yukun and Ashanti texts examined below. The great novelty of the present story is to have entirely suppressed any role that the dissociated son (or his ally: mother, magician, friend) might have played.

The trick or fraudulent act of the child rejected by the father is passed over in silence and supplanted by a relative *fault* of the preferred child (Ekouagha delays in carrying out the paternal command).

Though the story speaks of the father's blindness (following the Bible), this element is of no use here, since the other son does not conceal his identity. At most it provides the narrator with a literary device to express the father's perplexity (as he asks twice if his commission has been carried out). Thus the lesson of the story is reoriented toward a less fatalistic explanation of inequality. The real responsibility falls back on the black ancestor himself, who sins through filial disobedience, a serious fault in a social structure that accords economic and political preeminence to the elders in general and to the father in particular.

To the contrary of the outcome of the Ekoi tale (text no. 8), here the trial seems to result in a neatly Manichean vision of humanity. Even the differentiation of the descendants' skin colors is decided by the trial.

It will be noticed that the very disposition of the trial undergoes a curious transformation. In all the other African elaborations of the story of Isaac's sons, the trial is founded on the mechanism of a symbolic gift, implying a countergift. This narrative element is prefigured in the Biblical model by the sale of the birthright for a plate of lentils. Here what the hunter brings has a different function. Besides, the element itself is transformed, since it is now a question of bringing a domestic animal. Finally, the animal is used not to *formally* provoke the expected endowment but to serve as a ritual aliment, a "talisman."

The Biblical story has also inspired African myths that do not oppose the destinies of blacks and whites. Nevertheless, all known variants develop the theme of the origin of social inequalities. A Yukun text, for example,[36] very close to the Genesis model, presents the transmission of royal power as the stakes. This power should go to the sovereign's eldest son ("descendant of King David"), so that all reference to a trial is eliminated. Only the intervention of a malevolent magician prevents the expected transmission of power. Without a trial, he fraudulently substitutes the younger brother for the elder before the father.

A myth of Ashanti origin[37] also discusses the diversification of social conditions of two tribal branches issuing from older and younger ancestors. The father's preference for the elder is justified by his more "obedient" character in comparison with that of his younger brother.

Here again the "maternal" role in the intrigue falls to a functional substitute, who is no other than the father's messenger (a goat). This intermediary's intervention favors the younger brother—the presumptive outcast—over the elder—presumptive heir to the best lands. It can be seen that, though the intermediary character differs considerably from the maternal figure, his function in the story, as inventor of the ruse, is identical to hers.

4. Overview

The study of this group of texts can be concluded with a résumé of the essential traits marking the structure of these stories. In all the stories, at least potentially, there are privileged relations between one of the parents and one of the children. These relations may imply, but do not require, the existence of privileged relations between the other parent and the other child. The result of these initial relations is the foundation of inequality between the descendants of the two children. There is intervention by a "structural mediator" between the initial relations and the outcome of the intrigue.

Figures 1 and 2 show one way of representing this fundamental form of generative structure, from which all the realizations that constitute the tales derive. The crossed-out arrows indicate "dissociation" or "refusal."

Translated by Carolyn Cates Wylie

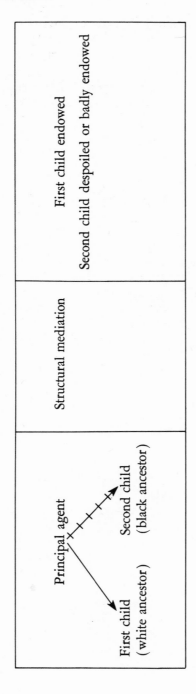

FIGURE 1

FIGURE 2

Texts	Initial relations	Structural mediation	Outcome
1, 2, 3, 4	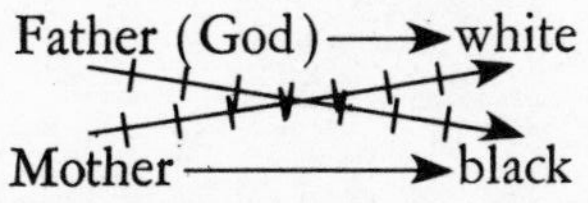 Father (God) ⟶ white / Mother ⟶ black (crossed)	No mediator / Oedipal relationship / Racial identification	White endowed (superior) / Black despoiled (inferior)
Hausa creation legend 5	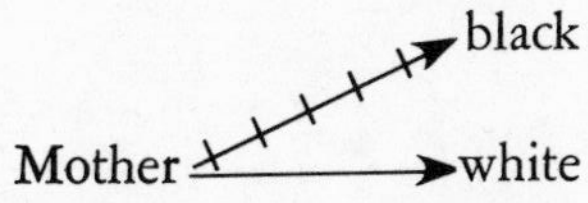 Mother ⟶ black / ⟶ white	Ecological mediator (lack of water) / Punishment by God	White superior (spirits?) / Black inferior
6, 7, 8, 9, and Yukun and Ashanti syncretic stories	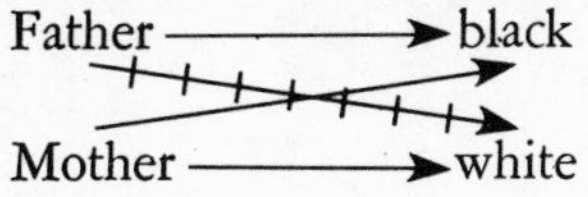 Father ⟶ black / Mother ⟶ white (crossed)	Trial with: / Trickery of the white and/or his ally / Accident / Fault of the black	Reversal of initial relations / White endowed (superior) / Black despoiled or badly endowed (inferior)

NOTES

1. V. Görög-Karady, *Noirs et Blancs: Leurs rapports à travers la littérature orale africaine* (Thèse de 3ᵉᵐᵉ cycle, E.P.H.E., Paris, 1973) (forthcoming).
2. D. Westermann, *The Shilluk People: Their Language and Folklore*
(Berlin: D. Reimer, 1912), p. 178.
3. In a Sonrai creation myth, "to hide" again means "to prefer": "After
having created the Universe, God created the first man, Adama, and the first
woman, Haoua. They had forty children. God had ordered them to bring
him the children, but Adama and Haoua tried to hide twenty of their
favorites from him. God became angry and said to the first couple, 'I am wiser
than you and I will put an impassable barrier between you and those of your
children that you hid from me, and you will never see them.' Those children
became the Holé, genies." (Cf. J. Boulnois and B. Hama, *L'Empire de Gao*
[Paris: Maisonneuve, 1954], pp. 74–75.)
In the different European and other mythologies, the term "hidden child"
means "child born with a caul." Such a child possesses supernatural powers,
but, in order for these powers to become effective, he must submit to a close
confinement. This seclusion can be analyzed as the symbolic equivalent of
gestation or reintegration into the parental body: the child "having a relationship only with his mother is completely comparable to the fetus hidden from
all eyes." (Cf. N. Belmont, *Les Signes de la naissance: Etude des représenta-
tions symboliques associées aux naissances singulières* [Paris: Plon, 1971], pp.
98–112.)
4. But too strong a connection between mother and son can be prejudicial
to the latter, not only in a concrete social context, in this case Shilluk society.
Indeed, the too strong tie established by the overly protective mother only
intensifies the Oedipal conflict and prevents the son from assuming his adult
role. It should be noted as a curiosity that Oedipus, who was blind, is associated with the color black and with night, which has a negative connotation
because it is associated with a curse.
On the Oedipal tie between mother and son in an African milieu, see G.
Calame-Griaule and P.-F. Lacroix, "La Mère vendue: Essai d'analyse d'un
thème de conte africain," in *Echanges et communications: Mélanges offerts à
Claude Lévi-Strauss à l'occasion de son 60ᵉᵐᵉ anniversaire*, ed. J. Pouillon and
P. Marenda (Paris: Mouton, 1970), pp. 1356–1380.
5. J. C. Cotton, "Calabar Stories," *Journal of the African Society* 18 (January 1906): 193–194.
6. Unfortunately, we are not familiar with the status of twins in Calabar
society. It should be recalled that, although in many African societies the
birth of twins is seen as a source of happiness, in others it brings misfortune,

a belief that can even lead to the murder of the babies (example: Boshiman society). The Guéré, according to a personal communication from Denise Paulme, welcome the birth of twins. "However, since such a birth entails an important loss of potency for the man, the arrival of a second pair of twins would be ill received, considered excessive; finally, male twins are thought to 'love their father too much,' a love that might quickly bring about their mother's death."

7. G. Calame-Griaule, unpublished manuscript, 1969. Informant: Ambara Dolo. Notes 8–13 are by Geneviève Calame-Griaule.

8. This is Haoua, Eve, whom the Dogo call Yakama. This tradition is therefore of "Musulman" origin but assimilated into Dogo tradition, as shown by the role of Nommo.

9. "Us," the blacks, the Dogo.

10. As she was black and her firstborn child was black, the white child appeared to be a bad omen.

11. The story shifts to the plural with the shift from the first white man to the white race.

12. *Dàbula*: manner, means, system; hence, science.

13. The strength of the Dogo is in their fecundity and their vitality. The race is vigorous and resistant in the face of difficulties. (Note the play on words between Dogo [name of the tribe] and *dogo*, "wild grass.")

14. In fact, Nommo receiving the child in the water and giving him a new birth is more like a feminine than a masculine figure. In connection with the hero thrown into the river, we should recall the initiatory tales in which the hero's or heroine's descent underwater and return with wealth or knowledge are the most common episodes. (Cf. Geneviève Calame-Griaule's study on the theme of the *Two Sisters*, forthcoming.)

15. This also agrees with the association of the color white and water (aquatic divinity).

16. W. Hofmayr, *Die Shilluk: Geschichte, Religion, und Leben eines Niloten-Stammes* (Mödling bei Wien: Anthropos, 1925), 2:241–242. Translated into English from V. Görög-Karady's French version.

17. A. J. N. Tremearne, "Bori Beliefs and Ceremonies," *Journal of the Royal Anthropological Institute* 45 (1915): 24.

18. "Eve has so many children that she is ashamed when God pays her a visit. She hides some of them and they fail to receive the blessing that God gives those in sight. Thus arises [*sic*] the differences [*sic*] in classes and peoples" (A. Aarne and S. Thompson, *The Types of the Folktale: A Classification and Bibliography*, 2d ed. [Helsinki: Academia Scientiarum Fennica, 1961]).

19. Eve is ashamed of the children who are closest to her, who remain (dirty) as they were at the moment of their birth. There is an allusion here to the original defilement of woman.

20. In other myths on the origin of inequality, the inferiority of Africans has often been explained by assimilation of the color black and dirtiness.

21. All were destined to be white after being washed?

22. This problem cannot be fully discussed here, but it should be noted that there is much evidence that the identification of dirt and blackness is a purely arbitrary cultural phenomenon. While it occurs in a number of African civilizations, it is far from being a general fact. In these "ideological" tales, one might even wonder if it is not a case of feedback from the ethnocentric (i.e., biased) European conception of the semantics of colors.

23. E. de Dampierre, *Un ancien royaume bandia du Haut Oubangui* (Paris: Plon, 1968), pp. 361–362.

24. Nevertheless, it is clear from their oral literature that the Nzakara do not condemn the use of trickery, which they equate with shrewd intelligence. On the contrary, they admire anyone who achieves his goals by the use of his wits, even if his means are not exactly legitimate. (One thinks of the cycle of stories whose hero is the deceiver Ture, or Tule.) Elsewhere, for example, in Kaffir oral literature, the weak but wily hare who escapes through trickery symbolizes the black man confronting the powerful, conquering white. This qualification shows, if that is still necessary, the "positional" value of the characters' attributes. (Cf. A. Mohl, "Sammlungen von kaffrischen Fabeln am unteren Sambesi," *Mitteilungen des Seminars für orientalische Sprachen* [1905], p. 2.)

25. R. Finnegan, *Limba Stories and Story-telling* (Oxford: Clarendon Press, 1967), pp. 261-263. Notes 26–33 are Finnegan's.

26. I.e., alive, on the earth.

27. Suriba exaggerates the length and high tone to almost ridiculous lengths to indicate that absolutely *everything* was there.

28. All things for which the Europeans are specially famous among the Limba.

29. This was spoken very quietly and surreptitiously, depicting the father's desire to conceal it from his children.

30. A few words here and later are missing owing to a fault in the recording.

31. It is not clear if it was the hoe or the child that the father mistook. In any case the book was given to the wrong son.

32. A usual question asked by a friend or visitor, often only half-seriously.

33. I.e., someone unable to become well off or gain honour. The word itself, *kuyakayakan*, is thought a funny one.

34. P. A. Talbot, *In the Shadow of the Bush* (London: W. Heinemann, 1912), pp. 387–389.

35. V. Largeau, *Encyclopédie pahouine: Congo français* (Paris: E. Leroux, 1901), pp. 400–403.

36. C. K. Meek, *A Sudanese Kingdom: An Ethnological Study of the Yukun Speaking Peoples of Nigeria* (London: Kegan Paul, 1931).

37. A. Cardinall, *Tales Told in Togoland* (London: Oxford University Press, 1931), pp. 48–50.

The Performance of the Gbaya Tale

PHILIP A. NOSS

INTRODUCTION

The Gbaya *to* or tale is an art form that has been transmitted from antiquity to the present.[1] It is an art form through which ancient values and mores find expression and validation. It is a comment on Gbaya social order, a statement about relationships in the home, in the village, in the garden, and on the hunt. It is relevant and meaningful, as the performer stated, "If it is without meaning, it is not worth telling."[2]

The context of the tale is one of entertainment and pleasure. The audience is not captive and will not listen long to pure didacticism however instructive.

The role of the folktale artist may be compared with that of the actor in a dramatic production. The narrator in telling the tale is a performer acting out before his audience an ancient play. But he is at the same time the producer, concerned not only with entertainment but also with interpretation. In the tale are found the words of the ancestors; in the performer is found the link between the past and the present.

Within the Gbaya tradition of the tale everyone is a performer.[3] One person may be a more skilled artist than another, but everyone has at least one tale that he can tell. These are, of course, prerequisites to a performance; namely, the teller and the tale. There must also be an audience. Then, as the individual begins his tale, he becomes the actor on stage. For the moment, this person, be he five years old or seventy, is the voice of tradition. When his tale comes to an end he recedes into the audience and another takes his place.

In his performance the artist uses all the skills of speech and mime at his command. Experience and natural ability are important, likewise creative imagination. But these are all expressed through four major

This paper was first presented at the meetings of the American Folklore Society held in Atlanta, Georgia, November, 1969. The collection of tales on which it is based was made while conducting research in Cameroun under a grant from the Foreign Area Fellowship Program from 1966–1968.

devices upon which the artist depends for his success. He may not always choose to use all four, but the skilled performer will not hesitate to make maximum use of each. The artist's tools are (1) personalization, (2) song, (3) ideophone, and (4) conclusion.

The formulas with which the tale may begin and end exemplify its twin functions of entertainment and meaning, together with the four devices through which these ends are attained. At the beginning there is a song:

Narrator: Young men, listen to a tale!
Audience: A tale for laughter, for laughter,
            Listen to a tale, a tale for laughter.
N.   Young men, listen to a tale!
A.   A tale for laughter, for laughter,
            Listen to a tale, a tale for laughter.
N.   Great men, listen to a tale!
A.   A tale for laughter, for laughter,
            Listen to a tale, a tale for laughter.
Narrator: Here it comes with a crash![4]
At the end of the tale there is the statement,
   My tale is set right under the *kolo* tree *gbat*![5]
or the following:
   Strike the *kolo* tree with the boar spear *rok*![6]

In the formula the artist begins his performance by addressing the different segments of his audience, the young men and the elders. He may single out the young women, the children, the old people, or even "madame," "monsieur," or a personal friend.[7] Through this initial formulaic exchange, rapport is established between performer and audience. The narrator begins in song and the audience responds in chorus. The themes of the song are "listen" and "laugh."" The word for laughter is an ideophone *zɛkɛɗɛ* which describes light, merry chuckling. "Here it comes with a crash!" is expressed by two ideophones, *rrrrr* and *kpingim*. The first, or its full form *hirrr*, describes moving a heavy weight.[8] The latter, *kpingim*, describes the thud of something heavy crashing to the ground. The tale is weighty, it is a burden, it is meaningful, and therefore at the end of the performance, the artist sets his burden under a *kolo* tree, a large shade tree that grows on high waterless plains providing a place of rest for the hot and weary traveler. If he is a hunter, he will set his spear into the tree *rok* to be ready again when he needs it.

1. Personalization
The first of the four devices exemplified in the formulas is personaliza-

tion. The tale is personalized for the audience by addressing its various members, but also by presenting the plot with characters and places that are familiar to them. The tale about a brother's search for his abducted sister may be told about Samari and Zɛk Gbai or about Jean and Margeurite.[9] Samari is a word borrowed from the Hausa language meaning "young men."[10] Zɛk Gbai is two names from the first and second leaders of a girls' initiation festival called *zaabɔlɔ*. The names Jean and Marguerite belong to two young people in the audience, the children of a friend of the speaker. In the tale about Samari and Zɛk Gbai, the girl is captured by Rain and taken to his abode in another world; in the second tale Marguerite is taken by men from N'gaoundéré, a city two hundred miles away, from where Fulani slavers long ago attacked Gbaya settlements. Thus one tale is given a universal setting, while the second with the same theme is given a domestic context.

However, the narrator is careful even in the universal setting to bring in the local so that Samari is shown playing a game calling out the names of Bongoya girls in the absence of his own sister, the Bongoya being a family in the town where the tale was told. When Samari reached the city of Rain and was asked where he came from, he answered that he came from Bétaré, the commercial center and government post twelve miles from the scene of the performance. And when Samari returned with his sister, he was depicted returning to the very town and even section of town where the audience was gathered.

The ultimate in personalization occurs in the rare instance when the performer himself enters the tale as a character. A common plot in Gbaya tales is that of two orphaned children living alone in the bush.[11] The boy goes hunting and wounds a buffalo which attacks him. He flees toward home calling to his sister to open the door. She does, he dashes inside, and the buffalo falls dead outside. But eventually she eats too much buffalo meat, falls asleep, and fails to hear his cries.

One boy about ten years old told this tale about himself:[12]

Listen to a tale. My father was dead, my mother was dead, all my people had died. The only one that death hadn't killed was myself, and my sister.

The boy went hunting, wounded a buffalo, fled to his house and was saved. They ate the buffalo meat and he went hunting again. He wounded a buffalo and he fled.

And then my sister, the buffalo fat had made my sister fall sound asleep *kengeleng* and she was just sleeping soundly away.[13] I went around the house again and again and then the buffaloes surrounded me and gored me to death. That's the end of it. When she got up, I was already dead. Here was my body, here was the buffalo body, the way the buffaloes had gored me to death. That's the end of my tale. The stark realism of the boy telling about his own dead body lying beside the corpse of the buffalo is a shockingly effective literary device.

2. Song

The second device is the song. The Gbaya distinguishes between the tale and the parable primarily on the basis of whether or not it has a song.[14] A parable is didactic; it is told to make a point. It does not include a song, it does not seek audience participation. A tale almost always includes at least one song and an unusually good performer may include several songs in his tale. The narrator who includes ten or twelve different songs is truly extraordinary. If a tale has no song, the performer may apologize:

Listen to a tale! (Yes.) The tale I'm going to tell has no song. It's like a parable but it isn't a parable.[15]

If the performer forgets his song, there is an obvious void even if he tries to disguise the omission and include other songs. If the song is very pleasing, the audience may ask to sing it again at the end of the tale.[16]

The performer's greatest challenge and test lies in the execution of the song. In narration he manipulates audience reaction, but in the song he invites the audience into full participation, participation which must be controlled if he is to be able to continue his tale. The old woman who picks up sticks to beat out the rhythm can be permitted to do no more than complement the performance. She must not steal the stage. The four-year-old boy who breaks spontaneously into dance must not be allowed to disrupt the performance. The artist must control the audience without stifling it. He must stimulate enthusiasm without permitting it to take control. If he is not able to develop and control this tension, the rapport between audience and performer is certainly impaired, and sometimes shattered.

In addition to encouraging audience participation, the song functions as an integral element within the tale. It is through the song that the emotion of the tale most clearly comes into focus. As the hero dances to the rhythm of fish bubbling in the water, the melody is light and quick.[17] When the little bird bears the message of death, the song is sung in a minor key, and each time it is repeated, it is raised half a note.[18] The song may be used for comic relief, may indicate passage of time or repeated action, may remind the listener of what has happened, may suggest what will occur, and may indicate the height of triumph or the depths of fear and defeat. But above all, it draws the listener into the performance.

3. Ideophone

The third feature of the tale is the ideophone. Linguistic definitions and descriptions based on formal criteria or on semantic criteria can be given for ideophones, but in a tale their function is description.[19] Through the ideophone the listener sees, hears, or feels what is being described whether it is a sound, sensation, emotion, color, texture, movement, state, quality, or anything else that is describable. And if it cannot be described there will be an ideophone to describe its state of indescribability.

The ideophone may be used in the tale purely for description. Wanto the hero shuffles *sor . . . sor . . . sor* until he begins to dance with rattles on his feet *ser . . ser . . ser . . ser . . ser . . ser . . ser.*[20] The old woman with the fruit on her body runs *hukuru hukuru* and plunges *gurumm* into the water.[21] The fat rodent runs *wurwurwurwurwurwurwurwurwur* and the old hunter follows *babababababababababababababababababa.* As he tries to keep from running down the steep bank too fast he goes *tititi* on his toes, and on the way back up he pants *hɛk hɛk hɛk hɛk hɛk.*[22] When Wanto's adversary suddenly determines *harak* to fight, Wanto gets his head pounded *kpim kpim kpim* against the rock. When the enemy later returns for another fight, his calls for Wanto are met with nothing but silence *selele.*[23]

The ideophone may also occur as part of the plot. The comic hero Wanto comes upon the house of two women.[24] He sees all their food and is hungry, but they refuse to share it with him until he identifies them by name. He goes away but sends his dog to spy on them. As they see the dog, they call out, "Boyaŋmawi! Boyakemo! I've got myself a dog! Boyaŋmawi! Boyakemo! I've got myself a dog!" They feed the dog and he runs off singing a song about Boyaŋmawi and Boyakemo, but at a stream he is thirsty and pauses to drink, *la-kpak . . . la-kpak . . . la-kpak . . la-kpak la-kpak,*

La-kpak la-kpak, la-kpak la-kpak.
La-kpak la-kpak, la-kpak la-kpak.
La-kpak la-kpak, la-kpak la-kpak.

The dog sings this song to the rhythm of its gait and when it arrives home it tells Wanto that their names are "La-kpak la-kpak." Wanto goes and tries it, but they laugh at him and he returns to beat the poor dog nearly to death. He then sends his second dog who is careful not to forget the women's correct names. Thus the ideophone representing the sound of a dog lapping water becomes a song describing the rhythm of a running dog and is finally given as a name.

In another tale Wanto's son Gūwɛ goes to the home of the man-swallower to recover his lost brother-in-law.[25] The monster has great respect for his guest and decides to kill him in his sleep. As they prepare for the night he asks Gũwε what kind of noise he makes when he is sound asleep. Gũwε is wise and says that the host should answer first, then the guest, and the monster complies:

Hɔ́ sɔ̃̃́, dɔng ɗɔng pɔsɔp.
Hɔ́ sɔ̃̃́, dɔng ɗɔng pɔsɔp.

Gũwε replies that his sound is,

Fio fio, fio fio fio.
Fio fio, fio fio fio.

The sounds obviously represent snoring, but the monster's snore indicates what he intends to do with his guest. He will eat him *pɔsɔp pɔsɔp*, he hopes. Gũwε's snore has a threefold meaning. First, it is the whistle he makes as he snores. Secondly, it is the whistle that calls his dogs when he is in danger. And thirdly, it is a rare tonal pun. The whistle *fio fio* is high tone; the word for death is low tone *fio*. The song foretells the manner of the monster's eventual death. He will be killed by Gũwε's dogs.

The ideophone may be the climax of the plot. The Gbaya used to mark off areas of grassland to be burned late in the dry season long after all the rest of the land had been burned clear. When all the animals had fled into those last patches of grass, they would be surrounded by hunters and burned. Lion once called the carnivores together for such a hunt and Wanto was to perform the sacrifice required before the hunt.[26] On the way to the place of burning he was delayed by a dance and never arrived. Animal after animal was sent back to capture Wanto, but all were overcome by the wonderful rhythm of the new dance. Finally, Lion himself returned, but not even he could resist the dance. Suddenly, in the distance they heard, "My name is Gbĩ́ĩ́ĩ́!" What was that? Nothing, keep dancing! Again they heard it, "My name is Gbĩ́ĩ́ĩ́!" And then *yεn yεn yεn, yεn yεn yεn, ɓirawandu, lɔkup! loɓoto loɓoto loɓoto loɓoto.* The plot of the tale builds to the point where the dancers hear the distant rumble of thunder *gbĩ́ĩ́ĩ́.* Lion tells them to dance on, and they hear it again. Then the storm clouds billow over *yεn yεn yεn,* there is a mild oath *ɓirawandu* to emphasize the suddenness and severity of the deluge *lɔkup,* and the hunted animals scatter *loɓoto loɓoto loɓoto loɓoto* through the mud and water. The grass is wet, the game has scattered. There will be no burning and no hunt.

Samarin writes, "I dare say that a masterful use of an African's language is probably always correlated with a generous use of ideophones."[27] This is very true in the performance of the tale except that the criterion for excellence is not merely the generous use of ideophones. They must be chosen carefully and used imaginatively.

4. Conclusion

The final opportunity and test for the performer lies in the topical conclusion which may occur at the end of the tale.

The tale of Wanto's son was told by two brothers. Their versions were similar, but their conclusions were quite different.[28] The one emphasized Gũwɛ's near catastrophe when his mother tried to keep him out of trouble by hiding his magic weapon. The artist explained that a mother should not restrain her son or interfere with his heroic efforts. The second brother made it an etiological tale. Because of Gũwɛ's God-given prowess in killing the monster man-swallower, the world today is inhabited by all kinds of people, Moslems, black people, and white people. Except for Gũwɛ there would be no people on earth, no towns, and no bird would sing.

In another tale Wanto gives the honeyfood that he received from his mother-in-law to the baboons thinking that it is nothing but the usual cassava stick. He arrives home with one piece, and when he tastes it he realizes that he has given away a real treat. He determines to punish the baboons for eating his delicious honeyfood. He tricks them into his house and kills all but two little ones that had remained outside to play. One narrator interprets this tale to explain the presence of baboon in the bush today.[29] Another performer gives the tale as an example of how evil and vengeance never end.[30] A third concludes that one should only play little tricks.[31]

The conclusion appears to be an explanation of an origin, the reason for a belief or practice; it seems to be a moral or lesson that links the tale and its interpretation to the wisdom of the Fathers. It does serve this function, but this is only surface structure. The optional nature of the conclusion, the fact that the audience may request it, the fact that different performers give differing explanations for the same tale suggests that the conclusion is not serious didacticism. It is basically one more opportunity and test for the performer's creativity. The deeper meaning of the tale is to be found within the tale itself, within the characters and their relationships.

Summary
The presentation of the Gbaya tale is a dramatic performance in which the performer is completely free to create and interpret. The four devices —personalization, song, ideophone, and conclusion—represent the esthetic principles underlying the performance of the Gbaya tale. They are tools for his creativity and a standard against which he is measured.

On these four criteria rests the success or failure of his tale as a meaningful and entertaining performance.

FOOTNOTES

[1] The Gbaya of Cameroun and the Central African Republic were traditionally a hunting and farming people. They form part of the linguistic-culture complex called Gbaya-Mandja-Ngbaka.

[2] Peđangkao Michel, Tape VIII, No. 1.

[3] This paper is restricted to nonprofessional performers, although the four criteria to be discussed are important to the professional as well.

[4] Abel Waa, Tape II, No. 48. The Gbaya text is the following:

Ngai nɔɔ, zii to!
Too zekeđe zekeđe,
Zii to, too zekeđe.
Ngai nɔɔ, zii to!
Too zekeđe zekeđe,
Zii to, too zekeđe.
Gasa-wi nɔɔ, zii to!
Too zekeđe zekeđe,
Zii to, too zekeđe.
Rrrrr kpingim!

[5] Abraham Yelem, Tape V, No. 8. The ideophone *gbat* describes setting something down abruptly and forcefully.

[6] David Poro, Tape V, No. 6. The ideophone *rok* describes striking the tree solidly with the spear. The symbol *r* represents an alveolar flap or trill.

[7] In this way the entire audience is invited to participate. Specific attention may also be directed toward one individual who will function as a prompter or answerer. Cf. Ruth Finnegan, *Limba Stories and Storytelling* (Oxford: The Clarendon Press, 1967), pp. 67–68.

[8] *Hirr* is part of a chant used as men attempt to move a great weight.

Leader: Hirr ya!
Chorus: Ya!
L.   Hirr ya!
C.   Ya!
All: Heeee!

[9] Adamou Marcel, Tape III, No. 12. Published in Philip Noss, "Gbaya Traditional Literature," in *Abbia*, 1967, xvii/xviii, pp. 35–67. Pierre Danghausa, Tape III, No. 23.

[10] Samari is the plural of the Hausa word *saurayi* meaning "young man." It is a common boy's name among Gbaya, Duru, and other peoples of Cameroun who have been influenced by Hausa merchants.

[11] Elisabeth Sumai, Tape IX, No. 15.

[12] Ber Poro, Tape IX, No. 4.

[13] *Kengeleng* is an ideophone describing the girl's prostrate form stretched out in sleep.

[14] The Gbaya have a complete set of terms, although they are not rigidly defined, for their various literary genres. The parable is called *lizang*.

[15] Ngɔzɔ, Tape VI, No. 26.

[16] David Poro, Tape V, No. 2. Popular songs from tales are also frequently used to accompany young people's dances.

[17] Alim Jean Marc, "Wanto's Termites and the Fish," from a collection of tales recorded by Philip Noss in 1962.

[18] Daniel Ndanga, Tape II, No. 35.

[19] For a discussion of ideophones from a linguistic approach see Paul Newman, "Ideophones from a Syntactic Point of View," *Journal of West African Languages,* 5, ii (1968).

[20] André Yadji, Tape II, No. 42. Published in Noss, "Gbaya Traditional Literature."

[21] Martha Adama, Tape VI, No. 30.

[22] Samuel Dɔɔka, Tape VIII, No. 6.

[23] Joseph Doko, Tape II, No. 30.

[24] Djauro Doa, Tape II, No. 2.

[25] Peɗangkao Michel, Tape VIII, No. 1.

[26] André Yadji, Tape II, No. 42.

[27] William J. Samarin, "Perspective on African Ideophones," *African Studies,* 24 (1965), 117.

[28] Paul Dua, Tape V, No. 28.
Peɗangkao Michel, Tape VIII, No. 1.

[29] Joseph Yɔngɔrɔ, Tape VII, No. 24.

[30] Be'oy Pierre, Tape II, No. 14.

[31] Martha Dari, Tape III, No. 10.

The Black Loincloth and the Son of Nzambi Mpungu

WYATT MAC GAFFEY

A Kongo dilemma tale collected by K. E. Laman some sixty years ago is similar in structure to Bernard Dadié's story "The Black Loincloth."[1] The resemblance is interesting but not surprising, since Dadié's story, though a work of art, is based on folk materials and the indigenous cultures of Ivory Coast and western Zaïre share a recognized though somewhat distant kinship through their common participation in the West African forest zone.[2] In this essay comparing the two, I take that kinship for granted.

Because the Kongo story is less well known and less readily available than Dadié's, I reproduce it in full. It is the product of a society divided into matrilineal clans (*mvila*). Although an individual is ascribed membership in his mother's clan at birth, his success in life, including his ability to withstand the internal rivalries of his clan, depends on a spiritual relationship to his father's clan somewhat like the Ashanti *ntoro*. Father is patron to the son, both materially and spiritually, and is particularly expected to protect his son from witchcraft. Formerly, fathers would make sure that their sons were initiated into appropriate cults and endowed with useful magic; nowadays they are considered spiritually responsible, and are also often financially responsible, for a child's success in school and later in finding work. The term Nzambi Mpungu, which usually means God, is applied in the story to a prototypical father, a person commonly said by BaKongo to stand as "God on earth" to his son. The word *mvila* carries the special sense of the *name* of father's clan, that is, its praise-name, which serves as a protective charm.

THE SON OF NZAMBI MPUNGU

Nzambi Mpungu married a woman who bore him a son. The boy grew up to be very kindhearted to his playmates. One day he followed the others down to the water to swim. When they were ready for the plunge, each of them had to recite his mvila and that of his father. The child of Nzambi Mpungu did not know his father's mvila and became deeply grieved when the others teased him, saying: "E, maybe you were cut from a tree and not born, seeing that you don't know your father's mvila." Thus they provoked him and he was very sad. One day, somebody said to him: "E, look your cane plantation is devoured by a nduutu rodent and you do nothing." He answered: "Let him eat. Do I know the mvila of my father?" Another person reported: 'Your pigs have been carried away by the crocodile." He answered: "Let them go. Do I know the mvila of my father?" Yet another came and said: "Look, the thread of the nzambi spider is wound around your face." He: "Be it so. Do I know the mvila of my father?" Another came: "The meat that you brought home has been invaded by bluebottle grubs." He: "I am not surprised to hear it. Let them do so. Do I know the mvila of my father?" Somebody told him: "Alas, the posts of your house have been hollowed out by the boring beetle." He said: "Let it do so. Do I know the mvila of my father?" One of them came back to report: "E, your bananas and your maize have been ruined by the storm." He: "E, he is not allowed to do so. Am I to recite the mvila of my father?"

Some time went by and then he decided that he should travel to the sky to make the acquaintance of his father and his mvila. No sooner said than done. He met the nduutu that asked him: "Where are you going?" He: "On my way to the sky am I to see my father and ask him about his mvila." The nduutu helped him and, walking ahead, he cleared a wide road for him all the way down to the Nzadi. Arrived at the river, he found no canoe to carry him to the opposite bank. Instead, the crocodile came and ferried him across. On the other bank, he searched for the way to the sky but could not find it. Then the nzambi spider brought his thread and helped him. The spider ascended to the sky and fixed a loop of the thread there. Returning to the earth, the spider said to the boy: "This is the way leading to the sky" and so both climbed up into the sky.

When the dwellers of the sky descried the boy, they asked him: "Why have you come?" He answered: "To see my father, Nzambi Mpungu, to inquire about my mvila." On hearing this, they said: "Well, be seated." They went away to palaver. They agreed to let him sleep in the lion house where he would surely be devoured. They did not realize, however, that he had brought a nyanzi fly. The fly overheard their plotting and reported their decision to the boy. E, the boy was sadly grieved, but the borer beetle helped him by penetrating the main post of the lion house and making a large hole in it.

In the evening, the villagers showed the boy his sleeping quarters. He went straight into the hole made by the beetle and hid himself. The villagers let the lions into the house and closed it. But the lions had no idea that a human being was in their midst. In the morning, the villagers let out the lions and, finding the house empty, they assumed that the boy had been eaten hair and hide. But then, to their astonishment, the boy appeared.

Again the villagers had a palaver. One of them was told: "May you be changed into a small boy with mpele sores, sitting on the rubbish heap. Meanwhile, we shall dress up in splendid garments and when the stranger comes we shall say: Look here, if your father is present select him from our midst. If he selects one of us, attired in our finery, he shall be killed." Again the fly overheard them and informed the boy. When they sent for him, he was told: "Select your father, who is among us." He chose the boy with the sores seated on the rubbish heap, and said: "You may disguise yourself like this, but you are still taata." The people were struck with amazement. Then the villagers said: "Well, we hear he is your father. Go then, tomorrow, and fell a big tree in one single stroke of the axe. If you are unable to fell the tree, he is not your father and you shall die." When he heard this, the boy thought: "How am I to do it? I cannot possibly fell a tree in one stroke." But the borer beetle heard him and went away to help the boy. He bored and bored until the tree was hollowed out clear to the bark without leaving any traces on the outside. All night long he bored and bored and did not sleep.

Came morning, the people called the boy and gave him an axe to fell the ma-hogany tree in one stroke. He went up to the tree, struck an impressive attitude in front of it and struck it, "mapoo." A strong gust of wind helped him so that the tree shuddered and fell to the ground. All who saw it were overwhelmed with wonder. Again the people congregated and called the stranger, and his father appeared, saying: "Yes, I am indeed your father. You have creditably completed the search for the prohibition in your mvila." The son rejoiced. He was also told about his father's mvila. Then he travelled back to earth by the thread of the nzambi spider. The crocodile carried him across the river and the boy returned to his village.

He was very happy and grateful to those who had helped him. He had a full sister whom he wished to give in marriage to one of his helpers. But at this point a quarrel arose among his neighbours. Some of them declared, that the nyanzi fly was to marry the girl, seeing that it had helped him. Others said: "No, the borer beetle is to have her." Others said: "No, the nzambi spider." Others again: "No, the crocodile." Others said: "No the nduutu rodent." Still others, finally, thought the storm should marry the girl—Well, what is your opinion? Who had worked hardest and so should receive the girl in marriage?

The form of the story, although moderately complex, is highly sym-metrical and presents no special difficulties. Analysis of the symbolic content, however, cannot be done on the basis of information contained in the story itself but demands a more general knowledge of Kongo culture.

Inability to recite the praise-name of his father's clan renders the hero vulnerable to a host of difficulties, all of which in the Kongo idiom are conventional images of witchcraft, based on the following general princi-ples. First, because witches are considered to "eat" their victims, there is an analogy between people and foodstuffs. Witches are neighbors and kinsmen who eat their relatives, instead of eating with them, and thus break down normal boundaries, as do wild animals that eat crops intended for domestic consumption. Secondly, men are thought of as being like trees, as a proverb puts it: "God made us like living trees."[3] The analogy is extensive and complex, but for present purposes its main features are that trees, like men, have souls that can be eaten by grubs boring within, like witches; and that trees stand together in the forest as men do in the village, the forest being regarded in various ways as the village of the dead. In the story itself, being cut from a tree (like an ancestor figure) is mentioned as an alternative mode of human existence.

Thirdly, spiritual forces in general, whether approved or disapproved, are said to resemble breeze or wind and are called by the same term, *mpeve* (from *veva*, "to blow"). Birds and flying insects, equipped with wings (*maveve*), personify such forces. Lastly, the verb *kanga*, "to tie," describes the effect of witchcraft; to dream of being corded is to be warned of witchcraft attack and impending death. In addition, although the connection between Nzambi (God) and *nzambi* (spider) is not clear, "the thread of Nzambi" is a conventional expression referring to the inevitability of death.

The agents of the hero's afflictions are divisible into those of the above, or sky, and those of the below, or land, corresponding to two important cosmological categories (*ku zulu, ku nsi*):

> cane eaten by *nduutu* rodent
> pigs eaten by crocodile
> spider thread around face
>
> meat eaten by fly grubs
> houseposts bored by beetle
> bananas and maize ruined by storm.

When the hero sets off to find his father he is assisted across the three intervening zones by rodent, crocodile and spider, each in its own habitat, the last providing a bridge between earth and sky and thus giving the hero access to a village not only *distant* but *elevated* with respect to his own. The rest of the hero's erstwhile persecutors, all of whom are natural denizens of the sky, help him to pass the three ordeals prescribed by the sky people:

> risk of being eaten by lions—fly, beetle
> identification of father—fly
> fell tree with one blow—beetle, storm

In the course of this sequence the hero is transformed from a condition of vulnerability and impotence to one of autonomy and strength. The same images that formerly suggested malevolent witchcraft, notably the beetle boring into wood, become signs of his power. This reversal is consistent with Kongo notions about the ambivalence of power, especially the power to kill (*kindoki*), which is illegitimate if used by witches for their own benefit but legitimate and necessary as used by chiefs for the public good.[4]

The first test is a test of the hero's ability merely to defend himself. The critical shift in his fortunes occurs in the second test when he makes contact with his father by seeing through his disguise. In passing the third test he demonstrates his own destructive capability.

The father's disguise, as a small boy, covered with sores, sitting on a rubbish heap, is a complex one. Throughout Central Africa the rubbish heap is a metaphor for the grave, a point of contact with the world of the dead. Skin diseases, especially those that temporarily or permanently mottle the skin, indicate contact with or a visit to the other world; the dead change their skins completely and become white. The small boy who is really a grown man belongs to a large class of Kongo liminal figures which express the relationship between this world and the other as a difference of generation, that is, as a relationship between father and son, combined into a single figure. The same relationship has already been expressed in the conventions of space by representing father as inhabiting another village (he belongs to a different clan) and as being "in the sky" (of superior generation).

Besides its manifest meaning as a conversation piece, the story has latent meaning both sociological and psychological. The setting is cosmological, employing the symbols of the Kongo universe divided by a river into the two worlds of the living and the dead. Sociologically, the story expresses the banal truth that a man can expect to succeed in life only by exploiting patrilateral links (*kitaata*). As a member of a matrilineal clan his position is in principle fixed by genealogy; as a client of his father's clan he may be able to obtain special privileges. In practice, in Central African societies generally, a man will choose whether to live in the village of his matriclan or in another village where he has patrilateral relatives, depending on the opportunities available to him. The outcome of the story shows the hero transformed from a small boy into the head of his lineage, competent to give his sister in marriage as a reward to one of his clients.[5] Psychologically the story reflects the oedipus complex, both in the sense that the hero achieves maturity by identifying himself with his father and in the sense that recovery of the lost and now deified father restores the balance in a matrilineal society from which father has been "eliminated."[6]

In "The Black Loincloth" the plot is inverted. We find a persecuted *girl* who has lost her *mother* and who undertakes an *involuntary* journey towards an *unknown* goal. This theme is appropriate to a patrilineal society in which children are linked with their polygynous father's lineage through the household of their mother. The heroine's task is to wash a black loincloth until it becomes "as white as cotton." (The French text specifies "kaolin," which in KiKongo would be *mpemba*, a chalky white clay, found in stream beds, which is a sign of the dead and a name for the other world. Undoubtedly "chalk" would be a better translation than "cotton.") Her journey takes her to four different waters which mark the progress of the plot.

Aïwa, the heroine, first reaches a perfectly ordinary stream. The fact that its waters refuse even to wet the cloth is the first sign that this is no ordinary task. Frogs by the stream would perhaps like to speak to her but are unable to.

The second water Aïwa encounters lies in the crotch of a huge silk cotton tree (Ceiba pentandra). It is surrounded by extraordinary signs: the tree itself; a phenomenal vulture perched in the tree; and a society of gigantic ants, talking among themselves. Presuming upon the cultural continuity of the West African forest zone, we may venture to interpret these features from a Kongo point of view. All are immediately recognizable, particularly the figure of the vulture (*mbemba*) on the silk-cotton tree (*m'fuma*). The vulture, which feeds on carrion, is associated with witchcraft, and *m'fuma*, its favorite perch, is conventionally spoken of as a meeting place or market where witches plan their kills or exchange victims (*fumana*, "to assemble, conspire"). The society of ants is likened, on a number of grounds, to the village of the dead. Pools in general are places for communicating with the other world, and hollow trees are both the origin of mankind, in some myths, and the abode of the ancestors, in some rituals. In short, this water is marked by signs of death.

The third water is a stream in a village of sympathetic apes who are distressed by Aïwa's story but unable to help her. Kongo folklore too provides for a village of apes, or else of dogs, on the way to the village of the dead.

The fourth water is reached only after a complex traverse marked by totally abnormal locomotion, both much slower and much faster than usual, through a trackless forest in which all the vegetation talks. After hearing her name called, Aïwa miraculously arrives at a central clearing where there is a banana tree by a small pool, and all is completely silent. The water of this pool accepts the black loincloth but much scrubbing produces no change of color. Aïwa lifts up her voice in song addressed to to her mother, as she did at both the first and the second water. Her mother appears, gives her a white cloth in exchange for the black one, and returns to the sky without saying a word. When Aïwa's wicked stepmother sees the cloth she recognizes it as one of the burial cloths of her husband's first wife.

As in the story of Nzambi's son, the fourth phase of the adventure brings in the vertical dimension representing the difference of generation, although in Dadié's story it is the mother who descends, instead of the child ascending. Moreover it is apparently the parent who names the child, not the reverse. The assistants are missing, as are the overt references to power, in either its illegitimate (witchcraft) or legitimate form (chiefship). Instead, the heroine achieves a passive kind of social recognition as her mother's and more importantly her father's daughter. In this connection the "loincloth" would, in Kongo terms, be highly appropriate, because of its association with the generative organs, but alas! the *pagne* of the French text simply means a woman's wrap or dress, and not a loincloth at all. It does, however, obtain in its white form a specific identity as the shroud of the dead woman, not merely the generalized whiteness of the other world.

In both stories, despite their differences, the basic problem is the same, that of establishing a valued social relationship expressed as a form of communication. In each case a naming is the critical event, hindered by the father's disguise in the Kongo story and in Dadié's by *noise*. As the first water Aïwa hears only frogs croaking. At the second, there are talking ants, but they talk only among themselves. In response to both, Aïwa sings an appeal to her mother. At the third water, the sympathetic apes do talk to her but are unable to communicate anything useful. The fourth water, reached only by crossing a cacophonous jungle, is surrounded by silence, following upon the first significant communication addressed to Aïwa, her name. In Kongo rituals recorded by Laman, the banana tree by the water's edge is a common representation of a soul at the juncture of life and death. The banana "tree" itself, by the abundance of its fruit and the brevity of its life, stands throughout Central Africa for the cycle of human existence.

I have shown that these two stories, one a recent literary work from Ivory Coast and one a Kongo folktale of the turn of the century, have a common structure. They presume similar cosmologies, and their symbolic contents lend themselves in large measure to a common and consistent interpretation derived from Kongo rules. The comparison enhances the interest of the stories.

FOOTNOTES

[1] K. E. Laman, *The Kongo*, Vol. III, Studia Ethnographica Upsaliensia, XII (Uppsala: Almquist and Wiksells, 1962), pp. 61–62. B. Dadié, "The Black Loincloth," in *The African Assertion: A Critical Anthology of African Literature*, ed. A. J. Shelton (New

York: Odyssey Press, 1968), pp. 40–55; originally published in B. Dadié, *Le pagne noir, contes africaines* (Paris: Editions Présence Africaine, 1955).

[2] J. Vansina, "Les zones culturelles de l'Afrique," *Africa Tervuren*, 7, 2 (1961), 41; M. J. Herskovits, "African culture areas," *Africa*, 3, 1 (1930), 47.

[3] "Nzambi Mpungu uyidika beto minti dimoyo." J. Van Wing, *Etudes Bakongo*, 2nd ed. (Brussels: Desclée de Brouwer, 1959), p. 298.

[4] W. MacGaffey, "The religious commissions of the BaKongo," *Man*, N.S. 5 (1970), 27–38.

[5] W. MacGaffey, *Custom and Government in the Lower Congo* (Los Angeles: University of California Press, 1970).

[6] E. Ortigues, "Le message en blanc," *Cahiers internationaux du Symbolisme*, 5 (1967), 75–93; R. Fox, "Totem and Taboo reconsidered," in *The Structural Study of Myth and Totemism*, ed. E. Leach (London: Tavistock, 1967).

Poetic and Gnomic Forms

Iwì Egúngún Chants – An Introduction

OLUDARE OLAJUBU

Iwì Egúngún,[1] a form of Yorùbá oral poetry, is an important genre of the traditional verbal art of the Ọyọ́ Yorùbá.[2] In many ways it is very similar to ìjálá and rárà, two other genres of Ọyọ́ Yorùbá verbal art. It is chanted exclusively by members of the Egúngún cult during the annual Egúngún festivals and during other Egúngún ceremonies and performances. Since iwì is closely linked with Egúngún and the Egúngún cult, some information about both is necessary for the understanding of iwì.

Egúngún[3]

Ancestor worship is an important feature of Yorùbá religion. The worship is based on the firm belief that the spirit of man never dies, but that after death, his spirit continues to influence the life of the community from another sphere. In times of crises or in the face of a challenge, the Yorùbá, like most Africans, summons and invokes the spirits of his ancestors. He swears by the name of his dead father. He ascribes all success in his human endeavors to the support he receives from his ancestors. Every year there is a festival in honor of the dead. During this festival, the spirits of the ancestors are reincarnated and materialized in the form of masquerades known as Egúngún.

The Egúngún appears under a costume known as agọ̀ or ẹ̀kú, a big garment made of beautiful, bright-colored cloth which is worn to cover the head and body. Sometimes an allowance is made for sleeves. A net is fixed to the face to allow the wearer to see. He also wears a pair of trousers and a pair of shoes made of tough cloth. The edges of the shoes are sewn to the edges of trousers so that no part of the leg is exposed. Sometimes leggings of cloth are also worn on the trousers. The form of the agọ̀ varies from one type of Egúngún to the next. But what is essential is that an agọ̀ should be made to cover the entire body of the wearer. No part is left out.

The wearer of the costume is usually a man, never a woman. He always carries a whip, and he speaks in a disguised voice, a coarse, croaky voice which resembles that of a frog. The wearer is usually a seasoned artist and is called an *Òjè*. He should not expose his face or any part of his body in public. His identity is usually kept a top secret. While everybody, male and female, knows that it is a living human being who wears the agọ̀ and is called Egúngún, he is regarded at the same time by the very same people as *ará ọrún*—a being from heaven, one of the ancestors who has come to visit and bless the people. He is referred to as *bàbá* (father). Everybody in the society, old and young, pays him deep respect. It is believed that he can pray for the people to bring them good luck, cure their diseases, give children to the barren woman, and stop an *abiku*[4] from dying. In times of social crisis—drought, famine, epidemics—Egúngún is called upon to appear and carry away the ills of the people. Egúngún is also used to execute criminals and to expel dangerous people from the community. Though Egúngún is the reincarnation of the spirits of the dead ancestors, a particular Egúngún does not necessarily represent the spirit of any particular dead individual. Each Egúngún is symbolic representation of each and all the ancestors.

Egúngún performs various functions among the Yorùbá; apart from those enumerated above, the Egúngún also entertains people, dances, chants poetry and dramatizes. For this reason, there are different forms of Egúngún, each designed to perform specific functions. For instance, there is a form known as *alabẹ̀bẹ̀* (the one with a fan) that dances; a type known as *pàaràká*[5] (the one that goes about) that runs after children and young people flogging whomever he meets; another known as *alágbo* (the one with medicinal concoctions) who goes about praying for people; and yet another form variously known as *onídán*[6] (dramatist), *alárìnjó*[7] (one who dances as he walks) and *agbégijó* (one who dances with wooden masks) who combines dancing with poetry chanting and drama. But in whichever form, all egúngún are regarded as representatives of the ancestors and are therefore revered by the people.

Of all the various forms of Egúngún, the Egúngún *onídán* calls for special mention. While all the other forms of Egúngún appear and perform only during the festival periods, the *onídán* performs all the year round. Such performers go about in groups of six or eight with their children and wives and a troupe of drummers who are usually permanently attached to the group. At each town or village they visit, they stage public performances of dance, poetry chanting and acrobatic display. Because of this, the *onídán* performers become the greatest exponents of Iwì Egúngún chants, and among members of the group and their wives and daughters can be found the best artists of Iwì Egúngún. They are motivated to sing well because members of the group supplement their living with earnings derived from the shows. Nowadays some groups of

Egúngún *onídán* live entirely on the earnings of their performances.

During the shows, the onídán makes use of wooden masks which depict various characters in Yorùbá society which the *onídán* tries to caricature and satirize. The most popular characters include Tápà (the Núpeman), Aṣẹ́wó (the prostitute), the Policeman, Oyinbo (the white man), and Ìyá Ọmọ (a mother). As he wears the mask that depicts each character, the *onídán* dances in a funny manner and imitates some of the odd behavior for which the character is known. For example, the Oyinbo (white man) speaks through his nose in a way that makes it difficult for anyone to understand what he says. This is to ridicule the British and American expatriates in Nigeria whom most Nigerians, including some highly educated persons, find very difficult to understand. They just cannot pick up his words! It is the changing of the *onídán* into these masks that is called *idán* (wonders or magic). The audience would say "o ńpìdán" (He is performing wonders or "making scenes").

Apart from performing from town to town, the *onídán* also performs for important individual members of the society, either voluntarily or by invitation, on festive occasions.

At each show, iwì chanting plays a very major part. The onídán chants as he moves onto the open stage in the marketplace or under the shade of a tree, introducing all his dances and punctuating all his activities with iwì. He depends on these chants to move his audience to give him generous gifts. He also winds up his play with iwì before going home.

There is a secret organization charged with the responsibility of organizing the appearances of the Egúngún and keeping secret the identity of the wearer of the agò. This organization is known as the Egúngún cult. It is essentially a male cult, and no women except an *ato*[8] can be admitted. New entrants into the cult usually undergo an initiation. Every member must swear on pain of death to keep the secrets of the cult and must assist in the effort to make people believe that the man under the costume is not an ordinary human being but one of the ancestors who has come from heaven. The cult is under a titled head known as Alágbààà. He is assisted by other officials, among whom are Alápìnni, Eéṣọrun, Àrẹòjẹ̀, Ọlọ́pọndà, Aláràn and Ọlọ́jẹ̀.

The Egúngún festival comes up once every year between March and June and lasts between a week and three months, the duration varying from place to place. During the festival various types of Egúngún appear in the streets in large numbers in their multi-colored dresses. Each is attended by drummers and surrounded by a large crowd of people made up mostly of wives and daughters of cult members and scores of whip wielding youths. Civic leaders and cult chiefs hold feasts for the Egúngún in rotation. During these feasts, the Egúngún and his followers entertain the patrons and the general public with music, dancing, poetry, drama, and parades in their colorful costumes. Each day of feast is preceded by an all-night iwì poetry chanting during which leading chanters compete for honors and distinction, and amateurs and apprentices try out their voices and skill.

Iwì and other Genres of Yorùbá Oral Poetry

All forms of Yorùbá oral poetry draw from a common source of oral materials for their composition. These oral materials include oríkì (praise names of persons, animals and other things), orílè (praise poems of various lineages and settlements in ancient Yorùbá kingdoms), ìbá (salutes to powers, natural and supernatural, that rule the Yorùbá world), proverbs, incantations, wise saying, clichés and prayers. These verbal formulae are set and cannot be altered or amended by individual artists. All artists are expected to memorize and chant them correctly during public performances. Members of the audience are always eager to reward correct renderings in cash and kind and to punish faulty renderings by way of cold reception and refusal to offer gifts.

Since all artists draw from this common source to compose the different genres, it follows that all the genres would have similar texts. In that case, what then distinguishes one genre from the other?

This brings up to the question of classification of Yorùbá oral poetry and the criteria for distinguishing one form from the other. Many Yorùbá scholars have written on this.[9] The main distinguishing features are as follows: each genre is chanted in a distinct tone of voice which is recognized by the audience; each is chanted by different types of people and on different occasions. For instance, ìjálá is chanted by hunters and devotees of Ògún (the Yorùbá divinity of iron and war) at their meetings and during festivals connected with Ògún. It is usually chanted by men only. Iwì is chanted by members of the Egúngún cult and their wives and daughters during the annual Egúngún festivals and during public performances of the Egúngún *onídán*. Rárà is chanted by professional beggars, minstrels and eulogists and can be chanted at all places and at all times by both male and female. But certainly the most important feature as far as the reader is concerned, since he is concerned with the printed texts, is the content of the texts of each genre. Each genre can be recognized by the type of information that dominates the text and by the order of arrangement of such information. The text can also reflect the nature of the audience, providing a clue to which genre it belongs. Therefore, though iwì shares some measure of similarity with other genres of Ọ̀yọ́ Yorùbá poetry, it is the special methods of composition and the special techniques of performance discussed below that distinguish it as a distinct genre of Yorùbá oral poetry.

Iwì is chanted exclusively by members of the Egúngún cult but not by every member of the cult because it is chanted in a special tone of voice which can only be achieved by talent, practice and skill. For instance, a chanter should be gifted with a sweet voice, and he should have a long repertoire of praise poems of the principal lineages in Yorùbáland. He should have a rich wealth of proverbs, wise sayings, incantations and jokes to draw from. Above all, he should have grown into the art by practice from childhood to adulthood. He should also be familiar with the principal personalities in the society.

There are two categories of chanters. The first category consists of the men who wear the agọ̀.[10] They are known as Ọ̀jẹ̀. Most of them belong to the onídán type of Egúngún. The second category consists of the talented members of the Egúngún cult who do not wear agọ̀. They are called Ẹlẹ́ṣà. A woman can also chant iwì if she is either a wife or daughter of a male member of the Egúngún cult and if she possesses the requisite talents and skill. During the annual Egúngún festivals, and during any Egúngún performance, it is usual for a crowd of men, women and children to accompany each Egúngún. During this time talented male and female members of the crowd chant iwì in praise of their ancestors, the Egúngún. This is the principal time when iwì is chanted. Iwì chanting is also an integral part of any public performance of an Egúngún onídán. Needless to say, in modern times iwì poetry can be chanted for entertainment during civic ceremonies like marriages, burial, and conferment of titles.

Iwì as a Poem: Composition and Performance Techniques

Iwì is a piece of verbal artistic creation having a beginning, a middle and a clear end. The beginning is made up of *ìbà* (homage or salute to powers that be) and other introductory chants. Such introductory chants include the signature tune of the chanter and his personal introduction. The middle is made up of salutes to individuals (oríkì), salutes to lineages (orílè), and comments on various aspects of Yorùbá life. The end is made up of the closing chants and the closing song. It is the duty of the artist making an iwì composition to harmonize the three parts of the iwì poem to produce a distinct form of oral poetry.

For the purpose of study, it is essential to view each iwì performance at a given social occasion to a given audience at a given time as one complete unit of iwì poetry. The length of such poetry can only be conceived in terms of the length of time employed in its performance. This ranges from two to ten hours, depending on the importance of the occasion, the size of the audience, the availability of refreshments and the ability of the artists. For instance, during the festival periods, iwì is chanted all night and all day, but only for few hours on other occasions. But whatever the length of an iwì performance, the structure of its text remains the same.

The iwì artist learns his chants by imitation. The art is usually a family art so that the artist grows into it, learning from the many public performances which his group gives every year. By the time he becomes a master artist, he should have in his repertoire the praise names of all members of the community, the praise poems of the important lineages, proverbs, wise sayings and incantations, all of which he has learnt by imitation over the years. He should also have learnt the sequence and technique of iwì performances. It is essential that he keep strictly to the traditional pattern and content of the chants in his public performances.

But the iwì artist is not a mere carrier of oral traditions or a mere performer reproducing by rote what someone else has composed. He is a creative artist—both a composer and a poet. His is a difficult job for he composes and performs at the same time. There is no time for rehearsal because his composition and performance are both conditioned by the circumstances of the performance.

Iwì is performed in the presence of large audiences in markets and public places. The audience is usually made up of chiefs, elders and nobles, craftsmen, farmers and traders. Some of them come early and stay till the end of the performance, while some leave early. But throughout the performance, people keep on coming and going. To the iwì artist, every member of the audience is important and worthy of his attention. Their patronage is the main impulse and motive behind the whole performance. The instability and variability of the audience, therefore, requires a marked degree of concentration on the part of the iwì artist. It also tests to the utmost his dramatic ability, his narrative skill and his ability to keep his audience for a long time.

Though the iwì artist has a set pattern or order of composing his poem, he must keep his eye on the audience, in composing and performing his chants. He must know the oríkì and orílè of each member of the audience, the names of each member's wives, children and parents. He must be conversant with the current gossip, jokes and happenings. As each guest arrives or departs or offers a gift, so also must he react by singing the praise of the particular guest. In the process of doing this, he may remember a joke which we would like to make, a social misbehavior which he would like to satirize or a moral lesson which he would like to give. He would digress a little to include these. In the process, he may forget to return to his former topic and go on to new themes.[11]

The chant continues for as long as the audience is willing to stay and as long as the audience can sustain the performance by giving gifts of money and drinks to the artists.

The iwì text has a characteristic pattern. Every iwì chant opens with introductory chants which form the beginning of the poem; these consist of the ìbà and the self-introduction of the artist. The ìbà is a set of verbal salutes to the powers that rule the Yorùbá cosmos. To the iwì artist, these powers include the Olódùmarè (the almighty God, usually referred to in iwí as Qlọ́jọ́ òní), the most important Òrìṣà, leaders of the Egúngún cult and the society in general, witches, veteran artists, medicine men and the artist's father.[12]

The body or middle of an iwì is the longest and most important part of the chant. It consists of salutes to members of the audience and their line-ages (called oríkì and orílè), proverbs, fables, prayers, incantations, wise sayings, songs, and jokes. Pieces of these are woven together to form episodes and plots in the chant. Every plot or episode in the chant is di-rected at particular individual members of the audience to please, praise or amuse them.[13]

An iwì chant does not end abruptly. Every performance is rounded off with a valedictory note from the artist. The note, which usually includes prayers and thanks to the audience for the goodwill and gifts, is con-cluded with a fitting song.[14]

An iwì is rendered in two voice patterns. The first is a high tuned voice which is very near to that employed in song. This is usually used by the Egúngún onídán and the eléṣà so most performances of iwì are done in it; in fact, it is the only voice pattern known to many. The second voice pat-tern is a croaky voice, regarded by cult members as the real voice of the Egúngún. Anyone speaking in the second voice speaks only as an Egún-gún and not as a human being. For this reason, the second voice pattern may not be uttered in public except under an agọ̀ by an Egúngún. This voice pattern is difficult to make; therefore, only specialists can chant iwì of any appreciable length with it. However, special talent, training and skill are required to produce any of the voice patterns.

An iwì is performed by a group of people who organize themselves into an orchestra or an ensemble. The orchestra consists of the solo, the chorus and the bàtá drummers. The solo is made up of men and women, usually two or three in each orchestra who have acquired specialization through long years of practice and have developed the longest repertoire. They alternate in singing the lead parts of the chant and from among them the leader of the orchestra is chosen.

The chorus is the group of chanters who sing the songs raised by the lead chanter. It consists of young boys and girls who are usually children or close relations of the lead chanters. Women who are wives or children of the lead chanters are also included.

Each iwì orchestra is homogeneous. Both the solo and the chorus belong to the same *ẹbí*.[15] The fathers, mothers or aunts become leaders— solo singers, while their sons and daughters serve as apprentices—chorus singers. When the leaders become too old to sing or when they die, their children take their places so that each member of the orchestra grows up and gains experience in performance. The drummers may not belong to the same *ẹbí* as the chanters but they must have permanent attachments with the chanters. The role of the drummers is to supply musical accompaniment to the songs raised in iwì. The chief drummer also aids the memory of the lead chanter by supplying him with hints and he encourages the lead chanter by shouting his praise names with his drum.

Every performance is opened by the leader of the orchestra and he chants the lead parts throughout the performance. He is however relieved and complemented by the other solo chanters at various stages of the chant. Sometimes the performance assumes the form of a dialogue among two lead chanters. At the end of each plot or episode in the chant, it is usual for the soloist to raise a song and for the chorus to sing the refrain. If the soloist likes, he can stretch the song for some time. Thus it can be seen that an iwì chant is the result of the joint effort of a team, every part of the team playing its part to build a single poem. This makes it unlike rárà which is a solo effort of an individual singer or ìjálá which is the work of rival artists each struggling to outclass the other.

Language

Iwì, being exclusively a verbal art of the Ọ̀yọ́ Yorùbá, is chanted in the Ọ̀yọ́ dialect and only Ọ̀yọ́ people or those who claim ancestry from Ọ̀yọ́ people chant it. This means that if there are Ìjẹ̀ṣà or Ìjẹ̀bu who chant iwì, they must have descended from Ọ̀yọ́ stock, and such people chant their iwì in Ọ̀yọ́ dilect. Apart from this, there is nothing special about the language of iwì. It employs and enjoys all the known characteristics of the Yorùbá language such as tonal manipulation, lexical matching and lexical borrowing from other languages, particularly from Hausa and English. Above all, the iwì artist employs all the poetic devices of Yorùbá oral poetry—e.g., repetitions and ready-made expressions to fit into particular situations.[16] The situation of the performance of iwì chants and the varied and unstable nature of the audience impose on the iwì artist the temptations of digression and the inconveniences of interruption. The iwì artist, however, tackles all these problems within the framework of his chants. He devises ready poetic expressions with which he answers questions, checks noisemakers and wards off other interruptions without having to stop his chant.

Content

The content of iwì consists mainly of a sequence of praise poems about individuals, gods, and lineage groups, these being interspersed with incantations, benedictions and commentaries on various aspects of Yorùbá life. The content of two other related genres of Ọ̀yọ́ Yorùbá poetry—namely, ìjálá and rárà—is similar. A close examination will, however, reveal that the content of iwì is clearly different from that of other types of Yorùbá oral poetry. For example, apart from the praise poems about individuals, gods and lineages, ìjálá chants also include praise poems about birds, animals, and plants; relate the exploits of hunters in the bush; and devote much attention to Ògún—his praise, his might and his deeds. Rárà, on the other hand, is concerned mainly with the praise and flattery of particular individuals, with the sole aim of attracting gifts from the respective individuals who are the targets of the chants. Hence rárà is a sequence of vivid character sketches and profiles. But iwì is concerned solely with the praise of man—living and dead—and his society. It gives prominence to persons and interpersonal relationships and to attitudes and values derived from the chanter's conception of the world of the Yorùbá. Iwì also tells of the glorious days of the lineages, of heroes of past wars, and of current events and happenings. Unlike ìjálá, iwì is not concerned with animal and plant life nor does it put any particular emphasis on the praise of any particular òrìṣá. And unlike rárà, iwì is not concerned only with particular individuals in isolation but with man in relation to his total environment.

The content of iwì, therefore, consists mainly of salutes: salutes to the gods and the superior beings known as ìbà, salutes to lineages known as orílè, and salutes to individuals known as oríkì. The ìbà consists of salutes to the major òrìṣà like Ṣàngó, Ògún and Èṣú, salutes to the supernatural beings like mother witch and medicine men, and salutes to parents (ancestors), leaders of the cult and of the society, and the forerunners of the artist. The orílè consists of salutes to the major lineages or rather settlements of the old Ọ̀yọ́ Empire. Such lineages include Ìkòyí, Ìrẹsà Ògbojò, Ọ̀fà, Ìkìrun and Ẹ̀rìn. These salutes are made up of praise names and cognomens of the progenitors of the lineages, detailed descriptions of the general habitat of the original home of the lineages and narratives of major events in the history of each lineage. The oríkì (salute to individuals) consists of a series of character sketches and praises of certain individuals. These individuals include the artist himself, his parents, his patrons and members of his audience and of the society in general. Such individuals also include the dead and those who are not physically present at his performance. Each individual has a special poem formed around his person. The salute to an individual invariably ends up or leads to the salute of the lineage to which he belongs. Thus oríkì and orílẹ̀ are closely related.

Oríkì and orílẹ̀ have fixed contents. Though no two artists can chant a given oríkì and orílẹ̀ the same way, yet there is a hard core or recurrent information running through each oríkì and orílẹ̀ which is known to the artist and the audience.[17] All the artist has to do is to recite correctly each oríkì and orílẹ̀. No artist is expected to amend the known content of an oríkì or orílẹ̀. Such amendments are treated as errors on the part of the artist and are frowned on by the audience.

Oríkì and orílẹ̀ form the largest and most important part of iwì. They are regarded by both the artist and the audience as the real chant. But the iwì artist punctuates the various orìkí and orìlé, with another group of chants, the subjects of which are many and varied. They include prayers, songs, witty sayings, jokes and comments on Yorùbá life, and they come in at the end of long chants of oríkì and orílẹ̀, serving as interludes, asides and commentaries. They also afford the artist the opportunity to educate, amuse, thank and pray for his audience. One important feature of the content of this group of chants is that they are original compositions of the artist expressing his own independent views of life and representing his personal contribution to the content of his iwì chant. They are also evidences of his understanding of Yorùbá philosophy. The quality of an iwì artist is measured largely by the content of such compositions.

Though iwì is a form of traditional oral poetry, its content is not static or stereotyped. It keeps changing with different situations. For this reason, no artist can repeat verbatim a chant he has chanted before. Every performance yields a new poem, created on the spur of the moment to satisfy a new audience and a new situation.

Conclusion

Iwì is a distinct form of Ọ̀yọ́ Yorùbá oral poetry, not only because it is chanted exclusively by a special group of people in a special tone of voice but because of its distinct content and style of performance. Its distinctiveness also lies in its elaborate techniques of composition and performance, which blend the poetry with drum music. By employing all the known techniques and devices of Yorùbá oral poetry, iwì emerges as a highly artistic and rich genre of Yorùbá oral poetry.

FOOTNOTES

¹ Iwì Egúngún is known by two other names: Ẹ̀sà and Ògbére. The word iwì should not be confused with *Ewì* which is the general term for all types of Yorùbá poetry.

² Ọ̀yọ́ Yorùbá: a subtribe of the Yorùbá with headquarters at Ọ̀yọ́ and with Aláàfin as the paramount ruler. They inhabit the following administrative divisions: Ọ̀yọ́ North, Ọ̀yọ́ South, Ibàdàn, Ìbàràpá and Ọ̀ṣun, and in Modákẹ́kẹ́ and parts of Orígbó in Ifẹ̀ division, all in the Western State of Nigeria. They can also be found in Ọfà and Ilọrin districts of Kwara State of Nigeria. Both the people and their language are known as Ọ̀yọ́.

³ There are two types of Egúngún connected with ancestral worship in Yorùbáland. The first, known as Egúngún Adó is that type of Egúngún found in Èkìtìland whose costume is a combination of cloth, palm fronds and feathers. The second, known as Egúngún Ọ̀yọ́, is that type of Egúngún found among the Ọ̀yọ́ people whose costume is made mainly of cloth. This paper refers exclusively to the latter.

⁴ In Yorùbáland there is a belief that certain children are born to die, that such children keep coming to the same mother and dying. Any woman who loses her babies consecutively is said to be suffering from Abiku. Such children are given special names—like, Igbékòyí, Dúródolú, and Kòsókọ́. See R. C. Abraham, *Dictionary of Modern Yoruba* (London: University of London Press, 1958), pp. 7–8, and A. B. Ellis, *The Yoruba-speaking Peoples of the Slave Coast of West Africa* (London: Chapman and Hall, 1894), pp. 111–14.

⁵ Meaning, literally, one who roams or wanders about—i.e., one who parades the streets.

⁶ A magician in the sense that the Egúngún is believed to be able to metamorphose into various characters—e.g., ape, royal python, crocodile, policeman, Tapa and prostitute. The idán (magic) is achieved by the Egúngún putting on masks and costumes that would make him look like caricatures of these characters.

⁷ Meaning, literally, "one who dances as he walks or travels"—i.e., a member of a travelling theatre group.

⁸ Name given to the third of the triplets, if female. She is dedicated to the Egúngún and has the privilege of knowing Egúngún secrets. But since women who know Egúngún secrets usually go barren, most Ato wait till menopause before they avail themselves of this privilege.

⁹ Cf. Ulli Beier and B. Gbadamọsi, *Yoruba Poetry* (Ibadan: Government Press, 1959); S. A. Babalọlá, *The Content and Form of Yoruba Ijala* (Oxford: Clarendon Press, 1966), p. 23; E. L. Laṣebikan, "Tone in Yoruba Poetry," *Odu*, No. 2 (1956), p. 35; and Ọlátúndé Ọlátúnjí, "Classification of Yoruba Oral Poetry," (Paper at the Weekend Seminar of Yoruba Language and Literature, Institute of African Studies, University of Ife, December 13–16, 1969).

¹⁰ Also known as èkú—the Egúngún costume.

¹¹ See Appendix II below.

¹² For an example of ibà, see Appendix I below.

¹³ For an example of the middle of an iwì chant, see Appendix II below.

¹⁴ For an example of the end of an iwì chant, see Appendix III (a) and (b) below.

¹⁵ Blood relation.

¹⁶ Cf. Adébóyè Babalọlá, "The Poetic Characteristics of Yoruba Ìjálá Chants," (Seminar paper, Institute of African Studies, University of Ife, Ibadan, 1964); Ọlátúndé Ọlátúnjí, "Tonal Counterpoint in Yoruba Poetry," (Paper presented at the 8th Annual Conference of the West African Linguistic Society, Abidjan, March 1969); E. L. Laṣebìkan, op. cit., pp. 35–36, and "The Structure of Yoruba Poetry," *Presence Africaine*, 8, 10 (1955), 43–50.

¹⁷ Cf. Babalọlá, *The Content and Form of Yoruba Ijala*, p. 25.

APPENDIX I

Ìbà o o o ò ò ò.
Mo ríbá lónǐ, mo ríbàa bòge.
Babàa mi ìbà,
Mo ríbà Eṣu, mo ríbàa Ṣàngó.
Mo ríbàa pẹ́lẹ́bẹ́ ọwọ́.   5
Mo ríbàa pèlèbè ẹsẹ̀.
Mo ríbà àtẹ́lẹsẹ̀ tí ò hurun.
Tó fi dé jọgbọlọ itan.
Ìbà ìyáa mi ọ̀sọ̀rọ̀ngà.
Apamáránkú olókìkí oru,   10
Afínjú àdàbà tí í jẹ lárìn ásà.
Afínjú ẹyẹ tí í jẹ ní gbangba oko.
Ìbà ọmọ afòrurìn.
Ibà Èṣù Láaróyè aràgbó,
Láfián ọmọ ẹlẹ́bọ tí i jorí ẹran.   15
Ọkàkà tí í ṣobìrin yàngìyàngì.
Èṣù dákun má ṣe mi lóde ilẹ̀ yí láéláé.
Mo wá ríbà ríbá.
Mo wá ríbàa babaà mi.
Ọlọ́jọ́ òní mo ríbà lọ́dọ̀ rẹ,   20
Kí n tó máwo ṣe.

ORIN

Ọ̀jẹ̀:   Mo ríbà o
         Mo ríbà a.
         Àtawo àtọ̀gbẹ̀rì
         Mo ríbà a.
Ègbè: Mo ríbà o, mo ríbà a
         Àtawo àtọ̀gbẹ̀rì mo ríbà a.

APPENDIX II
EXAMPLE OF THE MIDDLE OR BODY OF AN IWÌ CHANT

Ọ̀JẸ̀ KǏNÍ:
         O ṣé láyé Ọmọ Abílódeṣú.   *Signalling his take-over*
         O ṣé láyé o ó gbádùn ara.
Ara yíò gbǎdùn rẹ.
Bóyìnbó ti ṣe gbádùn-un bàtà
Báwọn alágbàṣé ṣe gbádùn ilẹ̀ tó bá kún. ⌐ *A witty saying.*   5
Bẹ́ẹ̀ lèmí í ṣe e polódùmarè mi.   ⌐
Adéyẹmí Ọmọ lóógun.
Àkànjí Àgbé, ọba asọ̀lùdẹ́rọ̀.
Àkànjí tó gbárẹ̀mọ rè Bàdàn   *Salute or*
Tó gbákìrun bọ̀ wá núu lé.   *praise to*   10
Adéyẹmí lọ Ámọ́làóyè.   *Adéyẹmí, the*
Òmọ Erínjogúnọlá Ọjọmu ọdẹ.   *Ọba of*
Ọmọ àpèwáàjoye láti wájú o   *Ìkìrun*
Àkànjí nlẹ́ ọmọ ọjà obì.   *(Akìrun)*
Adéyẹmí ọkọ Ṣègilọlá   15
Ọkánjúàa ṣòbìyà, in ṣá lÀkànjí.
Tí ndá mọ lọ́rùn ẹsẹ̀.
Ọmọ Oníkòkò.
Babaa wọn àgbà,

APPENDIX I
EXAMPLE OF THE BEGINNING OF IWÌ–ÌBA

Homage!
I pay homage today, I pay homage to Bòge
Homage to you my father.
I pay homage to Èṣù and to Ṣàngó
I salute the flatness of the palm.   5
I salute the flatness of the feet.
I salute the sole of the feet that grows no hair,
Till the smooth fat part of the thigh.
Homage to, Oṣoronga, my Mother,
Who kills without sending for death. The famous one of the night.   10
An elite of a dove that feeds among hawks.
An elite of a bird who feeds in the open farmland.
Homage to the offspring of the one who walks in darkness
Homage to Èṣù Láaróyè Aràgbó,
Láfian, child of the offerer of a sacrifice who eats the head of the sacrificial animal.   15
Òkàkà that makes a woman rather restless.
Èṣù, please never use me in this town.
I again pay homage.
I again pay homage to my father.
Ruler of today, I pay homage to you,   20
Before I embark on my art.

SONG

Òjè: I pay homage,
          I pay homage.
          Both the initiated and the uninitiated,
          I pay homage.   25
Chorus: I pay homage,
          I pay homage.
          Both the initiated and the uninitiated,
          I pay homage.

APPENDIX II

FIRST ÒJÈ:
Thank you offspring of Abilodeṣu.
Thank you, may you enjoy your body.
May your body enjoy you
As the white man enjoys his shoes,
As the laborer enjoys very weedy farmland.   5
That is how I salute my Lord.
Adéyẹmí, offspring of the brave one.
Àkànjí Àgbé, the king who brings peace to the town.
Àkànjí, who went to Ibàdàn as an Arẹmọ,
Who came back home as an Akinrun.   10
Adéyẹmí, Amọla-Oye, has gone.
Offspring of Erínjógunọlá, the Ojọmu of the hunters.
Offspring of the one who was invited from afar to take a title.
Hello Àkànjí, offspring of the owner of the kolanut market.
Adéyẹmí husband of Sègilọlá.   15
A covetous guinea worm, that was Àkànjí,
That attacks one on the ankle.
Offspring of the owner of the Pot.
Their grandsire

Ló gbé kòkò dénú igbó tán.
In náà ló dirúnmalẹ̀ tí ńgbé Kìrun   *Oríkì orílẹ̀*   20
Nílé ọmọ Erínjogúnọlá ojọmu ọdẹ̀.   *Ìkìrun.*
Àgùntonílàá ọmọ ọjà obì.
ỌJẸ KEJÌ:
E má jẹ́ ó ju méjìméjì lọ
Àlàbí oníbàtáà mi.
Bààmú–ọwọ́–òsì–tẹ́ẹ́rẹ́ baba Kàrímù.   *Personal*   *Salute to*   25
Ọmọ Igbólẹ́rù atìdímu.   *Oríkì*   *Àlàbí*
Òmọ Igbólẹ́ké ojúupa.
Ọmọ èyọ̀ọ, mi èyọ̀.
Ọmọ èyọ̀ tó ti mú Kìrun dòkun   30
Ọmọ èyọ̀ tó ti mu Kìrun dòsà.
Ọmọ èyọ̀ tó ti mú Kìrun dùn gbọ́ngbọ́n.   *Salute or*
Aláìsí ewúrẹ́.   *praise to*
Wọ́n sọgbà síloro.   *Àlàbí my*
Àìsí àgùtàn,   *Bàta Drummer.*
Wọ́n sọgbà á yàrà.   *Orílẹ̀ Ìkìrun*   35
Àìsínlé Inálowúwà
Wọ́n sọgbà Sọ́ńtokí
Lánùmí, mọ oníkẹmbẹ tí í légún-ún lọ.
Mo gbàaròo n ò sebẹ́ nisàlẹ̀ Isán.
ỌJẸ̀ KÍNÍ
Òótọ́ ni bẹ́ẹ náà ni.   *Signalling his take-over*
Bẹ́ẹ ni mo se ńpe Adé'ẹmí,
Àkànjí àgbé.   *More salutes to*
Ọba díẹ̀ k'Ákirun.   *Adeyẹmi the Ọba*
Ọmọ oníkeníirin   *of Ikìrun* (Akirun)   45
Àgbà àgùntonílàá ọmọ rọjà obì.
Alóólódù ọkọ Sẹ̀gi.
Adéyẹmí ọmọ lóógun.
Àkànjí àgbé ọba asòlúdẹ̀rọ̀.
ỌJẸ̀ KEJÌ
Ẹ má jẹ́ ó ju méjìméjì lọ.   *Signalling his take-over.*   50
Òkété-sa-bi-ó-le-gbé Adédìjí.   *Oríkì of his grandfather Adédìjí*
Babaà mi àgbà ló kọ́ mi lọ́fọ̀ kan àjímọ́ọrọ́.
Ẹ tún wá bi mí ẹ ní kí ni?
ỌJẸ̀ KÍNÍ
Bó bá ti rí o làdí ẹ̀ han ni.   *Introducing an*
                                     incantation.
ỌJẸ̀ KEJÌ
Wọ́n ní, alóló alòló.   55
Àtirọ̀run àkàlà.
Ojú ro wọ́n tòkí.
Ló dífá fún olómitútù   *Incantation*
Tí ńsobìrin Àgbọnìrègún.   *and*
Èdìdì àlọ̀.   *Prayer*
Ifá ò ní polómitútù kó pupa.   60
Ẹ ẹ̀ ní bá wọn kúkú ọ̀wọ́wọ̀ láéláé.
ỌJẸ̀ KÍNÍ
Èmi gàan ó máa sàmín àsẹ
Mo ní, nítorí péyín téégún fí í jobì
Abẹ́ asọ ló ńgbé.   65
Eyín tókètè fí í pakurọ.   *Commentary*
Ọmọ rẹ̀ ní í fí í hàn.

Carried pots to the forests.   20
Which later became spirits that lived at Ìkìrun.
In the household of Erínjogúnọlá, Ọjọmu of the hunters.
Àgùntọnílàá, offspring of the owners of the kolanut market.
SECOND ỌJẸ̀:
Don't let it exceed two at a time.
Àlàbi my bàtá drummer,   25
One with a mark across the left cheek father of Kàrimù
Offspring of the dreadful forest.
Offspring of Igbólẹ́kẹ́
Offspring of Ẹ̀yọ̀, my Ẹ̀yọ̀
Offspring of the Ẹ̀yọ̀ that turns Ìkìrun to an ocean.   30
Offspring of the Ẹ̀yọ̀ that makes Ìkìrun very sweet.
Without goats,
They made a fence across the lane,
Without sheep,
They made a fence across the ravine,   35
Because Inalowura was absent,
They made a fence across Ontoki
Lámùmí, offspring of the one with big trousers that pursues an army.
I hired a fireplace, I made no soup down there at Isàn.
FIRST   ỌJẸ̀:
It is true, so it is,
That is how I salute Adé'ẹmí
Àkànjí Àgbé.
Akìnrun is no little king
Offspring of possessor of both plastic and iron.   45
Àgùntọnílàá, the old one, offspring of the owners of the kolanut market.
Owner of both money and safe husband of Sègi
Adéyẹmí son of the brave one
Àkànjí Àgbé, the king who restores peace to the town.
SECOND   ỌJẸ̀:
Don't let it exceed two at a time.   50
Adediji, a rodent who selects its own abode.
It is my grandfather who taught me an incantation, useful for daily recitation.
Now ask me, say, what is it?
FIRST   ỌJẸ̀:
Explain how it is.
SECOND   ỌJẸ̀:
They say, alóló alòló   55
When the àkàlà was to go to heaven
It was very painful to them.
That was the divination that came for Olómitútù
Who was wife to Agbọnìrègún.
Èdìdì àlọ̀.   60
Ifá will not kill Olómitútù and make it red
You will never die of smallpox.
FIRST   ỌJẸ̀
I too will say "amen so let it be"
I say this because the teeth with which the masquerade eats kolanut
Abide under the mask.   65
The teeth used by rodent to break the palm
It is to its child it will reveal them.

Eyín tí babaà mí fí í jobì,
Mé fi han-ẹnì kan.
Àkànjí Àgbé mọ Ìrán-dùn-tó-tó-ó-jó.   **70**
ỌJẸ KEJÌ
Ọmọ Abílódeṣù máa gbọ́ wàsíì mi.   *Announcing his take-over.*
Wọ̀nrànwọnràn ní òṣùká ⎤
Ọmọ àyán-án-fìlù-ọ̀tẹ̀-pẹ̀ ⎬ *His personal Oríkì*
Bí kò bá sí ikú,   ⎦
Àdìsá, máa gbọ́ wàsíì mi.   **75**
Ẹni mẹ́ta ni ìbá pe'raarẹ̀ l'Ọ́lọ́run ọba.   *Introducing an Epigram; note the dialogue style.*
Ẹ wá bi mí, ẹ ní ta ni?
ỌJẸ KÍNÍ
Eléwo ni
Bó bá ti rí o làdí ẹ̀ han ni.
Torí àṣípayá lóbìnrínn í ṣílẹ́kùn éémọ.   **80**
ỌJẸ KEJÌ:
Olówó ìbà pẹ'raarẹ̀ l'Ọ́lọ́run Ọba
Olóògùn ńkọ́?
Ibá pe'raarẹ̀ l'Ọ́lọ́run Ọba.
Àlùfáà ńlá ìbá pe'raarẹ̀ l'Ọ́lọ́run Ọba.   *An epigram.*
Níjọ́ ikú ó bǎ polówó.   **85**
Owó ò ní ṣiṣẹ́.
Níjọ́ ikú ó polóògùn,
Agádágodo ni,
Gbètugbètu ni,
Àkáábá ni,   **90**
Àbà ni;
Àní gbogbo ẹ̀ níí ó mà wọmi.
Ijó ikú ó pààfáà ńlá,
Ẹ̀fúúfù lẹ̀lẹ̀ a máa gbé tákàààdá ẹ lọ.
ỌJẸ KÍNÍ:
Òótọ́ ni bẹ́ẹ̀ náà ni.   **95**
Ikú pa babaláwo,
Bí ẹni tí ò kọ́ Ifá.
Ikú polóògùn
Bí ẹni tí ò lóògùn.
Ikú ló pààfáà ńlá,   **100**
Bí ẹni tí ò ké s'Ọ́lọ́run Ọba.   *Wise saying.*
Mo wòkè,
Mo wòsàlẹ̀.
Mé è rọ́ba méjì tí í j'Ọ́lọ́run Ọba.
Kò sọ́ba bíi Bàlárátù tí í jóńṣẹ́ ńlá.   **105**
ỌJẸ KEJÌ
Òótọ́ ni bẹ́ẹ̀ náà ni.
Ẹ má jẹ́ ó ju méjì-méjì lọ. ⎤ *Signalling his take-over.*
Ó dorí Ráájí Àjàlá ọmọ ewé ojúmọ́lá.
Ǹlẹ́ Olóbùró òdodo
Èdè ilé Òbùró mọ gbẹ̀bìọ̀kúnọ́là,   **110**
Ọmọ agbẹ̀bí ile gbẹ̀bí òde.
Mọ agbẹ̀bí ẹranko gbẹ̀bí èèyàn.   *Oríkì*
Ọmọ ọsán pọ́n ganrínganrín.   *Orílẹ̀*   *Salute to*
Kẹ́ni má kò tòde àwọn lọ.   *Olóbùró*   *Ráájì Àjàlá*
Ọmọ oòrún kan tàrí gbọ̀ngbọ̀ngbọ̀n   **115**
Kẹ́ni má gba t'Àágberí.

The teeth used by my father to eat kolanuts
I don't reveal it to anyone.
Àkànjí Àgbé, offspring of the grand show that befits one's participation.   70
SECOND ÒJÈ:

Offspring of Abílódeṣù, listen to my words.
One with disordered head pad.
Offspring of one who the drums hail with rebellious strains.
But for death,
Àdìsa, listen to my sermon.   75
Three persons would have designated themselves, God the King.
Now ask me, say, who are they?

FIRST ÒJÈ:

Who are they?
However it may be, explain it
Because a woman will always open wide the door of the feared one.   80

SECOND ÒJÈ:

A rich man would have designated himself, God the King.
What of the medicine man (the Doctor)?
He would have designated himself, God the King
The great priest, would have designated himself, God the King.
On the day death would kill the rich man   85
Money would be of no avail
On the day death would kill the medicine man
The charm that locks up man's intentions,
The one that stupefies one
The one that makes one look like a fool   90
The one that arrests one's movements.
Indeed, everything will perish.
On the day death will kill the great priest,
Gentle winds will carry off all his papers.

FIRST ÒJÈ:

It is true, it is perfectly so,   95
Death kills a herbalist
As if he learns no Ifá
Death kills the medicine man
As if he possesses no charms.
Death kills a great priest   100
As if he does not cry unto God the King.
I look up
I look down below
I see no two kings known as God the King.
No king like Bàlárátù who is called the doer of great deeds.   105

SECOND ÒJÈ:

It is true, it is perfectly so.
Don't let it exceed two at a time
It is now the turn of Rááji Àjàni offspring of a certain leaf.
Hello Olóbùró the true one
Knowledgeable one of Òbùró who takes child deliveries free.   110
Offspring of one who takes child deliveries both at home and outside the home.
Offspring of one who takes child deliveries for both man and animal.
When the sun is high up in the sky,
Let no one walk across the front of their house.
When the sun is directly at the center of the head,   115
Let no one pass through Àágberí.

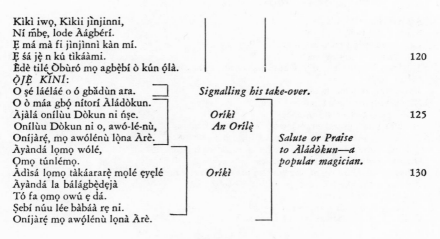

Kìkì iwọ, Kìkìi jìnjinní,
Ní mbẹ, lode Àágbérí.
Ẹ má mà fí jìnjìnnì kàn mí.
Ẹ śá jẹ̀ n kú tìkáàmi.
Èdè tilé Ọbùró mọ agbẹ̀bí ò kún ọ́là.
ỌJẸ̀ KÍNÍ:
O ṣé láéláé o ó gbǎdùn ara.   *Signalling his take-over.*
O ò máa gbọ́ nítorí Àládòkun.
Àjàlá onílùu Dòkun ni ṣe.   *Oríkì*
Onílùu Dòkun ni o, awó-lé-nù,   *An Orílẹ̀*
Oníjàrẹ́, mọ awólénù lọ̀na Àrè.   *Salute or Praise*
Àyàndá lọmọ wólé,   *to Àládòkun—a*
Ọmọ túnlémọ.   *popular magician.*
Àdìsá lọmọ tàkáararè mọlé ẹyẹlé   *Oríkì*
Àyàndá la bálágbèdẹjà
Tó fa ọmọ owú ẹ dá.
Ṣebí núu lée bàbáà rẹ ni.
Oníjàrẹ́ mọ awọ́lénù lọnà Àrè.

120

125

130

APPENDIX III
EXAMPLES OF THE END OF IWÌ

a. Un ó ṣe
  Un ó relé
  Ọdẹ́ ńṣe gbérèé apó ńlé.
  Àgbẹ̀ ńṣe gbérèé òjò
  Iyáa mí ńṣe gbérèéè mi.
  Wọ́n ńṣe gbérèéè mi nínúu lée wa.
  Àgùnbẹ́ onílẹ̀ obì.
  Ọmọ iṣú jinná n sán bọnu,
  Òwè ṣe rẹ̀rẹ̀ gbilẹ̀ n'Isàn.
Orin
  Ọ̀jẹ̀: A ó lọ,
      Kẹ́ ẹ mọ́ pá ò dá-gbére mọ́.
  Ègbè: A ó lọ,
      Kẹ́ ẹ mọ́ pá ò dá-gbére mọ́.
  Ọ̀jẹ̀: A ó lọ o.
      Kẹ́ ẹ mọ́ pá ò dá-gbére mọ́.
  Ègbè: A ó lọ.
      Kẹ́ ẹ mọ́ pá ò dá-gbére mọ́.
  Ọ̀jẹ̀: Akérébúrú ọmọ Jálugun
      Ijó inú ẹ̀kú, ẹrù niyọ̀
      Ọ̀jẹ̀ tí í jó bí alágbàálẹ̀.
  Ègbè: A ó lọ.
      Kẹ́ ẹ mọ́ pá ò dá-gbére mọ́.
  Ọ̀jẹ̀: Iwọ̀n-ọ̀n lú là á ṣèlú,
      Akérébúrú, bá a bá ti lówó sí,
      Leégún fi í jó fún ni í mọ.
      Mo níjó ọlọ́jà lọ́tò.
      Kẹ́ ẹ mọ́ pá ò dá-gbére mọ́.
  Ègbè: A ó lọ,
      Kẹ́ ẹ mó pá ò dá-gbére mọ́.
b. Ọ̀jẹ̀: Aláré mo júbà o
      Ìnlé o Àjèjé

5

10

15

20

25

All poisons, all maladies,
Exist at Àágberí,
Do not afflict me with any malady,
Just let me die on my own   120
The knowledgeable one of Òbùró offspring of the one who takes child deliveries free.
FIRST ỌJẸ:
Thank you very much, may you enjoy yourself.
Now listen for the sake of Àládòkun.
Àjàlá, he is Dòkun's drummer.   125
He is Dòkun's drummer, one who broke down houses.
Oníjàrẹ offspring of one who broke down houses at Àrè.
Àyàndá is the offspring of one who broke down houses.
Offspring of one who rebuilt houses.
Àdìsá is the offspring of one who on his own built a nest for pigeons   130
Àyàndá is the one who fought with the blacksmith,
And broke his hammer.
I think it is in your father's household.
Oníjàrẹ one who broke down houses at Àrè.

APPENDIX III
EXAMPLES OF THE END OF IWI

Ọjẹ:	I will now be done.
	I will go home.
	The hunter longs for the quiver at home.
	The farmer longs for the rain;
	My mother longs for me. 5
	They all long for me in our household.
	Agunbẹ, offspring of the owner of kolanut plantation.
	Offspring of the place where one waits for the yam to be done before eating it.
	Bean leaves blossom green at Iṣan.
Song:	
Ọjẹ:	We will be going, 10
	Lest you say we have not bade you goodbye.
Chorus:	We will be going,
	Lest you say we have not bade you goodbye.
Ọjẹ:	I say we will be going,
	Lest you say we have not bade you goodbye. 15
Chorus:	We will be going.
	Lest you say we have not bade you goodbye.
Ọjẹ:	Akereburu son of Jalugun
	Dance inside Ẹkụ, the ponderous one.
	An Ọjẹ that dances as one who has received an advance payment. 20
Chorus:	We will be going.
	Lest you say we have not bade you goodbye.
Ọjẹ:	The affairs of a town are managed according to its size.
	Akereburu, it is according to the strength of one's purse.
	That an Egungun performs for one. 25
	I have a special dance for the village head
	Lest you say we have not bade you goodbye.
Chorus:	We will be going,
	Lest you say we have not bade you goodbye.
Ọjẹ:	I pay homage to you singers
	Hello Ajeje,

```
                N ó máa fèyí ṣè lọ
                Kò búrú kò bàjé
                A ò ní féégún eléyì ṣàṣemọ                        5
                Ìpé tá a pé rèwerèwe
                Ìpò tá a pọ̀ ní mọ̀gbà
                Idùnmú la á kàn a à láburú ú rí
                Èmi Ọ̀jẹ̀ Àkànó mọ jìngín-là-á-gbọ́wọ́ọ-jó.
                N ó jéré délé                                     10
                Gbogbo yín ẹ ó jèrè délée tèyin
                N ó jéré délé tèyin
Ẹgbé          N ó jèrè délée tèmi
Ọ̀jẹ̀:        Èmi rábẹsá ọkọ Adédoyin
                Ọ̀jẹ̀ tí í sọ dídùn baba ọ̀rọ̀                  15
                N ó jèrè délé
Ẹgbé:        N ó jèrè délée tèmi
Ọ̀jẹ̀:        Èmi jìnnìjìnni l'Ágbé mọ Wòírà
                Nílé ọmọ abélépopọ́n
                Nílé ọmọ abélépopọ́n
                N ó jèrè délé                                     20
Ẹgbè:        N ó jèrè délée tèmi.
```

I will be going with this.
It is neither bad nor ill.
This egungun festival will not be our last.   5
As we gather here as youths,
As we are many here as elders,
It is gladness we shall meet, we have nothing evil to see.
I, Akano the Ọjẹ̀, offspring of one who gracefully raises his hand in dance
I will reach home with blessings.   10
All of you will reach your homes with blessings
I will reach home with blessings.
Chorus: I will reach my home with blessings.
Ọjẹ̀:   I, the plain-faced one, husband of Adedoyin
          The Ọjẹ̀ who says sweet things, the best of words.   15
          I will reach my home with blessings.
Chorus: I will reach my home with blessings.
Ọjẹ̀:   I, the feared one of Agbe, offspring of Woira
          In the household of one whose complexion is like palm oil.
          I will reach home with blessings.   20
Chorus: I will reach my home with blessings.

Pattern and Choice in Berber Weaving and Poetry

The genres of verbal art found in Tamazight, the Berber language of central Morocco, include several which have been collected and published as Berber poetry.[1] This paper develops a structural analogy between these genres and another element of the culture, the weaving, which seems to illuminate certain aspects of poetic structure. The analogy was originally proposed as an afterthought in the final paragraphs of a previous paper, where it was summarized as follows:[2]

> The novice weaver and the amateur singer approach their creative tasks with all the traditional patterns and units that they have encountered in daily use throughout their lives. The way in which they combine these materials and use the traditional patterns to create new compositions is a matter of individual talent and application. Poets (men) and master weavers (women) are distinguished from novice and amateur by their superior products, but the difference is one of degree, not of type. Their works are not signed, and the best work is added to the tradition. Singing and weaving are common activities, and the common traditions of the Imazighen

provide the means for singers and weavers alike to exercise whatever creativity they may possess in their pursuit.

It should first be made clear that recordings, transcriptions, and translations of "Berber poetry" are secondary representations of what is primarily an oral art, manifested in performance and stored in memories. Performance implies an occasion and an audience, and in Morocco it may also involve, depending on the genre, a more or less musical form, the use of instruments, handclapping, dancing, or other specific behavior by the performers and the audience. The "poetry" is only the verbal component of what is actually a complex event belonging to a genre which is defined and distinguished from co-existing genres by its total structure and function within the society, not only by its verbal form and content. For an outsider to define the genres and even begin to understand them, these complex events must be studied within their cultural context. The structural analogy presented here could hardly have been drawn from the poetry extracted out of context, since it depends on the manner of composition and performance as well as on the form and content.[3]

The two poetic genres of primary concern here are the popular song performances commonly called *izlan*, and the longer moralistic poems of the type called variously *tanš:at:*, *tamdiazt*, or *taif:art*. The following description omits many aspects, such as musical form, which are not crucial for the purposes of this paper.

In its broadest sense *izlan* (sg. *izli*) designates lyric couplets of several kinds: the more traditional *izlan n tarišt*, which have a ceremonial function,[4] and the nonceremonial *izlan n tairi*, or love verses. The same term, *izlan*, is also used to describe the performance of a constellation of the love verses with a refrain (*lya* or *tlaut*). In the *izlan* performance, the couplets are sung by two opposing persons or groups which alternate in singing lines and in introducing succeeding stanzas from a common stock of well-known couplets, interweaving them with the refrain in a complex performance pattern to be illustrated below. To call such a constellation "a song" would imply more unity and permanence than it actually has, since the same couplets may never again occur with the same refrain and with each other—unless, of course, the performance has been recorded.

Professional groups record *izlan* for the national radio agency and also for commercial 45-rpm disques, but their main medium is personal appearance at public and private festivals. A typical professional group consists of the leader (*šix*), a man who plays a stringed instrument, composes, and sings; his more or less regular male companion who plays drum and sings; and two to four female entertainers hired for the occasion, who sing "against" the men and also dance.[5]

Nonprofessional performances of *izlan* also involve two persons or groups, but they may be of the same sex. In a typical festival, these are local or tribal groups of two to as many as twenty young men, using the same type of drum but without stringed instruments. If the occasion is not too public, girls and women of the families may form one group of singers, or they may be in a separate house or tent, singing *izlan* with the *al:un* and the ceramic drum called *t:ariža*.[6] The element of opposition is always present, minimally in the two groups' alternation in choosing stanzas and singing alternate lines, more intensely when the groups compose stanzas against each other. Competition reaches its height in the formal battle of composers (*imṛyi imdiazn*) of different tribes, in the context of the circle dance–song event called the *aḥidus*. Here the most skilled poets compose on a given theme with lyric couplets composed *ad hoc* and laced with insult. In all of these contexts, it is vital that the basic unit, the lyric couplet or *izli*, be a self-contained unit, whether it be one of the well-known stock or one composed for the occasion.

The second genre of interest here, the *tanš:at:*, is a long (usually 60 to 90 lines) moralistic poem performed by its composer (referred to as *anš:ad*, but addressed as *šix*) with two companions. The *anš:ad*, as a tribal poet with a special gift or *baraka*, commands respect; his opinions, expressed in his verse, on religion, recent history, and current manners, morals, and politics, are considered to be quite influential.[7] In composing his poems without benefit of writing, constructing them in his head as he works at other tasks, the *anš:ad* often incorporates parts of previous poems. He may borrow a felicitous line, a successful introduction, or a larger block of lines developing a particular theme. When he performs, perforce from memory, he may rearrange lines or blocks of them from their order in a previous performance. This interchange is facilitated by the fact that the lines tend to be independent units, grammatically and semantically, or dependent at most on one adjacent line. No real stanzaic structure is apparent, although the poet breaks his performance into groups of three to five or six lines by having his companions repeat a line. This allows him to catch his breath and rest his voice very briefly, and "think into" the next line. Although the breaks usually come at suitable points in the development of his theme, they might come at different points in another performance.

Thus for a *tanš:at:* as for a performance of *izlan*, the process of composition continues in the performance as memory supplies the previously learned or created elements to be fitted into the performance structure.

With this background on the poetic genres involved we may examine more closely the suggested analogy between their composition and the weaving craft. The analogy is suggested by the poetry itself, in which the poet and his metier are frequently represented by images from weaving. In one *tanš:at:* the poet presents himself as a woman weaving, bringing to birth the next motif even as she finishes the one in front of her. In another, the topic about to be broached is described as a loom ready for the weft. Similar figures occur in the *izlan*; they are consistent with the general use of homely images drawn from daily life. The poet may refer to himself as a humble beast of burden carrying seeds to be sown, or put down an unskilled opponent as an untrained colt spoiling the fantasia game of the horsemen.[8]

The weaving imagery is particularly apt in that both weaving and the composition and performance of poetry are creative acts highly valued in the society and practiced frequently by a substantial number of its members, within the customary bounds of age and sex. Basically, weaving is done by women and girls, the tribal or professional poets are men, and the *izlan* are sung by the young men and by females of all ages. But the boundaries circumscribing these activities are breached in several ways. Women do compose poetry, both in these and other genres,[9] and both sexes and all age groups live with the products of both activities. Children are brought to the festivals and first feel the rhythms of the *izlan* on their mothers' backs where, tied in shawls, they bounce as the women dance.

As for the weaving, although men do not weave, they are deeply concerned with it. The highly decorative garments and coverings (shawls, djellabas, rugs, blankets, cushions, saddle blankets and bags, tent curtains, etc.) produced by the women of the household have economic and esthetic value, whether sold or used to furnish the home and clothe its members, or given as important gifts. The whole family shares in the pleasure and pride of possessing or giving these objects, or in acquiring a bride who knows the traditional motifs (*ilqḍn*) with which they are decorated.

These motifs are bands or rectangles of highly abstract geometrical design, identified by names which suggest their representational value: "Foot of the lion," "Tray and glasses," and the like.[10] They occur in infinite combinations, against the plain background color, usually dark red or natural wool, from which they are often separated by plain narrow bands of black or orange wool. The motifs themselves are executed in a wider variety of colors, including the home-dyed red, black, and orange wools, plus cotton floss purchased at the market in white, purple, and occasionally green. Smaller pieces, such as cushions and saddlebags, are often trimmed with small metal sequins (*muzun*) dangling from bright floss.

Thus the poetic references which compare the work of composing to weaving rest on parallels in the society's values as well as on the obvious fact that both are creative acts. But the full import of the poetic analogy becomes apparent only when the performance structures of the poetry are analyzed and compared to the weaving process and its product. The processes of composition in both the poetry and the weaving have some striking similarities:

    1. The existence of a stock of commonly known, more or less traditional elements (the couplets of the *izlan*; the weaving motifs).

    2. The practice of selecting elements from this common stock at will, and combining them with a unifying theme (the refrain of the singing performance; the background field of plain color into which the motifs are set).

    3. The uniqueness of the resulting constellation of elements and theme, which will probably not recur unless it is reproduced in other media (recordings of *izlan*; pictures of weaving).

    4. The unmistakable identification of such a unique constellation of independent elements and unifying theme, as an example of its genre, exhibiting the genre's characteristic duration or size, temporal or spatial rhythm, and properties of balance and tension which stop short of perfect symmetry.

The first three similarities have been suggested in the preceding discussion; the fourth must be substantiated by a deeper examination of the structures involved, with examples which will also serve to illustrate and perhaps clarify the earlier points. Let us focus first on the aspect of symmetry mentioned in (4), since it is particularly in this aspect that Berber poetry and weaving differ from Western expectations. If one looks for continuity between stanzas of an *izlan* performance, or bisymmetry in a rug or blanket, he may be led to make evaluations which are meaningless in the cultural context.

Taking first the *izlan*, one can discern a general theme of love and passion which characterizes the genre. Other than this there is no necessary connection in sense or story between one stanza of a performance and the next, except in contests with set themes. Even there the end result is not a unified "poem," but a completed event, a contest from which victor, vanquished, and audience carry away their personal satisfactions or chagrin, along with the more memorable of the couplets produced. In the non-contest *izlan* performance, the leader or first group to sing selects a refrain from those currently popular, or an old favorite. The refrain establishes a rhythmic and melodic pattern into which the stanzas are fitted. The choice of stanzas is apparently restricted only by the length of line, which must approximate that of the refrain, but words may be compressed or dropped, or repeated, or line-fillers added, and normal stress may be skewed, to accommodate the verbal content to the musical line.[11] The latter is inflexible, being marked strongly by drum, handclapping, or beating on any resonant surface available, all of which express the imperative internal rhythm experienced by the participants.

The thematic independence of the stanzas is exemplified in both examples of *izlan* performances which follow. The balance and tension appear only in the performance pattern: that is, the temporal order in which the lines of stanzas and refrain are introduced by the alternating groups. In the first example, recorded in Oulmes in 1965, three young men are amusing themselves in their quarters on a Saturday night by singing and drumming on suitcases. Only one is a good singer; the other two are from the Zemmour area, where contact with urban culture has greatly reduced the occurrence of *izlan* in comparison to the Middle Atlas regions. They do not know the refrain or enough couplets to provide a stanza, and so must take a passive role; the performance pattern schema which follows the verbal content indicates that they simply respond with part of the refrain. (In the schema, parts of lines are cited, but full lines are represented by their letter-number indices. Read from left to right for temporal order.)

First example of an izlan performance
Refrain:
    Ra   wa, hya! ay atay, aha! wa, hya! a n:ânaâ, aha!
    Rb   awa, yiwi-š ubr:ad; atay ur tḥlim s uaman.
           Hey, hey! O tea, aha; hey, hey, O mint, aha!
           O the teapot needs you; tea's no good with only water.
Stanzas:
    S1 a   a wayd-it:d:un, a Ṛb:i, dau uašal s amd:ak:ul;
        b   ayn:a xd:mn, ad as-t-iâaun, a ui.
        Would to God I were going underground to my friend;
        Whatever work he's doing, I would help him with it.[12]
    S2 a   haɣaš taunza g r:hn, ad ur š-in:-itf:ur
        b   umarg, ak:-zlin g ubrid ur ts:ind, a ui.
        Here's my forelock in pledge that passion won't follow you
        And cause you to lose your way on an unknown path.[13]
    S3 a   amarg am: r:ami; ad:ai d-ištg wul taṣ:iat:,
        b   yali âari ak:-id-inɣ, a luḥš, a ui.
        Passion is like a marksman; when the heart ponders the hunt
        It rises up to the summit to kill you, O wild beast.

S4 a   d:ix-d g ubrid, audx abr:m, an:aix iyrm
   b   u usmun; t:ut:in z:igi imṭ:aun, a ui.
        I went down the road, I came to a turn, I sighted the house
        of my companion; tears began to fall from me.

Performance pattern:

Group Z (2 males)	Unison	Group M (1 male)	
Ra.2 wa hya!		Ra.2 a n:anaa, aha!	
		Rb, S1	
Ra.1 wa hya!		Ra.1 ay at:ay, aha!	
Ra.2 wa hya!		Ra.2 a n:anaa, aha!	
	Rb	S2	
Ra.1 wa hya!		Ra.1 ay at:ay, aha!	
Ra.2 wa hya!		Ra.2 a n:anaa, aha!	
	Rb	S3	

and so forth, until the tape ran out, after the fourth stanza.

The second *izlan* performance was recorded in 1972 during the national holiday celebrating the Alaouite dynasty and the present ruler, King Hassan II, and incidentally the success of the preceding week's referendum on a new constitution. The professional musician, Lfn:an Mulay Driss, asked us to record the verses he had composed for the occasion, and took us to the house of a *šixa* (female entertainer) for the recording. As soon as it was her turn to initiate an *izli* she quite predictably introduced a well-known one on the usual theme of love, and from then on, the nationalistic theme was abandoned except in the refrain.[14] Here is the verbal content:

Second example of an izlan performance
Refrain:
   Ra   a, d:ustur, inžh, a ua;
   Rb   a, Mulay lḤasan, ifrḥ š:âb.
         The Constitution has succeeded, everyone!
         Milord Hassan, the populace is pleased.
Stanzas:
   S1 a   a Mulay lḤasan, d ib:atnx ay tgid!
      b   Ṛb:i at:-iâun, igas r:ay d yuk:!
           Milord Hassan, you truly are our father!
           God aid you and make your word indivisible!
   S2 a   a mid:n, may i-tbṭ:um d wayd-rix?
      b   wax:a ixḍa, rix nk: ad as-nt:ṣbar.
           O people, why do you part me from my love?
           Although he's wrong, I would keep on forbearing.

S3　a　mad ul-nš as-ax-tt:ud, a wayd-rix?
　　b　mad is il:a maun išučn tiḥrga?
　　　　Was it your heart's will that you forget me, love?
　　　　Or did someone make you forget by witchcraft?
S4　a　ay inžda, maun-it:ini wayd-rix?
　　b　is ax-ira, mad nk: ay t-iurz:un?
　　　　O passers-by, what does my true love tell you?
　　　　Does he want me, or am I the one who's seeking?

The performance pattern is quite symmetrical. After a short prelude (*tq:sim*) played by the *šix*, he and his drummer begin with the refrain; then they introduce their patriotic *izli* as the first stanza, feeding the first line to the *šixa*. She repeats it, and the men sing the second line; the *šixa* responds with the first line, and they repeat the exchange several times, adding the refrain after each line, before going on to the next stanza. The schema is as follows:

Male group	Female
Ra, Rb; S1a; Ra, Rb	S1a; Ra, Rb
S1b; Ra, Rb	S1a; Ra, Rb
S1b; Ra, Rb	

Instrumental interlude: instruments, handclapping

	Ra, Rb; S2a; Ra, Rb
S2a; Ra, Rb	S2b; Ra, Rb
S2a; Ra, Rb	S2b; Ra, Rb

Instrumental interlude as before: audience cries approval: "tbark l̩:ah, a Mulay Driss" etc.

Ra, Rb; S3a; Ra, Rb	S3a; Ra, Rb
S3b; Ra, Rb	S3a; Ra, Rb
S3b; Ra, Rb	

Instrumental interlude as before: audience calls.

	Ra, Rb; S4a; Ra, Rb
S4a; Ra, Rb	S4b; Ra, Rb
S4a; Ra, Rb	S4b; Ra, Rb
S4a; Ra, Rb	S4b; Ra, Rb

Instrumental interlude, followed by Arabic song.

To compare this process of assembling independent commonly known units in an *izlan* performance, or the process of composing a *tanš:at:*, with the weaving process and its products, we must examine several typical pieces. Figure 1 shows a saddle blanket (*taytait*) in plain weave with continuous horizontal bands of different motifs characteristic of the lighter rugs and the blankets. Figure 2 shows a throw rug (*tauhnat*) of deep cut-pile with rectangular block motifs.[15] Both pieces have the dark red wool backgrounds commonly used in areas where Tamazight is spoken. The examples are sketched in loom position, the lower right corner being the beginning point. From here the weaver works horizontally to her left and back. As her work progresses to a point above her reach as she sits cross-legged on the floor, she rolls up the finished part onto the lower crossbar (*afg:ag*) of the loom and lets down more warp from the upper one. Thus while the immediate design is visible in the horizontal plane (from side to side), earlier motifs are lost sight of in the temporal process of weaving an object, which extends over two or three months or more.

In describing their work, several women have remarked that they "lay down" a band of one motif, and then select the next one.[16] Despite this casual approach, the finished product generally displays considerable balance between the beginning and the end of the work.

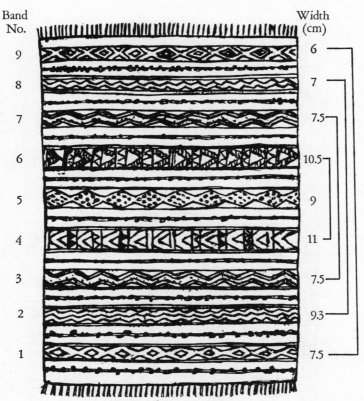

Fig. 1. Saddle blanket (*taɣtait*), 109 x 150 cm

The *taytait* of Fig. 1, for example, has nine wide horizontal bands balanced in pairs around the middle (fifth) band. Each pair is similar but only two bands (3 and 7) are identical. Horizontally the question of symmetry is moot; the motif simply repeats itself in the space allowed much as the stanza of the *izlan* performance is repeated until one group is ready to introduce the next stanza.

In the designs of block motifs such as shown in Fig. 2, horizontal symmetry is approached by balancing pairs of motifs around the center block. Usually the outer two match, while differing from the next two; these match each other but differ from the center block. The center block may match the outer two (as in rows 2 and 5), or it may match its flanking blocks except for color reversal (row 3); or it may differ completely from the other motifs in the row (as in rows 4 and 6). Note that the outer blocks in row 1 are different, and that the right border is twice the width of the left. Vertically the rows are approximately balanced in size (row 5 is the center) but not in motif.

Row

Fig. 2. Zemmour cut-pile throw rug (*tauhnat*)

Is perfect symmetry deliberately avoided, or simply difficult to achieve? Questioning on this point revealed little except that the weavers seem not to share my notion of symmetry. Indirect evidence that the concept is not active in the weaving esthetic was the reaction of weavers and their families, including the men, to some pictures of Navaho rugs. They expressed great admiration for the Navaho designs, which exhibit a high degree of symmetry and unity; but they found it difficult to say why they found them so appealing.

In both types of design exemplified here, the bands or blocks are at once separated and united by the intervening areas of plain dark red, which are punctuated by narrow bands of black or of tiny identical motifs. These plain background spaces and their identical accents, repeated at approximately the same intervals, serve somewhat the same function in the visual plane as does the refrain in the temporal dimension of an *izlan* performance. That is, they establish a rhythm, a sustaining field into which elements of similar size but of different motif are introduced from the commonly known stock within the genre. The choice of elements and of setting defines the range within which the ordinary person can exercise creativity.

To the more gifted, of course, belongs the privilege of extending the range by creating new elements for the common stock. This would include the professional musicians, but is not restricted to them; as we have seen, the performance structure of *izlan* permits anyone to initiate a stanza without claiming or denying authorship. This is the proving ground in which talented young men whet their verbal skills and master the intricate rhythms beat out with palms and fingers on the *al:un*. Those who dare enter the battle of poets, and succeed, may if they wish undertake the longer, more difficult poems of the *tanš:at:* genre; in any event they are *inš:adn*, composers.

In creating these more difficult forms of verbal art, the stock of fixed traditional elements is at least one stage earlier in the creative process than are the ready-to-sing *izlan* of the common stock. It consists of the figures, themes, symbols, grammar, idiom, and vocabulary of the poetic tradition, the composition of which into poetry requires the skill of a talented or at least a practised composer. The society seems to place great value on the skilled use of these traditional elements. Innovation is valued to the extent that it occurs *within* a traditional form, or modifies it with familiar elements from the national culture.

In a society in which art is not separated from daily life, a large part of the enjoyment of aural and visual patterns must lie in active participation in their creation and performance. For the Berber inhabitants of Morocco's Middle Atlas, learning to weave or to sing *izlan* involves the acquisition of a large repertoire of commonly known elements and the ability to combine them into pleasingly balanced patterns. It is not surprising that the poets should have noted the analogy and incorporated it into their stock of conventional images. It is worth noting that despite many changes due to increased modernization and decreased isolation, both the verbal arts and the weaving traditions still play a very active role in family and community life, thus validating the poetic imagery which relates them.

FOOTNOTES

[1] For a general discussion and references on Berber literature, see R. Basset [Ch. Pellat], "Berbères: VI. Littérature et art," *Encyclopedie de l'Islam*, 2e éd., 1960. For several examples from Tamazight, see E. Laoust, *Cours de Berbère marocain: Dialecte du Maroc Central* (Paris: Librairie Orientaliste Paul Geuthner, 1939), pp. 271–80.

[2] Jeanette Harries and Mohamed Raamouch, "Berber popular songs of the Middle Atlas," *African Language Studies*, 12 (1971), 52–70. It contains further examples of the genres given here and a more extensive description of the verbal art forms of the Middle Atlas. The present paper was originally presented in October 1970, at the Midwest Modern Language Association annual meeting.

[3] The author gratefully acknowledges the aid of Dr. Lois Anderson in observing and recording a number of such occasions, during our 1971–2 field trip sponsored by the U.S. Department of Health, Education and Welfare and by the University of Wisconsin Graduate School.

[4] *tariš* "saddle" refers to the highly decorated leather saddle of a fine horse or mule, and to the procession in which a bride is carried on such a mount to her new home. Certain *izlan* are appropriate at certain stages of the wedding.

[5] The stringed instrument may be a violin, a *luțar* (a three-stringed instrument fingered and plucked by hand, made of skin stretched on a deep bowl, with hand-hewed pegs; it is commonly available in Meknes), or a three-stringed guitar. The drum, skin stretched on a wooden cylinder about 5 inches deep and 12 to 18 in diameter, is commonly available. It is called *al:un*.

[6] Older men do not participate in *izlan* performances, since the lyrics are considered shameful (*ḥšuma*); they assemble at festivals in a separate tent to recite verses of the Koran or to listen to the moral poems described hereafter.

[7] In March, 1972, tribal poets were invited by the national radio-television agency to come to the capital and record new poems in support of the new constitution which was coming up for a popular referendum. The new poems were broadcast to the appropriate areas.

[8] The latter image occurred in a friendly contest between three poets who often perform together as the *šiux n Mrirt*; on this occasion they composed against each other on the theme of horsemanship, using it and the fantasia game as an image for their own game and their skill at it.

[9] Women sometimes whisper lines to male poets in contest. One woman recorded for me several *tinš:adin* of her own composition, which I am under oath not to play to her family or any men. In other genres, women compose the lyric cry called *lmait*, or *tamawait*, and *ihl:il*, short stanzas on religious, ancestral or tribal themes or personages, sung while weaving or grinding grain, etc.

[10] A detailed study of weaving in a representative tribe of the Middle Atlas appears in Mme. G. Chantréaux, "Les tissages décorés chez les Beni Mguild (avec XI planches hors text)," *Hespéris*, 32 (1945), 19–34. A general description is found in Jeanne

D'Ucel, *Berber Art* (Norman: U. of Oklahoma Press, 1932). The names, sources and variations of designs and the general esthetic of weaving is discussed by Father Ange Koller, O.F.M., in the chapter entitled "Son bon goût naturel dans son activité productive" of his *Essai sur l'ésprit du Berbère marocain* (Fribourg: Editions Franciscaines, 1949).

[11] That the choice of stanzas is not restricted by theme (save for the contests noted above) is apparent from examples and can be verified by questioning the performers. Asked how he chose the next *izli*, one talented young man (Tafrout Abderrahmane, of Zawia echCheikh) could only say that he knew a great many. Were there any that he could not use? His immediate response was affirmative: some were "not the right length." After some thought he distinguished four general categories of length and gave examples of each. To date I have found no vocabulary of metrics in Tamazight, but there are a number of terms designating different drum rhythms.

[12] Literally translated as "O one who is coming, O God, under ground to friend; that which they work, who will help him with it." This construction of a vocative phrase addressing an impersonal pronoun modified by a relativized verb phrase (two in this case) expresses a wish of the speaker; it is common in poetry.

[13] For the significance of a girl's forelock (*taunza*) as the seat of her *baraka* see James Bynon, "Riddle-telling among the Berbers of Central Morocco," *African Language Studies*, 6 (1966), 96.

[14] In some professional performances the women do not initiate new stanzas, but only respond. In nonprofessional group singing, only those poor in resources would fail to take their turn as initiators of new stanzas.

[15] Woven in Khemisset by Lalla Ghenou, and sketched from a photograph in which, unfortunately, the ends were obscured.

[16] Aicha Sibwi says (field book 15.52–3): "I tied my weaving, I raised the alternate threads in it, I wove in it a little. I laid down a motif. The motif I wanted, I would set down and so on until I finished my weaving."

Trends in the Content and Form of the Opening Glee in Yoruba Drama

J. A. ADEDEJI

Introduction

This article* will trace the origin and development of the Opening Glee as a theatrical art form and account for those factors which have brought about changes in the content and form of presentation. These changes will also be linked in general terms to changes in Yoruba society. Examples of Yoruba drama will be drawn from the theatrical presentations of the Yoruba Masque Theatre (Alá`rìnjó or Eégún Aláré) and the Yoruba Operatic Theatre (the Travelling Theatre Parties). These are the two theatrical developments in Yorubaland which are indigenous and are products of Yoruba cultural history. Both are professional theatres with travelling troupes or companies which developed from religious rites.

The Opening Glee

The Opening Glee is a theatrical form which, like the classical "prologus," is an entrance song or chant that precedes a play. In the traditional Yoruba theatre, the Yoruba Masque Theatre, the prologue or entrance song was called the Ìjúbà. This was a ritualistic opening scene between the leading or chief actor and the chorus. The Ìjúbà contained a pledge and was a form of salute. As a theatrical form it is believed to have been first used by Èsà Ògbín, the foremost Yoruba masque-dramaturg and professional entertainer, as a tribute to Ológbin Ológbojò, the "father" of the traditional theatre.

The Yoruba Masque Theatre emerged as a Court entertainment from the egúngún (masquerade) rites about the early part of the seventeenth century at the instance of Ológbin Ológbojò, an official at Court at Ọyọ Igbòho.[1] By the eighteenth century, it had become the people's theatre, with troupes plying the towns and villages of the Old Ọyọ empire. The theatre survived the collapse of the empire, but its existence has been

---

* This article is a revised version of a paper read at the conference on "Yoruba Language and Literature" held at the University of Ife, Nigeria, December 13th–16th, 1969.

marked by vicissitudes as a result of the onset of Western European culture in Yoruba society.

The following is an example of the traditional entrance song of the Yoruba Masque Theatre as presented by the Agbégijó troupe at Ọtta (recorded on tape February 16, 1965).

CHIEF ACTOR:

>Mo júbà, kí ibà mi ṣe.
>Ibà ni ngó kọ́ jú ná, aré mi d'ẹ̀hìn.
>Mo rí'bá, mo ri'bà Baba mi Àjànkoro Dùgbẹ̀.
>Òun l'eégún Aláré, a-bi-kókó l'étí aṣọ.
>Afínjú Òjẹ̀ tí í dún kòokò lórí Eégún.
>Baba mi má a gbóhùn ẹnu mi,
>Mo rí'bá, mo rí'bà.
>Jẹ́ k'óde òní yẹ mi o.
>
>Mo júbà pẹtẹ́ ọwọ́,
>Mo júbà pẹtẹ́ ẹsẹ̀,
>Mo júbà àtẹ́lẹsẹ̀ tí kò hu'run tó fi de gbọ̀gbọ̀lọ̀ itan.
>Ará iwájú mo túúbá,
>Jànmáâ mo bẹ̀bẹ̀ ẹ̀hìn.
>Ibà ẹnyin Iyàmi Òṣòròngà,
>Ẹiyẹ a-bọ́wọ́ winni,
>Ẹiyẹ a-bẹsẹ̀ winni,
>Afínjú ẹiyẹ tí í jẹ láârín òru,
>Mo júbà o, k'óde òní ó yẹ mí.
>Mo tún júbà Ẹ̀sù Láâlú Ọkùnrin ọ̀nà,
>Ọ̀ ṣa' mọ l'ógbẹ́, gún'mọ l'óbẹ́.
>Ẹ̀sù Láâlú mo juba o,
>Mo júbà j'óde òní ó yẹ mí.

CHORUS:

>Ojú Aiyé pé! (4 times)
>Ẹ wá wo gbẹdu àwa.
>Ojú Aiyé pé!
>Ẹ wá wo eégún àwa;
>Eégún àwa nfọ Tápà, ó nfọ 'Jẹ̀ṣà.
>Ojú Aiyé pé!
>Ìta pé!
>Ará pé!
>Ẹ wá wo gbẹdu àwa.
>Ò-ṣèré l'Adélọwọ.
>Ò-ṣèré l'Òdìgbo.

CHIEF ACTOR:

Olóde àgò o!
Òkúta àgò o!
Ẹnyin Olóde!
Ẹ bùn wá l'óde o
K'áwa ó rí bi jó.
Ó d'ọwọ́ Ìrèlẹ̀.
Ó d'ọwọ́ Ìtá,
Ó d'ọwọ́ Òsanyìn,
Ó d'ọwọ́ Ògbojò tó l'eégún.
Nítorí Ògèdèngbé ló d'ójẹ̀ 'lẹ̀,
Sọungbé ló ti kọ́ awo ó ṣe.

SONG:

"Ibi ẹ rí, ẹ kí gbe mi lọ,
Ibi ẹ rí o ẹ kí gbe è mi lọ. (2 times)
Emi Adélọwọ̀ ọmọ 'Ṣábí,
Ibi ẹ rí o ẹ kí gbe mi lọ,
Ẹní ba ṣẹ l'aiyé mú. O-ṣèré l'Adélọwọ."

CHORUS:

Ojú Aiyé pé!
Ita pé!
Ará pe!
Ẹ wá wo gbẹ̀du àwa.
Òjíkí orúkọ
Ìyàmi Òṣòròngà.

SONG:

"Ẹmú Aiyé!
Ẹ má mà mú wa.
Ẹmú Aiyé o!
Ẹ má mà mú wa!
Ẹní bà ṣẹ l'Aiyé mú,
O-ṣèré l'Adélọwọ."

CHIEF ACTOR:

I submit my pledge, may my pledge be fulfilled.
It is the pledge I will first submit, my performance comes
at the end.
I behold a pledge, the pledge is to my father,[2] Ajankoro
Dugbe.

He is the masque-actor, with a concealed knot at the hem
    of his garment.
The scrupulously neat masque-histrione who is a threat
    to the existence of other masquerades.
My Father, hearken to my voice,
Behold the pledge,
Let me become worthy of this outing.

I pledge to you my open hand,
I pledge to you my flat foot,
I pledge to you the underfoot that grows no hairs, even
    as far as knee-high.
To you who have passed before me, I humbly bow.
From you my companions, I beg for courage.
The pledge is to you,
Iyami Oşoronga,[3]
A "bird" with divers hands,
A "bird" with divers legs,
The scrupulously neat "bird" whose sorties are at
    midnight.
I hereby submit my pledge;
Let me become worthy of today's outing.

My pledge is also to you Eşu Laalu who patrols the road,
Who slashes and inflicts wounds.
Eşu Laalu, behold my pledge.
I submit the pledge,
Let me become worthy of this outing.

CHORUS:

The eyes of the World are set!
Come and see our "gbèdu."[4]
The eyes of the World are set,
Come and see our masquerade;
Our masques speak Tapa, they speak Ijęsha.
The eyes of the World are set
Ita (the open)[5] is complete!
Brethren are assembled!
Come and see our "gbèdu."
Adelọwọ is a player;
Odigbo is a player.

CHIEF ACTOR:

You owner of the Open, make way!
You owner of the Open, give us a space,
A space to put on our show.
We consign ourselves to the deity Irẹlẹ;
We consign ourselves to the deity Ìtá;
We consign ourselves to the deity Ọsanyin;
We consign overselves to Ologbojo, the owner of the masquerade.
Because of Ogedengbe,[6] he introduced masque-dramaturgy.
He first learnt the secret at Sọungbe.

SONG:

"Shout my name, wherever you may,
Shout my name wheresoever you may. (2 times)
I am Adelọwọ, son of 'Ṣabi,
Shout my name, wherever you may.
It is he who offends that the World catches.
Adelọwọ is but a player."

CHORUS:

The eyes of the World are set!
Ita is complete!
Come to see our "gbèdu."
"Early homage" is your name Mother-Superior, Ọṣoronga.

SONG:

"You catcher of the World, do not catch us.
You catcher of the World, do not catch us!
It is he who offends the World catches.
Adelowo is only a player."

Modern Yoruba society has witnessed the emergence of a new form of entertainment, the Operatic Theatre.[7] It developed from the "Native Dramas" popularized by guilds and societies of the Secessionist Churches in Lagos in the early part of the twentieth century. Later, encouraged by its popularity and success as a theatrical art form, some of the Choirmasters involved with the production of the "Opéra," as it was then called, organized their own drama groups outside the Church and held public performances at the Lisabi Hall, Ebute Metta and the Glover Memorial Hall, Lagos. With developing interest in concerts and amateur theatricals growing out of the remnants of the Variety Shows or the so-called Concerts of the 1880s, the organizers of the Yoruba Opera began to operate with artistic modifications that derived from traditional and foreign sources.

It was the Lagos Glee Singers, an established group of prominent Lagosians and veteran performers of European Operettas,[s] who were the first to use the "Opening Glee" to describe its entrance song. The term was later adopted and popularized by the Operatic Theatre in their operations in Lagos and the provinces. But what is most significant in the early examples of the Opening Glee was its focus on departure from the traditional ijuba. The following example is that of the Ogunmola Travelling Theatre in the late forties:[9]

CHORUS:

Eré dé, eré o.
Eré tó gbámúṣẹ́n,
Eré tó lárinrin,
À-rí má le è lọ,
À-wò-pádà-séhìn.
Ẹ f'ara ba'lẹ̀ kẹ́ rí ran o e!

CHIEF ACTOR:

Alága wa o, àti 'gbákejì,
Ẹnyin iyáa wa,
Ẹnyín bàbáa wa,
Kí a tó má a b'ére wa lọ,
Bí babaláwo bá jí,
A júbà l'ọ́wọ́ Ifá.
B'oníṣègùn bá jí o,
A júbà l'ọ́wọ Ọsanyìn.
Onígbàgbọ́ tó bá jí o,
A f'ìbà f'Ọlọ́run.
Ọba òrun, ar'áiyé-rórun,
Awá mà júbà l'ọ́wọ Rẹ o.

CHORUS:

Òní a dá'jọ́ eré,
Òla a f'ọkàn s'ọnà.
Ọjọ́ tí a dá pé l'óni o,
Ẹ f'ara balẹ̀,
K'ẹ f'ara balẹ̀ wò ran l'ójọ́ òní o.
Agbe t'ó l'aró, Kì í rahùn aró.

Alùkò t'ó l'osùn,
Kì í rahùn osùn.
Lékeléke t'o l'ẹfun, Kì í rahùn ẹfun.
Kí ẹ má rahùn owó,
Kí ẹ má rahùn ọmọ,
Ohun t'ẹ́ ó jẹ, t'ẹ́ ó mun
Kó má wọn nyín o.

Òní a dá'jọ́ eré,
Ọla a f'ọkàn s'ọnà.
Ọjọ́ tí a dá pé l'oni o
Gbogbo ènià.
L'ọ́wọ́ ìkẹ́kùn Aiyé,
L'ọ́wọ́ ìkẹ́kùn Èṣù,
L'ọ́wọ́ alákobá Aiyé o
Abáni-wá-kún-tẹni,
Èdùmàrè kó gbà wá o.

Àwa l'elére Ilẹ̀,
Àwa l'elére omi,
Egbére, Òṣùpà, Ilẹ̀, ilẹ̀ aiyé o. (2 times)
Bí're ló bá mọ̀ ọ́ ṣe,
Ko múra o kíkan-kíkan.
Bí'bi ló bá mọ̀ ọ́ ṣe a,
Ko múra o kíkan-kíkan.
A, Párádísè la ó ti ṣè 'dájọ́,
A, Párádíse!

CHORUS:

We are here to present our play.
This is the time for the play,
A play that is gripping,
A play that is entertaining,
A play that one would see and would not like to leave,
A play that one would like to see backwards.
Be patient and see a real show.

CHIEF ACTOR:

Our Chairman and his supporter,
Our mothers,
Our fathers,
Before we go on with our play, when the priest of the
    Ifa cult awakes,

He places his pledge in the hands of Ifa.
When the physician awakes,
He places his pledge in the hands of the deity Ọsanyin.
The Christian, when he awakes pledges to God,
King of Heaven, One who oversees earth and heaven,
This is our pledge to Thee.

CHORUS:

Today we announce the date of our performance,
Tomorrow we look forward to it.
But today completes the announcement,
So be patient to see our show this day.
The bird "agbe,"[10] who is the possessor of the indigo,
    never lacks the dye.
The bird "aluko," who is the possessor of the "osun,"[11]
    never lacks the dye.
The cattle-egret who is the possessor of the chalk,
    never lacks the color.
May you not lack money,
May you not lack children,
May you never be short of what to eat and what to drink.

Today we announce the date of our performance,
Tomorrow we look forward to it.
But today completes the announcement
To all people.
From the snare of the World,
From the snare of "Eṣu,"[12]
From the World's troubleshooter who increases one's
    misfortunes,
May the Almighty deliver us.

We are the players on the Land.
We are the players on the Waters,
You Spirits, Moon, Land, of this World.
If doing good is your accomplishment,
Be steadfast at it.
If evil-doing is your accomplishment,
Be steadfast at it.
It is in Paradise that we shall face judgement.
Yes, in Paradise!

Hubert Ogunde, regarded as the "father" of the Yoruba Operatic Theatre, popularized the Opening Glee at the early part of his professional career. It was his remarkable and spectacular entrance song that became the model for many others who came after. But as time went on, his Opening Glee acquired more foreign characteristics and sloughed off its traditional elements. Recently, the tendency has been to replace the entrance song with an improvised "curtain-raiser" which has nothing to do with the total performance. Other contemporary practitioners have even abandoned it.

In his plays of the fifties, Ogunde used the Opening Glee as a commentary on the action of the play in performance or sometimes to tell the story of the play. The following is an extract from the Opening Glee of his play, *Journey To Heaven*:[13]

Aráiyé ẹ wá k'awá k'ọrin ọgo s'Olúwa.
Angélì ẹ bọ̀ k'awá k'ọrin ìyìn s'ókè o. (2 times)
Ará aiyé ẹ gbọ́ mi, ará ọ̀run ẹ gbọ́ mi.
Ọmọ l'ẹ̀hìn-ìwà, ọmọ l'ọ̀pó ilé.
Èdùmàrè fún wa l'ọ́mọ,
Tí yí o gbẹ̀hìn tún ẹ̀hìn ṣe o. (2 times)
Ẹni ọmọ́ sin l'ó bí'mọ, ọmọ ò l'áyọ̀lé,
Ẹni ọmọ́ sin l'ó bí'mọ o, ọmọ ò l' áyọ̀le o.
Èdùmàrè àwá mbẹ̀ ọ́ o dáríjì àwọn apànìa.
Aiyé l'ọjà, ọ̀run n'ilé,
Aiyé l'ọjà, ọ̀run n'ilé o.
Ẹnyin tí mbẹ l'áiyé,
Ẹ kú ọjà aiyé o,
Ẹnyin tí mbẹ l'áiyé, ẹ kú ewu ìrìnajò, etc.

O come, mankind, for us to sing a song of glory to the Lord.
O come, angels, for us to sing a song of praise to the Highest. (2 times)
Dwellers on earth hear me,
Dwellers in heaven hear me,
Child is after-life, child is the post that sustains a house,
May the Almighty give us children who will succeed us and clear up after us. (2 times)
He has children, whoever is buried by his children.
Until this happens, it is futile to put one's hope on them.
Indeed, he has children, whoever is succeeded by his children since their life is so uncertain.
Almighty we beseech Thee to forgive murderers.

The World is the market, Heaven is home.
Those of you in this market-like World, we greet you.
Those of you living in this World accept our greetings
  on the occasion of your pilgrimage.

In the entrance song of his play, *Yoruba Ronu* (1964),[14] however, Ogunde returns to the traditional role of the Yoruba dramatist. In it he offers a supplication:

SOLO:

Olúwa ló ni isẹ́ aiyé.
Ènìà mà ni 'ránsẹ rẹ̀,
Ẹdùmàrè t'ó rán mi ní'sẹ́ aiyé
O ní'ngbó o, o ní'ntọ́ o.
Ó ní'ndẹ̀ bẹ̀ 'tàn s'ẹ́hìn.
Ẹbẹ̀ mo bẹ̀ aiyé, Ẹ ma dàamú mi.
Ẹ mà jẹ́ njẹ́sẹ́ Ẹlẹ́dà rán mi o.

CHORUS:

Ẹní bá m'aiyé yío j'ogún aiyé.
Ẹni kò bá m'aiyé, Ẹ mà kú iyà ò.
Aiyé ni kọ̀rọ̀, aiyé ni gbangba òde.
Aiyé l'okùnkùn, aiyé yi ni'mọ́lẹ̀.
Àwa ò mọ bi aiyé mí lọ.
Ẹnìkan ò mọ bi aiyé ti ńbọ̀ o,
Ṣùgbọ́n a mọ bi a gbé ti bẹ̀rẹ̀.

SOLO:

Ìjì Aiyé bẹ́ni k'isu ẹni má jiná.
Ìjì ọmọ ènìà b'ẹ́ni k'ọ́bẹ̀ ẹni má sọkalẹ̀.
Ẹlẹ́da mi ní irọni.
Ó ní orí mi kò gbà ibi,
B'ẹ́ni àiyà mi kò gbẹ̀bọ̀dè.
Aiyé l'odò, odò l'aiyé.
Aiyé bí ẹ bá d'agbọ́n, Ẹ má ta mí,
Bí ẹ bá d'odò, Ẹ má mà gbé mi lọ.
Bí ẹ bá d'àgbàlá igbò, Ẹ má ṣe kàn mí.
Mo ti bá wọn ṣ'awo de'lé Olókun.
Gedegede l'ọwọ́ 'yọ ju orí.
Iṣẹ́ku òrun p'ẹ̀hìndà;
Ẹ mà jẹ́ njíṣẹ́ Ẹlẹ́da rán mi o.

CHORUS:

Olúwa ló rán mi.

Èmi a jíṣẹ́ Elẹ́da rán mi
Ọ̀gàràmilálẹ̀ o!

SOLO:

The works of this World is the Lord's.
Mankind is His Messenger.
The Almighty who has sent me on errand to this World
Says I must grow to old age, says my life must endure,
Says I must prosper and leave a record behind.
I beseech the World not to worry me;
Allow me to deliver the message of my Creator.

CHORUS:

The one who knows the World will inherit the World.
You who do not know the World accept my
    condolences on your suffering.
The World is the hidden places, the World is the
    open places.
The World is darkness, the World is the light.
We do not know whither the World is going
No one knows from where the World is coming.
But we know from where we set out.

SOLO:

If the World could have a wish, no one would wish
    one's yam properly cooked.
Human beings never wish that one's stew is
    properly cooked.
But my Creator says nay:
He says my head will withstand any evil
    designs that can harm me;
He says my heart will resist any conspiracy
    that can damage me.
The World is the lower layer of the Universe.
The lower layer of the universe is the World.
O World, if you become a wasp, do not sting me;
If you become a ram in a stampede, do not attack me.
I have joined them at the Olokun shrine for initiation,
I have sacrificed to the denizens of the Earth.
The hands outstretched project beyond the head.
You the ghost-mummer from Heaven turn your back;
Allow me to deliver the message of my Creator.

CHORUS:

> It is the Lord who has sent me.
> I will deliver my Creator's message.
> Behold my humble pledge!

In both the traditional and modern Yoruba theatre, the entrance song is significantly a theatrical device of social consequences. An analysis of its content and form yields evidence of its relevance to and consistence with the Yoruba ideational system.

The traditional Yoruba theatre (the Aláṛìnjó or the Masque Theatre) is a social institution with an indirect regulative function. It has two basic dramatic genres: the spectacle and the revue. The dramatic spectacles are designed to meet religious objectives and are based on Yoruba myths and totems. The revues are sketched out as comments on the state of or happenings in Yoruba society. In both types satire is a theatrical element.

In view of his role, the traditional Yoruba dramatist sees himself as one who has a sacred duty. To this extent, therefore, his entrance song or opening glee has an integrative function. His ijuba (pledge) is a social obligation, and it is his responsibility to open his show with it as a formal salute. In relating this practice to the social context, the ijuba is seen as a functional attribute of the performer.

The traditional Yoruba dramatist uses his art to explain his knowledge of the world through satirical representations. In this act he needs a sensitive participation of his spectators in the reality of his art. The spectators are an assortment of people who crowd round the arena of play to see the dramatist's performance. The arena of play, in fact, is an open space encircled by them. It is therefore the first duty of the performer to create an atmosphere that will rouse congenial feelings and to capture the necessary mood that will ensure friendly responses in his spectators. By design, the entrance song has a sense of beauty and is endowed with efficaciousness. The performer is aware that the Yoruba universe is sustained and animated by certain vital forces. Therefore his entrance song must inspire confidence, and at best, find an echo in the mind and sensitivity of his spectators.

The entrance song of the Aláṛìnjó or the Yoruba Masque Theatre, apart from clarifying the role of the dramatist in society, reveals the relationship between the performer's art and the import of what he communicates. The performer makes certain acknowledgements. His first pledge is to his "baba" (father) who is his source of inspiration. In the Yoruba social structure "father" is a classificatory rather than a descriptive term. The art of the Masque Theatre belongs to the Ọ̀jẹ̀ (a guild of histriones). Ológbojò, who is the acknowledged founder of the guild, is addressed as "baba" (father), likewise all his descendants. Since acting started as a lineage profession, the present dramatist is likely to have trained under his own late father.

During performance, the performer is confronted by the Yoruba cosmos which is believed to be inhabited by certain vital forces. Since his theatrical arena is an open space, the dramatist is obliged to acknowledge the presence in it of certain "unseen higher powers":

"Iyami Oṣoronga" is the Mother Superior who is head of the guild of witchcraft. According to Pierre Verger,[15] "Odù Ọ̀sá Méjì" describes the important position of womanhood in Yoruba society and says that Ifa has decreed as follows:

> Ó yẹ kí a má a f' ìbà f'óbirin,
> Nítorí ọgbọ́n aiyé ti wọn ni.

> It is fitting that we should give our pledge to women,
> Because the wisdom of the world is theirs.

Èṣù Láàlú is believed in Yoruba theology to be the lieutenant of Olo-dumare and acts as "a special relations officer between heaven and earth, the inspector-general who reports regularly to Olodumare on the deeds of the divinities and men, and checks and makes reports on the correctness of worships in general and sacrifices in particular."[16] The dramatist is anxious that he does not get into trouble through the agency of Èṣù. The deity is needed more for his benevolence and protection than for his capabilities in mischief-making.

Apart from his pledge, the dramatist seeks the cooperation of certain other deities and the express permission of the owner of the open space. The Yoruba universe in divided into three spheres: Ọrun (Heaven), Aiyé (World) and Ilẹ̀ (Earth). Ọrun is the seat of Olódùmarè or Olọ́run (High God or owner of Heaven). In Yoruba cosmology, Aiyé is an ordered structure whose stability is maintained by certain elements and vital forces. Its inhabitants are diverse and include human beings, animals and "ẹbọra" or visitors from the other spheres, namely, Ọrun and Ilẹ̀. Ilẹ̀ is believed to be the creation of Ọbàtálá, the arch-divinity, but its worship is enshrined in the rites of the Ogbóni cult. Onílẹ̀ is the earth-god. Both Olọ́run and Onílẹ̀ maintain a kind of surveillance over Aiyé through their emissaries and agents.

The Aiyé is a collective, and the traditional theatre is a functional institution within it. The dramatist submerges his own personality even as he uses his art to work for its stability and continuity. By informing and exposing certain deviant behaviors in society in an entertaining way, the dramatist is indirectly using his art to regulate the norms of society. Drama, whether as a presentational or representational art, is larger than life. In the acts of performance, it is not unlikely that the dramatist's designs become distortions of actuality and therefore offensive. Thus, he may incur the ire of his spectators, both humans and deities, as the case may be. His entrance song, therefore, is a pledge that ensures his safety.

In the modern Yoruba theatre (the Operatic Theatre), on the other hand, the content and form of the entrance song show evidence of modifications which are the direct consequences of westernization in the Yoruba society. The style and form of any theatrical art must reflect the sensibilities of the people with whom it communicates. In spite of its traditional links, the Yoruba Opera is a form of entertainment which developed as a result of Christian education and the influence of Western culture in the Yoruba society. Even though the traditional role of the dramatist has not changed, his world-view as well as his attitudes have. As a Christian, his concept of the universe is that which is dominated by the biblical Ọlọ́run (Lord of Heaven) and filled with angels who serve Him as messengers.

The place of performance is a playhouse, an enclosed physical structure, with a stage or a raised platform on one end and an auditorium on the other. The spectators comprise those who fulfil the necessary conditions of admission to see a show. At the head of the assemblage is a chairman whose duty is to oversee the orderliness of the spectators and the smooth running of the program. He is even allowed to make a speech and announce his donation.

The dramatist in his entrance song recognizes the category of peoples assembled before him and in anticipation of their gifts pays tribute to them. He does not stand in awe of his spectators and the consequences of the effect of his drama. He is aware that everyone has to give an account of his stewardship to God on the day of judgement.

But the attraction and prospects of Christian education and Western culture have not changed the personality of the Yoruba dramatist completely. The entrance song of Ogunde's *Yoruba Ronu*, as an illustration, represents the ambivalence of the "transitional man" in a changing society whose Christian faith is sometimes submerged by his apparent recognition of the existence of other forces in his universe. In it, in spite of his faith in God, Ogunde appeals to the vital forces and the elements who are the inhabitants of Aiyé (the World) to assist him in his mission to deliver his Creator's message:

> Olúwa ló rán mi;
> Èmi a jíṣẹ́ Ẹléda rán mi.

It is the Lord who has sent me;
I will deliver my Creator's message.

The modern dramatist believes God to be his only source of inspiration. His art is a product of missionary activities and westernization. He has not descended from a long line of traditional artists and attributes his success to doing God's will. He works with a view to creating a new dimension in society and relies on the esthetics and theatricality of a foreign form and style for accomplishment. But in spite of his faith, his new art form, and the security of his playhouse, the dramatist still entertains a nagging fear of Aiyé. It is this dynamic, yet complex phenomenon of the Yoruba cosmos that brings both the traditional and the modern dramatists to the same level of humanity.

Conclusion

The form of an art is affected by its function. The Opening Glee is a technique of approach, and it functions for the purpose of identification. Its content and form reveal that the role of the Yoruba dramatist, in spite of his creativity, is to communicate a message which he believes to be transcendentally inspired. However, in recognition of the nature of certain vital forces which exist within the Yoruba cosmos the dramatist pledges himself to them as a guarantee that while his performance lasts, he is safe. By using word and gesture, music and dance, as well as the means of the theatre, the dramatist evokes the image and rhythm which are the basic characteristics of performance.

In order to analyze the significant trends in the content and form of the Opening Glee, it has been necessary to discriminate between function and meaning in order to relate the value of the artistic form to its social context. Analyzing the data, there is evidence of the overriding concern of the dramatist, both traditional and modern, about Aiyé (the World). The role of the dramatist in the Yoruba society shows the importance of the theatre as a regulative institution. It seems probable that the dramatist originally designed the Opening Glee to serve an integrative function, but its concept and esthetic effect are found to be theatrically effective.

FOOTNOTES

[1] See J. A. Adedeji: *The Alarinjo Theatre: The Study of a Yoruba Theatrical Art From Its Origin to the Present Times*, Ph.D. Thesis, University of Ibadan, 1969.

[2] The reference to "father" is conventional. It is an implied recognition of the person who was the actor's source of inspiration and tutor. "Father" may, in fact, be the lineage-head from whom the actor has descended, acting being a lineage profession.

3 She is "Mother Superior," the head of the guild of witchcraft.

4 The expression is rhetorical. A pageant is implied and not the royal drums.

5 It is not the "open" that is being referred to but the owner of it, sometimes called Olóde (the Lord of the Open or the god Ṣọnpọná). The expression is to the effect that the god's presence has made the open whole.

6 Ògèdèngbé is one of the attributive names of Olúgbèrẹ́ Àgan, the first Yoruba mummer or masked actor.

7 This theatrical art is erroneously called the "Folk Opera."

8 See advertisement in *Lagos Standard*, May 4, 1910; May 31, 1911; and also the *Times of Nigeria*, October 9, 1917.

9 Ogunmola used this "Opening Glee" for all his shows in the late forties and early fifties before he modified the form.

10 "Agbe" is the Blue Touraco Musophagidac of the Cuckoo family.

11 "Osùn" is the African camwood which yields a dye used as cosmetics.

12 "Èsù" in this reference is the biblical devil, Satan or Lucifer. He is thought of as the malignant supernatural being capable of malevolent acts.

13 Hubert Ogunde, *Journey to Heaven* (Lagos: Sore-Masika Press, n.d.), pp. 1-2.

14 Hubert Ogunde, *Yoruba Ronu* (Yaba: Printed by the Pacific Printers, n.d.), pp. 5-6.

15 Pierre Verger, "Grandeur et Decadence du Culte de Iyami Osoronga," *Journal de la societe des Africanistes*, 35 (1965), 200-218.

16 Bolaji Idowu, *Olodumare, God in Yoruba Belief* (London: Longmans, 1962), p. 80.

Tone Riddles from Southern Mozambique: *Titekatekani* of the Tshwa

JOHN E. KAEMMER

INTRODUCTION

The term "tone riddle" has been used by Donald C. Simmons to describe a type of riddle he reports having found among the Efik and Ibibio of Nigeria. In these tone riddles the response to a query is a language string approximately as long as the query, and it is related to the latter by similarities in phonemic language tone (Simmons 1958:123). Simmons has noted that no tone riddles have been reported from other parts of Africa (1958:126).

In his ethnography, *The Life of a South African Tribe*, Henri Junod describes two types of riddles among the Thonga of southern Mozambique. The first type, *mhumhana*, actually involves guessing and refers to games of finding hidden objects, as well as to finding answers for questions. Junod calls these "riddles in one sentence" (1962:179). The second type of riddle is called *psitekatekisana,* and Junod refers to them as "riddles containing two statements" (1962:180). Junod gives examples of several types of these:

a) those of which "the inner meaning is not difficult to discover" (1962:180)
b) those which are "a comparison of two objects" (1962:182)
c) those "which refer to some historical event" (1962:183)
d) those which have "merely a similitude in sound" (1962:183)
e) "Lastly I would class in a final category *the riddles which are altogether incomprehensible,* of which there are quite a large number." (1962:184)

Junod suggests that the lack of meaning may be due to mistakes in transmitting the *psitekatekisana* from one generation to another (1962:184). He presents no hypothesis as to why such incomprehensible forms of folklore should continue in popular usage, and it would seem quite possible that these are in fact tone riddles, since Junod seemed unaware of the phenomenon of phonetic tone.

The Tshwa people, who are in the northern group of the Thonga, according to Junod, and who speak a related language, also have riddles of two types, although they use the term *titekatekani* (singular *litekatekani*) for both. The purpose of this paper is to study a number of the phrase-answer type of *titekatekani* in terms of tonal correspondence to see if the "tone riddle" is indeed extant in Southeast Africa, and also to discuss the theoretical implications of the tone riddle for the study of folklore and the language arts. The reason for studying the Tshwa *titekatekani* rather than the Thonga *psitekatekisana* is my own familiarity with the Tshwa language and the availability of a Tshwa informant, Mr. William James Humbané, who is presently studying in the U. S. A. He is of the Komari clan of the Homoine district of southern Mozambique.

The context in which *titekatekani* are used is essential in understanding them. The informant indicated that frequently both the question and answer have no meaning. When asked why people enjoyed them so if that was the case, he replied that the enjoyment is in the competition. Usually in the evening, after the meal and before bed, a group gathers around a fire. There is no distinction of sex, age or kinship. Sometimes tales (*tikaringani*) are told, but on other occasions competitions of *titekatekani* are held. The group is divided haphazardly and one side gives the query and the other replies. Sometimes one person challenges the group. This is a test to see who has more knowledge, since answers cannot be invented.

The formula for beginning a *titekatekani* session is to say *harateka teka teka*[1] . . . as long as desired, which gets everyone's attention. This formula can also be repeated while one is trying to think of another *litekatekani*, thus avoiding an awkward silence. The term *chelatembe* serves as a formula to challenge the correctness of an answer given by the opposite group. The side which fails to answer loses a point. If the side which gives the query can't provide the response, it loses a point also. Sometimes there is argument over the correctness of a response. Objections are voiced in terms of *hazvizwali khwatsi* ("they don't sound well") as well as *hazviyelani* or *hazvifambelani*, which are synonyms for "they don't go together." The session is ended when someone says "*phuu, xamina hiwurongo*," literally "phuu, my thing is sleepiness" or "as far as I'm concerned, I'm ready for sleep."

In addition to use in competitions, some *titekatekani* are quoted as proverbs (*mavingu*), such as this one:[2]

```
            kílá       xìmàngà              –khòtsà    –khòtsà
 1) Q: à kílá    wáxímángà   lòkù   wángákhótsà   wúkhótsílè
        the/tail/of cat/        if       /it is curled/it is curled

            nwínyí     mùtì                 –sùkà     –sùkà
    R: à nwínyí    wámútì   lòkù   ángásúkà   ísúkílè
        the/headman/of hamlet/if/he has gone/he has gone
```

ANALYSIS

Since the Tshwa do not distinguish the two types of riddles as the Thonga do with their terms *psitekatekisana* and *mhumhana*, I specified to the informant that I was particularly interested in the type of *titekatekani* in which the question and answer were of similar length. He had no difficulty in understanding what I meant. Seven of the *titekatekani* in this collection were recalled by the informant after he had seen some of the *psitekatekisana* collected by Junod and Jacques (1957:312–337).[3] For the remainder of this paper all references to *titekatekani* are only to those with the phrase-type answer.

In order to avoid a purely subjective impression of the tones in the *titekatekani*, the latter were studied in relation to the Tshwa tonal system. To the best of my knowledge the Tshwa tonal system has not been thoroughly described in the linguistic literature. Welmers includes examples from the language in his description of "terrace level languages" (1959: 5). He suggests that phonemic terracing takes the place of a descending intonation pattern, since a non-low can be lower than or the same as preceding non-lows, even if a low tone intervenes. Stevick, on the other hand, treats the terrace effect, or tone slip, as "a feature of area phonetics, functioning differently in different languages" (1965:92). Thus in Tshwa he considers the tone slip to be significant only in relation to the immediately preceding non-low (1965:91). He notes that in Tshwa "two level tones . . . account for what may be considered in some sense the 'basic' tones of all words, but contrastive downstep occurs at certain points within words in certain constructions" (1965:92). This broad scheme was used as the basic orientation for working with the Tshwa tones in the *titekatekani*. The basic tones of all words in the *titekatekani* seemed to be of two levels, with the one exception of a loan word, *màdáwàní*, in this one:

2) Q: gìgílígì gìgì wámágígì (no meaning)
   –phùngèlà   màdáwàní –kóká   nèngè
   R: lòkù (u)phúngélá kàmàdáwàní wàkókwá nèngè
   if/you are careless/with machines/you will have cut off/a leg
   If you are careless with mine machinery your leg will be cut off.

In order to provide tonal information to supplement that of the *titekatekani* themselves, I had the informant use the nouns and verbs of the *titekatekani* in a variety of sentence frames. The purpose of this was to divide the nouns and verbs into tonal groups, as suggested by Pike (1948:48). Nouns were given in three ways: 1) initially before a verb, 2) isolated as in answer to a question "who/what is that?", and 3) following a high verb. Verbs were put in frames with their infinitive forms as nouns both initially and following a high verb. The initial forms of both nouns and verbs did not involve a tone slip (with the exception noted above) whereas the other forms frequently did; thus the former were considered as the basic tonal forms. In the examples these forms are placed above the nouns and verbs as they appear in the *titekatekani*. Basic verb forms are preceded by a hyphen to indicate that they are stems only. The isolated stem, as the imperative, has different tones.

When making a tonal analysis of the *titekatekani* the following factors were taken into consideration: 1) the resultant tones of the queries and responses of the *titekatekani*, 2) the number of syllables in related queries and responses, 3) the parallel phrase structure, that is, the functional relationships of nouns, verbs and modifiers within the queries and responses, and 4) the basic tone groups of the nouns and verbs in the related queries and responses.

In the *titekatekani* themselves the tonal similarities between the query and response appear to be of three types, and, with two exceptions, each *litekatekani* fits in only one of these groups. In the first group are the *titekatekani* with exactly the same resultant tonal pattern in the query and in the response. Twelve of the twenty-seven *titekatekani* collected are in this category:

3) Q: hàràtékà   wátekélà   (no meaning)

   nhwànà –sùkà   wùkátí
   R: nhwànà   súkà   wúkàtíní
   grown girl/go from/marriage (i.e., leave your husband)

4)   xìhlòbyànà   mátí
      Q: xìhlòbyànà   khápà   nímátí
      small well/is full/of water

               –hlàmbà   –hlàmbà   núná
      R: lòkù (u)hlàmbà   hlámbà   nínùná
      when/you bathe,/bathe/with husband

(See also examples 5–10 below and numbers 20, 23, 25 and 27.)

For a *litekatekani* to fit in this group the query and response must have the same number of syllables. Nevertheless, there are only five of these in which the phrase structure of the query and response is parallel:

5)   símú   màhìlà   hwétí   kùbàsà
      Q: símú   légà   màhílà   R: hwétí   léyà   kùbásà
      field/of/millet   moon/of/whiteness

(See also numbers 8, 10, 25 and 27.)

There are six *titekatekani* in which we find identical basic tones of nouns and verbs where they occur in similar slots:

6)   –àlàkànyèlà   –vàtlà   pàlàlà
      Q: nzàháálákányélà   R: nzàhávátlá   pálálà
      I am still thinking.   I am sharpening/spear.

7)   xìkhòkwànà   (ideophone)
      Q: xìkhòkwànà   rwîî   (The vowels of *rwîî* are nasalized.)
      small coconut tree/straight
      The small coconut tree is straight.

         –ètlhèlà   (ideophone)   –ènzèlà
      R: nzìètlhèlà   léê   alternate: nzìènzèlà   léê
      I sleep/over there   I go visiting/over there

(See also numbers 5, 8, 25 and 27.)

There are only four *titekatekani* with both parallel phrase structure and identical basic tones:

8)   xìkhàtò   chùrí   lìkùlù   mànzá

  Q: xìkhàtò   xáchùrí   R: lìkùlù   lámànzá

      bottom/of mortar   large amount/of eggs

(See also numbers 5, 25 and 27.)

Three *titekatekani* have the same resultant tones with neither parallel phrase structure nor identical basic tones:

9)   mhùtì –tlúlá rìnzí   kàmbà –fénéngêta

  Q: mhùtì   tlúlá rìnzí   R: kàmbà   fénéngètá

      buck / jump / ditch   leaf / cover up

(See also numbers 3 and 23.)

The following is the only one with parallel phrase structure and different basic tones, yet which has the same resultant tones. This is brought about by raising the first tone of the query:

10)   lìràngà –mbétá mùtì   –nàvà

    Q: lìràngà lômbétá mútì híkúnávà

       pumpkin/of to spread over/hamlet/by creeping

       kókwànì –mbétá mùtì   –kàsà

    R: kókwànì wômbétá mútì híkúkásà

       old woman/of to spread over/hamlet by crawling

       old woman who gets about the hamlet by crawling

A second type of tonal similarity is represented by a group where query and response tones are different at the beginning but similar at the end. This group includes five *titekatekani* which have the same number of syllables (numbers 11, 12, 13, 14 and 24), and three in which the number of syllables varies (numbers 15, 21 and 26). The number of dissimilar tones at the beginning varies from one (numbers 14 and 11) to three (number 15). Numbers 11 and 12 are the only ones with parallel phrase structure and identical basic tones. In number 11 the query involves a meaningless string in which the first two syllables are different from those of the response; in number 12 the noun *sáti* (wife) differs from the noun *sáti* (woman) by affecting the imperative form of the preceding verb. Number 13 has parallel phrase structure, but number 14 does not. Neither has the same basic tones.

11)
              mùhàmbù
  Q: gìgílígìgí múhàmbù khúdùswá
     — — —   /sweet potato/big sized

       –fá   mùhànyì
  R: ùtàfá rìní múhànyì nzíwèná
    you will die/when/long-lived person/(tone of blaming or
      dislike)
    when will you ever die, you long-lived person?

12) –bánzá fúlà –xòkòlà
  Q: bánzà fúlà yíxòkólè múgìrìgìrì wàtìmàngwá
    break outer skin/nut/pry/– – –/– – –

    –téká sátì –hlàyìsà mùhlàngànyètì tìmbìtá
  R: téká sátì múhlàyísè múhlàngànyètì wàtìmbìtá
    take/wife/care for her/fire-keeper/of the pots
    Take a wife and care for her; it is she who keeps the fire
                       under the pots.

13) xìsùká tùvà –pèlùkà
  Q: xísùká xátúvà nwápèlúkà
    tail/of dove/waves in the wind

    lìráví kùhlù –tsèvàmà
  R: líráví lákúhlù nwátsèvámà
    branch/of fig tree/sags from weight

14) xìpfhákì –gègérélà   mámánì tínó
  Q: xìpfhákì xàgègérélé R: mámánì wàtínó gínwé
    ear of corn/it is hard and dry   mother/of tooth/one
                              a one-toothed woman

15) kànjú   mùlùngù xìjùmánì
  Q: kànjú gáxìbvòkótà R: mùlùngù wáxìjùmánì
    cashew fruit/of bigness   white man/of sudden
    large cashew fruit   appearance (as when
                            checking on a worker)

The third type of tonal similarity is where the succession of lows, highs and tone slips is the same, but where there can be a variation in the number of syllables at each level. This variation is never at the end of the *titekatekani*, so this could perhaps be a specialized form of what was described as the second type, especially numbers 16 and 19. Only number 17 has the same number of syllables in the query and response, and they vary in their distribution between tones. These variations may be schematized as in Table 1. It will be seen that the order of levels is the same, but that the number of syllables at a given level can vary.

16)   màhlálà   –hànyà   màkwérù
       Q: mbàmbàmba màhlálà R: hìhànyìlè màkwérù
       fallen/wild fruit   we have lived long/my brother

17)   mhùtì   wùtlúkùtlúkù   màngùlwè   lìsìha   khámbá
                                                 –fénéngètà
       Q: mhùtì yáwùtlúkùtlúkù màngùlwè wálìsíha khàmbà
                                                fénéngètá
       buck/zigzagging/small animal/of boldness/animal/take cover

       mùnhù   wùkómbèkómbè   –nyíkélá tìmbìlú
       R: mùnhù wáwùkómbèkómbè zvàkwè ángányíkélì
                                   zvàkwè hítímbìlú
       person/who begs/his things/he does not give/his things/due
                                           to selfishness

       A person who begs for what he has does not give away what
                                       has because of selfishness.

(See also numbers 1, 19 and 22.)

Table 1

1)	1	5	3	3	1	3	1		16)		4	1	1
	1	4	3	3	1	3	1				5	1	1

17)	2	1	1	1	1	1	4	3	3	2	1	1
	2	1	1	1	1	1	3	4	3	2	1	1

19)	3	1	3	2	1	2		22)	1	2	1	1	1	3	1
	4	1	3	2	1	2			1	2	2	1	1	3	1

(For each example the top line indicates the number of syllables at this level in the query and the bottom line indicates the number of syllables at this level in the response.)

There are two exceptions to these groups. Number 18 would be in group one were it not for the tone difference on the fourth syllable from the end. This may indicate another group of *titekatekani*, in which the tones are the same at the beginning and vary at the end. Only a larger sample could indicate whether this is so or not. The important fact is that of the fifteen syllables in this *litekatekani* there is only one in which the tone of the response varies from the pattern set by the query.

18)
            màsòkò   –fámbá
  Q: bhùrù másókwénì xákùfámbà hímágòngònzwá
      movement or sound/in small paths/go/ – – –
    –hànyà   –wóná   wùsíwàná
  R: nzìhànyílé ngúvù nzíngàwóná zváwùsíwàná
      I have lived/long;/I have seen/poverty

The other exception is number 2, which would be in group three were it not for the low tone on the seventh syllable of the response. It is not logical that this could be explained as another group. It may be that since the word in which this irregular tone occurs refers to machinery of the mines in South Africa, this *litekatekani* is of fairly recent origin. It may have been made by someone expressly as warning to children and young men about machinery, with the semantic function overshadowing the formal structure.

In both of these exceptions there is only one tone which keeps the *litekatekani* from one of the three groups, and in both cases the difference involves the tone on the syllable "ma," which is preceded and followed by a non-low. It is possible that this represents a change of tone which falls within the limit of acceptable variation, perhaps related to the nasal consonant. Because this hypothesis can explain both exceptions it is attractive, but additional tonal analysis is needed before establishing any definite rule in this respect. The fact remains that even in the exceptions there is an extremely close relationship between the tones of the query and those of the response.

It is not surprising that Junod and Beuchat found a great deal of sound resemblance in the *psitekatekisana* and phrase-answer riddles in general, even without considering tones (Junod 1962:183; Beuchat 1965:196). Of the twenty-seven *titekatekani* collected here, nineteen have the same number of syllables (numbers 3–14, 17, 18, 20, 23, 24, 25 and 27). There are also twelve pairs with parallel phrase structure, if the meaningless strings are excluded (numbers 1, 5, 8, 10–13, 15, 19, 20, 25 and 27). Of course the tonal correspondence would add to the subjective feeling of sound resemblance, even though one was not aware of the principle in operation.

In comparing the basic tones of nouns and verbs in relation to phrase structure we find that with only one exception (number 12) there are no cases where the basic tones and parallel phrase structure are the same in query and response yet produce differences in the resultant tones. In general, where the resultant tones are different it is because the phrase structure and/or the basic word tones are also different. There are many instances where the phrase structure and basic tones are different but the resultant tones in the query and response are the same. These are sometimes due to grammatical features, such as the fact that imperative forms of both high and low two-syllable verbs are usually high-low. By far the greatest correspondence is where the phrase structure, basic tones and resultant tones are the same.

A study of the *titekatekani* is incomplete without looking at their meaning, even though this has not been the principal aim of this paper. Out of the twenty-seven *titekatekani* twelve contain at least some strings described as meaningless by the informant. These are always in the query unless they occur in both query and response, as in number 19 and number 22 below.

19) Q: màpàpàrígwàní màtlùkà yáxènhé
    − − − / leaves/of the xenhe tree

    R: màhùpàni íkwìhí múphàhlì wámhàmbá
    − − − /where is/officiant/of the sacrificial offering?

It is possible that work on the field with older informants, and covering a wider area would provide meanings for some or perhaps all of these strings. There are certain fixed forms which would seem to provide for the tonal query without involving meaning. *Hàràtékà hàràtékà* in number 20 appears to be the opening formula made into a query:

20)
    Q: hàràtékà hàràtékà   R: khùmà súkà nzìlò tánà
                                ashes,/go;/fire,/come

There is probably some relationship here with the verb *kùtéká*, to receive or to take. *Ghubudu* appears in two tonal forms in number 21:

21) Q: ghúbùdù ghúbùdù ghúbùdúù   (no meaning)
    vúlá −nà mùmú

    R: vúlá yákùnà nímùmúù
    rain/which falls/with sunshine

Mr. Humbane did not have a meaning for the term, but I remember being told while in Mozambique that it represented the sound of shaking a blanket or mat. *Gigiligigi* or *gigiligi gigi* appears in several *titekatekani* with only the first three syllables of these forms having the same tones.

22) Q: gìgílígì gìgì wámágígì   (no meaning)
      R: màtsátsátá wáxìdhù hìxìfòkò   (no meaning)

(See also numbers 2 and 14.)

A study of the meaning of the *titekatekani* yields no sense of unity of the genre. One can only describe the types of meaning, much as Junod did. Only a few of the *titekatekani* appear to be proverbs, if the latter term is defined in terms of the presence of connotata as well as denotata. Such are numbers 1 and 23:

23)   ndlèlà   –lànzà mámáni
      Q: xódòdò hìndléla   R: xólànzà mámáni
          it persists/on path   it follows/mother

A larger number could be considered maxims or good advice:

24)   (ideophone) màrhámbú fènhè
        Q: kóngólókóxó márhámbú yáfénhè
          sound of things dropping/bones/of monkey
          (throwing divining bones)
          –àlàkànyèlà màlémbé ndlàlà
        R: àlákányélá málémbé yándláìà
          remember/years/of hunger

(See also numbers 2, 3, 4, 12, 17 and 25.)

In several *titekatekani* the query and response are metaphors:

25)   kùhlù   xìtshìtshì   mùti   vàlòyì
        Q: kùhlù wáxìtshìtshì   R: mùti wáválòyì
          fig tree/of fearsome   hamlet/of witches

(See also numbers 5, 10, 13 and 14.)

Numbers 18 and 26 appear to be forms of request:

26)   nkílá   xìmàngà
        Q: nkílá wáxímángà màbùbúngwàní
          tail/of cat/ – – –
          –phàmèlà   màkwénú
        R: phàmélá ngúvù mìná mákwénú
          dish up/much/to me,/your brother

A meaningful connection of query and response in terms of meanings is often impossible in translation. Whether such meanings can be accurately elicited from informants seems to be a matter of controversy, since probing can lead to statements which are unnatural (Simmons 1961:245; Messenger 1961:246). A thorough study of the meanings of the *titeka-tekani* would involve actual observation on the field of the social event and the social context.

Thorough study would also involve a complete analysis of the Tshwa tonal system, so as to find out whether either query or response have variations from the language norm, and if so, what they are. There are certain places where the *titekatekani* appear to vary the standard spoken language. Such is the case with *nímùmúù*, which is usually spoken *nímùmú*. Compare *mumu* here with the same word in number 21:

27)   hlókó hwàrí   −nónóhá
    Q: hlókó yáhwàrí kúnónóhá
        head/of partridge/is hard

        wúswá   mùmú   −nánzíhá
    R: wúswá gámùmú kúnánzíhá
        corn mush/of noonday/is tasty

The high noun *khámbá* is for some reason low in the query of number 17. This is a part of the question of permissible variation, and to deal with this demands thorough analysis of the tonal and expressive systems, and should involve a number of informants. The constraints which the query imposes on the response is the principal concern of this paper.

CONCLUSION
The analysis of the tonal relationships of the *titekatekani* leads to several important conclusions. In the first place, tonal correspondence between the query and response is too consistent to be attributed to chance. It occurs in 100 percent of the *titekatekani* of this collection. In 44.4 percent the correspondence is one-to-one. This is a greater proportion of correspondence than Simmons found among Efik tone riddles, where 17 out of 94 had "almost complete dissimilarity" (1960a:806). These Tshwa *titekatekani* can definitely be considered as tone riddles.

A second conclusion is that the tonal correspondence is the basic factor common to all of the *titekatekani* of the phrase-answer type. A similar length and phrase structure is also to be found. However the same number of syllables occurs in 70.5 percent and similar phrase structure occurs in 44.4 percent, whereas tonal correspondence is present in 100 percent. This includes five cases or 18.5 percent with neither parallel phrase structure nor equal length. The meanings are so varied and abstruse that the *titekatekani* cannot be considered a unified genre in those terms.

A third conclusion comes from the fact that these *titekatekani* are basically the same type of phenomenon as the Efik and Ibibio tone riddles, which indicates an extensive spread of this phenomenon in Africa. It also raises the question as to whether it might not exist in other areas of the continent between Nigeria and Mozambique. Beuchat (1965:195) gives riddles from Lingala, Lamba and Nyanja in which the answers are in phrases. Perhaps tonal analysis of these would indicate the same type of tonal correspondence. Junod (1962) and Messenger (1960) also report similar types of phrase-answer riddles, but they did not present a tonal analysis. These latter cases represent languages closely related to Tshwa and Efik, respectively.

A fourth conclusion is that in a sense the *titekatekani* are a type of poetry. They are good examples of style in the sense of "recurrence or convergence of textural pattern" (Freeman 1970:4). In the *titekatekani* the query establishes a tonal pattern, from which the response varies not at all, or only in certain ways. This is a structural constraint on the form of the response. Put another way, the content of the deep structure is restricted by the requirements of the surface structure. If we conceptualize a continuum with emphasis on deep structure, or meaning, at one pole and emphasis on surface structure or form at the other, we find the *titekatekani* closer to the latter pole, as is also the case with poetry. In this respect the *titekatekani* are more closely related to tongue-twisters and nursery rhymes than to regular riddles, in that the former are also closer to the form pole than to the meaning pole. Conventional one-word-answer riddles are farther from the formal pole than are tone riddles; that is, they are constructed basically in terms of the deep structure, with the surface structure possibly introducing ambiguity.

The phenomenon of tone riddles raises interesting methodological questions regarding the study of folklore and the verbal arts, and indeed, artistic activity in general. It is necessary to emphasize that the basis upon which the *titekatekani* of the phrase-answer type are called tone riddles is the result of linguistic structural analysis. It is not to be elicited from informants, as the work of Junod (1962) indicates. The whole science of linguistics is based upon covert linguistic structure, so that it does not depend upon folk evaluation of data for all of its conclusions. The scientific study of artistic activity in man also needs to turn at times to analysis of structure to discover covert patterning. The fact that in tone riddles a close correspondence of sound exists covertly indicates that the covert aspect of artistic behavior is of great significance.

The *titekatekani* are also important in that they bear upon the definition of poetry. Poetry is often defined in terms of meter and rhyme. This may be correct for European languages, but the *titekatekani* indicate that the patterning of tonal variations can possibly function in the same way in tonal languages. Kiparsky (1970:171) writes of the importance of considering the schema when analyzing poetry. It is possible that in tonal languages the schema upon which poetry is built is frequently related to arrangement of the language tones. Simmons cites this kind of schema in certain types of Efik poetry (1960b:1).

In referring to literary style, Bierwisch makes a distinction between the microstructure and macrostructure of verbal expression, the former dealing with linguistic form and the latter with the structure of ideas. He says that "a rational literary theory must encompass both realms" (1970: 112). In writing about folklore, Dundes makes a similar distinction between linguistic structure and folkloristic structure (1965:182). Thus when we find forms of folklore in which there is a constraint on output caused by the linguistic forms, or microstructure, it is especially necessary to study that linguistic structure. In Africa, where nearly all languages are tonal, that means tonal analysis. The sole consideration of idea structure and the failure to consider tonal analysis has resulted in inconclusive attempts to fully understand riddles with phrase-type answers.

Structural constraint on verbal output is not the only characteristic of literary style. Freeman cites, in addition, "deviation from the norm" and "a particular exploitation of a grammar of possibilities" (1970:4). It is possible to consider deviation from the norm as part of the grammar of possibilities, in which case these two merge into one, which is, in effect, the stylistic aspect of individual creativity. It is this which makes tonal word play in Yoruba different from the tone riddles, since in the former the tones are changed at will for special effect (Bamgbose 1970:110).

Since the *titekatekani* are fixed forms they are not subject to this latter aspect of style. They may have implications for it, however. Simmons has shown how tonal similarities are used in some types of Efik poetry (1960b:1) and how familiarity with tonal patterns of proverbs is used in drum signaling (1960a:805). If the Efik, with fixed tone riddles, also use tones in their poetry, it is possible that the Tshwa do the same. Further investigation needs to be done on this, among the Tshwa as well as all over Africa. Song texts need to be studied not only to see how they relate to the music but also to see if there are stylistic tonal arrangements within them.

It is possible that the tone riddles serve not only as entertainment, as among the Tshwa, or as indirect allusion, as among the Efik (Simmons

1958:124–5), but also serve a covert didactic function. They may instill in the younger members of the society an awareness of tone and the possibilities of its manipulation, thus providing them with the social poetic norms upon which later artistic creativity can be based.

> The very existence of poetry in a certain language has fundamental importance for this language. . . . By the very fact of foregrounding, poetry increases and refines the ability to handle language in general; it gives the language the ability to adjust more flexibly to new requirements and it gives it a richer differentiation of its means of expression. Foregrounding brings to the surface and before the eyes of the observer even such linguistic phenomena as remain quite covert in communicative speech, although they are important factors in language. (Mukařovský 1970: 54–55).

In other words, the *titekatekani* among the Tshwa may function in a manner similar to the way in which the nursery rhyme is a factor instilling an awareness of meter and rhyme in English-speaking children.

Phonemic language tone is for the most part a real headache for Europeans and Americans. It tends to be ignored except in those areas of Africa where there are so many contrastive pairs that intelligibility is drastically reduced by wrong tones. In southern Africa the number of such contrastive pairs is relatively small, so that ignoring tone is possible for ordinary language use, provided one doesn't mind sounding foreign. However, in the study of language arts, including folklore, poetry, and song, the tone in southern Africa is just as important as it is elsewhere, as is shown by the *titekatekani*. We cannot assume that tone plays no role in the African verbal arts any more than we can assume that it is the *sine qua non* of verbal art in Africa. The actual truth is probably somewhere in between. More research in this aspect will not only increase our knowledge of how the human mind works artistically, but it will also provide a corrective for those African artists and Western scholars who still think they need to follow European criteria of literary art.

FOOTNOTES

[1] In all Tshwa words in this paper conventional Tshwa orthography is used, except that prefixes are joined to stems. Sounds approximate English with the following exceptions: Consonants are unaspirated unless followed by "h." "x" indicates the sound of "sh." "r" is flapped. "v" indicates the bilabial fricative except where otherwise indicated. "tl" is a lateral stop, "hl" a lateral fricative. "g" is always hard. "zv" is a voiced sibilant fricative. "by" is a voiced sibilant affricated stop. Some letters have been underlined to show differences not indicated in the orthography: "*d*" and "*b*" indicate implosives. "*v*" is the labio-dental fricative. "*n*" is velarized.

² The *litekatekani* itself is indicated by "Q" (query) and "R" (response). The words above the query and response are the basic forms of the noun or verb with the basic tone markings. In marking the tones ` is used for all low tones, and ' for all non-low (high) tones except where a tone slip (stepdown or drop) occurs. This is marked by ' but the succeeding non-low tones on the same level are again marked '. An occasional downward glide is written as ˆ although further analysis might show it to be a rapid ' ` on a two mora vowel.

³ *Titekatekani* numbered 4, 8, 9, 10, 24, 25 and 27 in this paper are related to numbers 142, 101, 76, 65, 151, 105 and 91 respectively in Junod and Jacques.

REFERENCES CITED

Bamgbose, Ayo, 1970. "Word Play in Yoruba Poetry," in *International Journal of American Linguistics* 36:110–116.

Beuchat, P. D., 1965 (1957). "Riddles in Bantu," in Dundes 1965: 182–205.

Bierwisch, Manfred, 1970. "Poetics and Linguistics," in Freeman 1970:96–115. Translated by Peter H. Salus.

Dundes, Alan, 1965. *The Study of Folklore.* Englewood Cliffs: Prentice-Hall, Inc.

Freeman, Donald C., ed., 1970. *Linguistics and Literary Style.* New York: Holt, Rinehart and Winston, Inc.

Junod, Henri A., 1962 (1927). *The Life of a South African Tribe, Volume II, Mental Life.* New Hyde Park, N. Y.: University Books, Inc.

Junod, Henro Philippe and Alexandre A. Jacques, 1957. *Vutlhari Bya Vatsonga (Machangana); The Wisdom of the Tsonga-Shangana People.* Cleveland, Transvaal: The Central Mission Press.

Kiparsky, Paul, 1970. "Metrics and Morphophonemics in the Kalevala," in Freeman 1970:165–181.

Messenger, John C., 1960. "Anang Proverb-Riddles," in *Journal of American Folklore* 73:225–235.

———, 1961. "Anang Proverb Riddles and Efik Tone Riddles," in *Journal of American Folklore* 74:245–246.

Mukarovský, Jan, 1970. "Standard Language and Poetic Language," in Freeman 1970: 40–56.

Pike, Kenneth L., 1948. *Tone Languages.* Ann Arbor: University of Michigan Press.

Simmons, Donald C., 1958. "Cultural Functions of the Efik Tone Riddle," in *Journal of American Folklore* 71:123–138.

———, 1960a. "Tonality in Efik Signal Communication and Folklore," in *Men and Cultures*, Selected Papers of the Fifth International Congress of Anthropological and Ethnological Sciences, A. C. Wallace, ed. Philadelphia: University of Pennsylvania Press.

———, 1960b. "Tonal Rhyme in Efik Poetry," in *Anthropological Linguistics* II(6): 1–10.

———, 1961. "Efik Tone Riddles and Anang Proverb Riddles," in *Journal of American Folklore* 74:245–264.

Stevick, Earl W., 1965. "Pitch and Duration in Two Yoruba Idiolects," in *Journal of African Languages* IV (2):85–101.

Welmers, William E., 1959. "Tonemics, Morphotonemics and Tonal Morphemes," in *General Linguistics* IV (1):1–9.

Dramatic Forms

The Concert Party as a Genre:
The Happy Stars of Lomé

ALAIN RICARD

In the neighborhoods of Kodjoviakope or Lom Nava, two districts in Lomé, Togo, even the casual stroller might be attracted to a bar by the highlife rhythms of a Concert Party Band. Let him enter and remain for the evening and he will discover that the music is merely a prelude to a night of theater. What follows here is an account of what one could term the principles of the Concert Party—the four basic structural elements which allow us to define such entertainment as drama: setting, actors, media, and plots.

The "Ambassador" Courtyard.   The blackboard as mass media.

SETTING   Sunset is invariably accompanied by the first twangs of the head guitar. Music is responsible for the temporal division of the performance. In the monotonous progression of the day, the real beginning of the show occurs when the orchestra starts to play. A unique moment beginning at a precise time—day must end before the music begins. From 7 to 9:15 P.M. the musical prologue serves to attract passers-by into the bar and helps warm up both actors and public. The musical prologue resolves one of the essential problems of all theater: how to begin? On different occasions, we have arrived at 8:30, at 9:00, sometimes as late as 9:15. The bar fills slowly, but the band continues to play, as if it has to fill time until the entrance of the comedians, signaled by a particular rhythm, by an intensification of the communication.

Advertising tonight's show in Lomé.   The "Centre communautaire" courtyard.

1

2

In general, Concert Party troupes put on their plays in bars. These are often large patios with covered sides (see illustrations 1 and 2). One of the sides of the patio is always reserved for the actors. The actors carefully delineate their playing area. The space for the spectators is defined by the seats brought into the patio for the occasion. Between the seats and the stage, there is an empty space, often filled by children sitting on the ground. Actors dislike this usurpation and often attempt to push the children out of their space.

Most often there is no difference in level between the space of the actors and the space of the spectators. If the actors have the choice, however, they prefer a raised stage: this is the case in one of the bars of Lomé, Tonyeviadji, a bar highly appreciated by the actors for just this reason (illustration 3). Space is thus polarized—an area for the spectators, an area for the actors. There is no fusion of the stage and the public, but rather a dialogue between them which supports and re-affirms the duality between stage and public. Certain signals in the actor's play call for a response from the public because they bring into perspective the distance between the two. Thus, the pointed finger of the comedian towards the spectators is at the same time a sign of direction and a sign of indication: "You are there, I am here. Laugh!" It calls for an exchange (my gesture versus your laughter) and not for fusion.

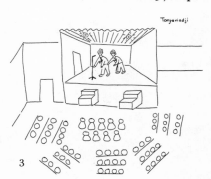

Tonyeviadji

3

Lucas and old father.

The opposite occurs when the spectators come on stage. However, their presence is not meant to dissolve the play into the anonymity of the festival. They come on stage to give the actor a visible sign of their approval, a coin which they place on the actor's forehead. The spectator doesn't touch the actor; he merely places his coin on the latter's forehead. The monetary exchange thus accomplishes the mediation between the actor and the spectator.

Dozens of spectators sometimes come on stage to place coins on a favorite's forehead. The crossing of the limit between the stage and the public does not signify the abolition of the distance, but on the contrary, is a tacit recognition of this limit. The gift of the coin represents a spatial parallel of the interchange provoked by the pointed index of the actor.

Lucas the playboy.

ACTORS　　　A special time and a special space are set aside for the exchange that will take place through the actors. Pascal d'Almeida, president of the Happy Star Concert Band, office clerk and versatile actor, presented himself to us in the following terms, when interviewed for our film:

> I was born in Kinshasa where my mother owns a bar. Many Mina live there as expatriates. In 1961 I returned to Togo, six months without work, then I found a good job at the SCOA (an important commercial firm on the West African coast); but you can't work all the time. So I began to play the guitar with Melo-Togo, a good band. I had learned in the Congo with Papa Noël.
>
> Often I would go to Aflao (a border town between Ghana and Togo) with a friend from the SCOA. We went to see Concert Parties. And we said to ourselves, why not us? Because the Concert Party has a larger public than the dance hall band: everybody comes—families, the young, the old, not only single young people and couples. In 1965, with some neighborhood friends, we started our own Concert Party. For two years, we didn't have much success. In 1967, we split into two groups. My colleague from the SCOA founded another troupe, "Togo Nouveau," and we split the public. Now, business has improved and there are many troupes of Concert Party, but the "Happy Star" is the oldest and the best.

Pascal d'Almeida, president of the "Happy Star," is the group's producer. The troupe exists legally, thanks to him. He is the one who arranged for the loan which permitted them to replace their minibus destroyed in an accident two years ago and, more recently, to buy a new sound system. At thirty-two, Pascal d'Almeida is also the oldest member of the troupe as well as the one with the most stable and prestigious job: office clerk. An accomplished actor, he is capable of playing many diverse roles and particularly excels in that of the wicked stepmother, in our opinion the most difficult in the repertory. A musician, he is also a singer and dancer and imagines himself an acrobat and magician as well. He likes to boast that his charms are the most powerful, and apparently he is right, for in the conflicts which have not ceased to divide the group, he has always been the victor. He wears several rings and often dresses in black. He is called "Type Noir" and he well recognizes the nickname's magical connotations.

Pascal is ill-at-ease in French and often has to search for words. Nevertheless, he is far from timid and never hesitates to give his opinion. In Ewe, his own language, he is considered particularly persuasive. In his relations with the other members of the troupe, Pascal is the uncontested leader; he makes all important decisions, although he has been known to yield to the pressures of Lucas, director, and Ben, vice-president.

Like the majority of the members of the troupe, Lucas lives in the neighborhood of Nyekonakpoe, one of the oldest districts of Lomé. The straw-thatched mud house in which he lives testifies to his poverty. Lucas is a professional actor in the sense that he has no other source of income and is not looking for another job. Certainly, his role with the "Happy Star" takes a lot of his time: at times as many as four plays a week, each requiring his presence from 7 P.M. to 1 in the morning, several afternoons devoted to parading the streets of Lomé advertising the evening show, not to mention rehearsals. For the moment, however, the life of an actor is far from easy. Lucas, as one of the stars, earns the most money after Pascal, but this amounts to barely 3000 CFA a month (12 dollars) and that only on a good month. With a wife and child to feed, this doesn't go far in a big city where life is notoriously expensive. Lucas is the principal male actor and often plays the father or the king, that is, the authority figure. His versatile talents include character roles such as in *Bob Cole*, in which he plays a playboy swindler. If Pascal is the producer, Lucas is the poet; he composes songs well-known throughout southern Togo, songs through which the popularity of the "Happy Star" grows.

Benjamin, "Ben," also enjoys great prestige among the theater-going public of Lomé. During the day he is a worker with a hard but good job at the Lomé brewery; at night, of all the actors, he is no doubt the most versatile. We have seen him within the space of the same evening interpret the roles of a comedian in the prologue, a playboy and a prostitute! His range of roles is thus larger than that of Lucas, who is limited by his physique and voice to masculine roles. Ben can play women. He is particularly good in character roles; thus his nickname "Nago," an allusion to his interpretation of policemen of Yoruba origin, famous for their severity. Ben is also a composer of numerous stories.

Benjamin, Lucas, and Pascal are truly the stars and the nucleus of the troupe whose member-actors fluctuate around twenty in number. These three are the oldest and enjoy, by their different and complementary skills, the respect if not the friendship of the other members. Lucas is twenty-seven, Ben twenty-six and the other members of the troupe are all between seventeen and twenty-two years old.

Several sub-groups exist within the "Happy Star." Three members are especially close by social origin as well as by affinity: Richard, Cyprien and Alex. Richard is head guitarist. Eighteen years old, he left a well-known band to join the troupe as leader of the rhythms section. He lives with his parents, as do many young Loméans. His father is a petty clerk, his trader mother has a small grocery store/bar in the family concession. Richard does not consider himself unemployed—an opinion not shared by his father. Alex, nicknamed "Zorro" or "Papa," lives next-door to Richard. Tall, slim, elegant, he recalls Lucas and, like Lucas, is talented in character roles. Although he also plays the drums, he is principally an actor. He plays the old man, an incarnation of the traditional wisdom of the Ewe people, even though he is only nineteen years old. Long study of old men in his village as well as thorough knowledge of classical literary works in Ewe, such as *Agbezuge* (a religious novel), give him the literary and visual understanding necessary for his role. He too has no other source of income; his grandmother is a petty trader and has a small bar in the family concession.

Of the three friends, Cyprien, called "Paouna," is the tallest and the handsomest. He is the playboy. But appearances to the contrary, Cyprien is the master of the transvestite role: on stage he is the Ashao, the prostitute. Cyprien's interest in his many girl friends has a professional bias: he copies their walk, their movements, their wigs, their make-up, even their nail-polish. All these stage accessories are borrowed from his girlfriends. The public knows that the seductive Ashao on stage is really Cyprien and appreciates in the best Brechtian tradition of distancing, the precision of his interpretation.

The prostitute is not the only feminine role in the Concert Party. The young, marriageable girl who sometimes becomes the unfaithful wife is another popular role. This is the specialty of Teobald Adjakpa, eighteen years old and a carpenter by trade. Short and stocky, he makes a charming but sometimes crafty wife.

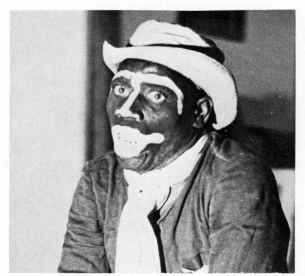

Dafiso is the clown, specializing in the roles of the comedian and of Scapin, that is, the steward. He is a talented clown and dancer. Unemployed, he expresses himself poorly in French which, by the way, is the reason Pascal gave for excluding him from the trip to France. He and Ben are the Two Bobs so highly ap-

One of the Bobs.

preciated in the prologue. Situated a bit apart is Vondoli who plays the clown on the top of the truck in parades through Lomé to advertise the evening show. He also participates in the prologue.

In addition to the permanent troupe, there are a certain number of young newcomers, who play small parts—minor prostitutes, stewards, etc. These have found a spokesman for their interests in the person of Simon de Fanti, nicknamed "Coins" because, as he explained, coins attract women. Thirty years old and once an intimate of Pascal's, Simon left the troupe some years ago after a conflict with Pascal. He has recently rejoined the troupe but there is still a certain coolness in his relations with Pascal. Like many members of the troupe, Simon has close ties to Ghana, where he was one of the stars of the "Happy Star of Accra" and where he acquired his trade. His considerable talents are especially evident in comic roles, for which his short stature and unusual features qualify him.

The members of the troupe are thus divided into three groups: the directors (Pascal, Lucas and Ben) and two teams. There is a good deal of conflict between the groups but we shall not go into detail here.

MEDIA The actors reach the audience using certain media such as music, song, poetry, ordinary language, make-up, etc. Led by Richard, the rhythms section is composed of six musicians: two electric guitars, one guitar, one bongo, a battery of drums and a pair of castanets. To these are often added various gourds and bells. The musicians are all capable of playing any instrument and there is often a certain rotation observable, although the head guitar is always played by Richard. Thus, the troupe is usually composed of seventeen members: eleven actors and six musicians. Actors and musicians take turns at the ticket office and many of the actors are also excellent musicians. It is not unusual to see Pascal and Lucas take turns at the guitar and Alex take the drums.

The Concert Party is a musical comedy: music is the support and often the vector. The Band doesn't use just any music drawn by chance from a cosmopolitan repertory but always plays "highlife." The Concert Party couldn't exist without this very unique rhythm. As a syncretism of traditional Akan rhythms, of calypso and of jazz, highlife has become the most popular music on the coast of Benin. It is a sort of West African jazz.

A stage entrance is effected in a very definite way. There is only one door leading backstage and all the actors exit and enter through this door.

The rhythm of highlife accompanies the entrance of each actor on stage. The slow entrance imposed by the rhythm of highlife, the music, the facing of the public, all give a hieratical aspect to these entrances. The entrance of the parents, of the marriageable young girl, of the beau, all are treated with the same solemn lightness: there is a tempo to the concert, an internal rhythm which must be respected. This is because the characters appear facing the public, static, like photographs. Their existence often ends with their appearance. The Concert Party is a theater of clichés and the music accompanies the projection of these pictures according to apparently invariable rhythms. There is a great and very modern sense of the *Image* in Concert Parties.

The audience dances to the rhythm of highlife and drinks beer. Highlife is the music of the good life, of the high-time in the bars of the big city.

Plays are not written: each text is the collective creation of the group which improvises around a storyline presented by one of its members. Plays are drawn from folktales heard in the village, from plays copied from other Concert Parties (usually Ghanaian), from newspapers and popular novels. The text is theatrical in that it calls for participation of the public; it is open-ended and permits the actor to insist on a comic episode or to draw out a sad scene. The text produced by the troupe is in the language of Lomé: this vehicular language is at the meeting point of two languages, Ewe and Mina, which for certain linguists are merely dialectal variants of the same language complex. It is highly probable that a homogenization o fthe different dialectal variants is occurring, to the advantage of the variant spoken in Lomé. The radius of performance of the "Happy Star" troupe furnishes striking evidence of this process. Their area covers all of southern Togo, that is, a region including at least four dialectal variants. The troupe is understood everywhere. The language they speak borrows numerous expressions from French and English.

The Concert Party has a very powerful visual appeal, thanks to its creative use of color in costumes and make-up. The playboy, frequent protagonist of the plays, tosses around "that's right," wears a hat, glasses and carries a briefcase. He smokes and flashes about a thick wallet. This "accoutrement"—such is the word used for the costumes—is of great importance. The playboy automatically seduces women, inducing them to leave their husbands. To lose the costume is no longer to be, and this is precisely what happens to Francis the Parisian. Loud-mouthed and egotistical, Francis seduces Cecilia with his handsome clothes, but as bad luck would have it, his clothes are reclaimed in the presence of Cecilia. All his prestige evaporates after such a debacle. The costume functions here as a true theatrical costume. Hat, long pants, coat are the signs of opulence accompanying the status of *fonctionnaire* (civil servant but also business man). An unemployed man doesn't wear an elegant hat but rather native dress with shorts. It is the elegance of Francis which leads to his success. The theatrical action is here based on a game of appearances, a game which the costumes set up. Glasses, cigarettes, hat, coat, long pants constitute the gentleman (illustration 4). Their disappearance reduces the personage to insignificance. Drawings of the different characters of the Concert Party illustrate the use of the costume and two or three accessories to define a type. The old man often has a lantern hanging around his neck and leans on a cane (illustration 5). It is out of the question to go to the store and buy a real cane; any board will do. The beautiful young girl always wears a suit cut in the latest fashion (illustration 6), or, if the girl is dressed in the traditional mode, she is tastefully and elegantly garbed (illustration 7). The steward or rustic is always in rags, wears a cloche hat or bandanna and often holds a rag swung over one shoulder (illustration 8). The comedians of the prologue are in imitation tail suits (illustration 9).

We also present in an appendix masks drawn as lines on each face. The actor is black-faced and traces his masks with white shoe polish. Of all the masks the most unusual are no doubt those of the comedians. The mouth is ringed

10   11

in white and so are the eyes (illustrations 10 and 11). These masks
are the first to appear before the
spectators for they are the ones who
open the show, and the effect is indeed striking. The eye surrounded
by white shoe polish, white accent-
ing the lines of the nose, and white
around the mouth—all these offer
numerous possibilities with interesting variations. Thus, we can have a
twin pair which are mirror images.
One of the pair will have a sort of
monocle (illustration 11) on the
right eye and the other will wear his
monocle on the left eye. The masks
vary from none at all (the young
girl or the prostitute—illustration
12) to the old woman or ugly young
girl covered with white "pock-
marks," to the moustache of the
gentleman (illustration 13) to the
enormous mouths and noses of the
clowns. The Concert Party imposes
a universe of masks codifying visual
expression and adding a very important dimension of structured spectacle to the plays.

12

13

PLOTS   All these elements—setting, actors, media—are combined in plots dealing mostly with family life. Let us not forget that the Concert Party is the only living channel of creative expression for most Loméans. Here are two typical plots.

Francis the Parisian

—Apprentice locomotive driver, John, is involved in a train accident.
—John's two wives, Marie and Elise, meet Francis the Parisian fanning himself with a fistful of banknotes. Marie is impressed.
—Francis departs with Marie, leaving faithful Elise alone.
—John returns home after his accident. Elise comforts him.
—Marie and Francis live it up.
—Marie rebuffs John. "I don't know you."
—Francis returns and the highlife continues.
—John tells Elise about Marie.
—Elise, alone, laments John's fate. She meets a gentleman who turns out to be a friend of John's with a new job offer for him.
—Elise tells John the good news and carries him off to the pharmacy to be cured.
—A "Nago" reclaims the coat, hat, dark glasses, shirt and tie rented by Francis. Marie is perplexed.
—A steward reclaims the pants rented by Francis. Francis is left in ragged shorts.
—When Marie enters, Francis explains that he's training for a boxing match.
—Marie clothes him in native dress. She brings food to him. There is a marathon eating scene with the saleswoman in the background. Francis has no money to pay.
—Marie enters wearing ragged native dress. The saleswoman has taken her skirt in payment for the food Francis has eaten. Marie leaves Francis.
—Francis laments the fickleness of women.
—John is now cured and living the life of a gentleman with Elise.
—Marie in ragged native dress begs for forgiveness and is taken in as a maid.
—Francis in rags is hired as a steward. Francis and Marie plot against John and Elise. But their plans are overheard.
—Marie denounces Francis. Elise and John beat Francis and chase him away. Marie is also driven out.

The African Wife from Paris

—Mr. John explains how his success in school has resulted in his being sent to Paris, where he has married an African living in Paris. Now back home, Mr. John has married the local girl who paid for his early studies.

—Mr. John tells Cecilia, his native wife, and his steward that the Parisian wife will soon arrive.

—Mr. John brings Monica home from the airport. The next day he leaves for work.

—Cecilia and Monica have difficulty communicating. Monica speaks no Ewe and Cecilia speaks no French. Cecilia wants to learn French and Monica teaches her some simple phrases. Cecilia teaches Monica the native dances and Monica teaches Cecilia the latest Parisian styles of dancing.

—When Mr. John returns home, Cecilia tries out her French on him. Mr. John doesn't understand a word.

—Dinner is served. The food is too spicy and Monica develops stomach cramps.

—The doctor is called, but he can do nothing for Monica. Monica dies.

—Monica is buried with much ceremony. Mr. John laments the sad fate of his Parisian wife.

—Monica appears to haunt Mr. John.

—Terrified, Cecilia leaves Mr. John.

—Mr. John is left alone.

The repertory of the "Happy Star" consists of about thirty different plays. New ones are added, drawn frequently from local incidents: the latest one we saw describes the murder of a police officer by his wife's lover, the arrest and subsequent public shooting of the wife and lover. Stories and pictures giving full details of the case appeared in Dahomean newspapers last year. Most stories concentrate on family life and the numerous problems caused by polygamy, one of them being the frequent fostering of children. The most popular story is *Agbeno xevi*, the story of the orphan, which takes its title from a well-known Ewe proverb: As long as there is life, there is hope. The female version of *Agbeno xevi* is the story of Cinderella, shown in a few sequences of our film.

CONCLUSION   The Concert Party can be viewed from many different angles. To the sociologist, it provides valuable data on the functions of voluntary associations. As one of the most popular cultural activities among school leavers, apprentices and the unemployed in Ghana and Togo, the Concert Party no doubt plays a role in filling an emotional vacuum for the newly-urbanized. It is conceivable that the Concert Party could become a powerful medium of change since it draws so much empathy from the audience and requires a strong emotional involvement.

The Concert Party is no less interesting viewed through the theory of diffusion of innovation in culture. K. N. Bame has shown how most of the Concert Party groups in Ghana can be traced directly to the original group in Sekondi.[1] The "Happy Star" of Lomé is no exception: in Aflao, members of the group saw and heard Ghanaian groups performing in Akan. At least one of their actors was a member of the "Happy Star of Accra," a Ghanaian group. The catalyt for the birth of the Concert Party in Togo was no doubt the meeting between Pascal, an excellent guitar player and organizer, Lucas, an actor and a poet, and Ben, an actor and a composer. These innovative personalities must be given the credit for establishing a new medium of communication in Togo. And thus, the Concert Party can be studied from the angle of the theory of communication.

And finally, the Concert Party could possibly increase our understanding of the relationships between ritual and drama. For instance, the Concert Party apparently has nothing to do with the cult of "Vodun" practiced in the same area. Yet members of the group are reluctant to explain the meaning of the facial masks and are equally reluctant to paint their faces in broad daylight.

The Concert Party belongs partly to tradition but also shows how new problems can be posed using the creative impulse of tradition. To young creative writers in Africa, the Concert Party is probably an important repository of forms waiting to be used.

[1] K. N. Bame, "Comic Play in Ghana," *African Arts/Arts d'Afrique*, I, 4 (1968), 30–34, 101.

LIST OF ILLUSTRATIONS

Drawings by B. Ricard

For the last four years, we have had the opportunity of working closely with the Happy Star Concert Band of Lomé. Four years ago, we started recording their performances; casual acquaintance grew into friendship and we decided to film the activities of the troupe, with their collaboration. In May 1973 the Happy Star Company was invited to the World Drama Festival of Nancy, one of the rallying points of the avant-garde. That year's Festival proposed a confrontation between avant-garde and popular theater. For the first time the Happy Star Concert Band undertook rehearsals and performed on a stage. We were with them and our understanding of the Concert Party deepened. Then, in the summer of 1973 we spent two months in Togo, to analyze the present condition of the group and the possible impact the trip to Europe might have made on their performances. Our film, *Agbeno xevi*, is available for purchase and rental from the UCLA Media Center, Royce Hall, UCLA, Los Angeles, California 90024.

Tragedy – Greek and Yoruba:
A Cross-Cultural Perspective

ROBERT PLANT ARMSTRONG

INTRODUCTION

I argue the existence of a cultural dynamic—pre-conceptual, pre-affective
—which we learn with splendid, vast and rapid talent. This dynamic,
which I call the mythoform,[1] is a monitoring function of the human
consciousness and it builds the cognitions of populations into cultures,
those highly particular and characteristic systems of negative entropy
which we encounter from people to people. The mythoform enables any
individual in any culture to encounter a novel stimulus in terms which are
recognizable and acceptable to him and to his culture—in other words in
terms which *are* his culture.

It is further the case that in the work of affecting presence the mythoform is celebratively enacted—for the sake (the joy, the utility, the awe)
of its own forms. The affecting presence derives its unique power from
this simple fact, namely that it incarnates the very conditions of man's
consciousness. The conditions of its existence are culturally variable, and
they are both general and specific.

Now the work of affecting presence may incarnate the mythoform in either or both of two respects: first, the mythoform may be incarnated into work as actors; and second, the mythoform informs—indeed it constitutes—the dynamics established by the networks of interaction among its parts. All works of affecting presence do the latter; those which also do the former I refer to by the special term *myth*.

I further posit the existence in European and Yoruba cultures, at least, of two different mythoformal dynamics. One of these is consequential—which is to say that actions entail consequences—or *synthetic*; while the other is sequential, or *syndetic*.[2]

Against the background of these elementary assumptions, I propose to examine two tragedies in order to determine whether one can come to a definition of tragedy that will enjoy cross-cultural validity.

Oedipus Rex

In European culture, the cultural mythoform is constituted at least in part by a dialectic of oppositions. Now "opposites" are defined in quite specific though variable ways. What are opposites in some instances may not be so in others. Two people who belong to different political parties are thus political opposites. If they are of the same sex, however, they may not be viewed as opposites—traditionally at least—with respect to sexual relationships, which, since by definition these must occur between opposites, are forbidden them. In some instances even when two people are of opposite sexes, they are even so not social opposites, and so sexual relationships are forbidden between them as well. It is for this reason that neither parent and child nor brother and sister may engage in intercourse.

If any of these forbidden relationships—which we may understand to be alien to the best interests of proper synthesis—occur, the force of the law is brought down upon those individuals who perpetrate them. So, in literary practice, for instance, has it typically been the case that in homosexual novels happiness was impossible, and suicide was the typical end ordained for the fictional homosexual. The case is not wholly different with respect to incest—witness *Oedipus Rex*, for instance, where suicide and mutilation of the chief and offending characters occur.

There is an abyss of difference between a novel of the homosexual genre and the *Oedipus Rex*, however. This difference derives not only from magnitude of view about the nature of man, nor from language—although these are both factors of critical differentiation—but from the fact that in the homosexual instance "righting" of the askew dialectic is worked upon the characters, who become mere pieces in an enactment of a morality which is based upon our mythoform, while in the other instance that mythoform itself splinters into terms and enacts itself, wears itself out *through* itself masking as characters. The characters of Greek tragedy are so little individuated because they are archetypal principles! Those masks they wore were for more than mere cosmetic effect!

We have come to the point where it is possible to hypothesize that *Oedipus Rex* is a tragedy because it enacts the dialectic of synthesis gone awry. The more general proposition is that it is a tragedy because it perverts the dynamic of the mythoform. Indeed we may perceive in this a new principle in the definition of tragedy. In fact, if we view the case in these terms, we may make the concept of tragedy *cultural* rather than merely a convention of European literature.

If such actions as are regarded within a culture as perversions of the mythoform are not done but merely jested with, the ludicrous—man, or more often animal: the trickster, for example—then the literary or dramatic form that results is comedy. Anansi sleeps with his mother-in-law. And in Java, where the mythoform—whatever it might be—must exist within the terms of the discipline of extension, comedians characteristically elicit laughter by threatening to commit some of the sins of extensionality, which involve the extremities—touching the head, putting one's posterior area (which, when he is sitting, is an extremity) near the face of another. In the ordinary conduct of one's life, such actions would evoke serious and perhaps even mortal consequences. It is not accidental that in our culture, in a convention deriving from ancient days, the masks of comedy and tragedy are shown as but different aspects of the same face. The trickster is as importantly involved with the vitality of the mythoform as the culture hero is. The mythoform must flex itself if it is to remain healthy. It must maintain itself through the rejection of its alternatives.

Thus it is that in such literary forms the mythoform in its uncorrupted essence presides over the whole through its straightforward enactment in both the general dynamics of enactment and in particular details as well. That this is the case represents a culturally normative function of the mythoform. Therefore, I should like to show how it is that in the *Oedipus Rex* the work itself, as an organism with both form and process, enacts not the perversion of the cultural mythoform but the straightforward reality of it. Thus while the tragedy's substantive dimension cries out one swearing of the myth, the structural dynamic insistently swears the other. This fact reinforces the victory at the substantive level of the mythoform writ pure which characterizes the endings of—at least—European tragedies.

The substantive dimension of *Oedipus Rex*—its *aboutness*—may be viewed as occurring in six phases, though the work is not formally divided into scenes and acts. These phases are the beginning, or introduction; the phase which occurs between Oedipus and Tiresias; that among Oedipus, Creon, and Jocasta; the one between Oedipus and the Corinthian messenger; the phase of the herdsman; and the ending. Each of these phases ends with a major chorus and with the withdrawal or introduction of a major actor. But these phases also have a significant dramatic function. They do more than constitute convenient blocs for the consideration of the work, as we shall see finally. But we must not think that they fragmentize one world. For the fact of the matter, of course, is that the unflagging dedication of Sophocles to the disciplines of the unities of time, place, and action makes an uncompromising oneness of the work.

The mythoformal reading of the *Oedipus* is, most basically, a presentation in polar continuity, involving in serial plan cataclysmic oppositions among successive pairs of polar actors. Its particular significance, to be sure, derives from the overriding bonds of value which should have held these oppositions in dynamic stasis, for oppositions are good and necessary to social, ethical, and empirical progress. But some oppositions pervert this good—all the more horrible when, unbeknownst to one, what he conceives to be good is in fact evil—when what should by the law of man have proved to be enduring, ennobling, humanizing, proves instead to be quite the reverse. Our view of the simple though infinitely tyrannical order of the universe which for us validates the polar nature of all things would appear to have been suspended in the case of man, who by integrating the oppositions of his parents is in himself, if not in his roles, the ultimate synthesis.

Yet as Freud saw, this synthesis is more apparent than real. It is a beguiling illusion, and the individual consciousness must define itself in the only way it can, which is to say in opposition to all others. This is the myth of consciousness which enacts itself in the *Oedipus*. A horrible incest has produced, in dreadful synthesis, the Sphinx, offspring of Echidna and her own offspring, Orthus, the dog.[3] The deformity which is the Sphinx, issuing from this heinous union, expresses nonetheless the integration of its dam and sire. Mankind can be safe only if the Spinx is destroyed, and so Oedipus, who because of his own deformity of the foot is ritually appropriate for it, undertakes this task in behalf of mankind. His awareness of his own crippledness, whether it makes him especially apt to answer the Sphinx's fatal riddle or not, is—we assume—at least not irrelevant to the puzzle about man based only upon the nature of man's pedality.

Oedipus slays the Sphinx because he has rendered it powerless, having resolved the paradox of its riddle, and so he must go the rest of the way in the unraveling of this monstrosity of integration by also engaging in precisely the same kind of union which produced the Sphinx. Thus, he marries his own mother and begets not a monster but two sons and two daughters. Through this inevitable sacrifice of himself and his kind, for he destroys either one life or the happiness of all his people, he analyzes being once again into its identity of whole and unmonstrous selfness, and mankind is again safe. Once the seed of incest that bore evil has spent itself—perpetrated by gods and destroyed by a hero—Thebes is purged and mankind is released to its natural destiny of utter selfhood.

So much for the myth. But what of the tragedy, which is a special way of viewing the mythoform? In his tragic conception Sophocles takes a moral view of the story of Oedipus, which seems to be a definitive characteristic of the tragedy. This is signified by the fact that the Thebans are suffering a plague of sterility, and by the fact that the conception of the play is in terms of guilt and atonement. In Sophocles' view the destruction of an evil does not justify the commission of another evil, irrespective of the social good derived from the first action. But at the same time, Sophocles cannot escape the force of his own insistent mythoform, and the deep fact remains that this evil is so profound an evil as it is—sufficiently profound indeed to cause all the people to suffer—owing to the fact that what has occurred between Oedipus and Jocasta is a perversion of the dynamic mythoform itself. The deep answer to the question "Why is incest wrong?" must differ from culture to culture. But surely in the Greek culture it had to do with a violation of the synthetic imperative. Sophocles' overriding cultural purpose in writing this work, at least as the evidence of the work itself leads us to believe, was to show the horror resulting from a morally repugnant (and mythoformally perverted) state of affairs.

It is the orderly process of the proper enactment of the mythoform, which moves inexorably against such offenders as Oedipus and Jocasta, with the force of the rightness of the culture, which brings these offenders down.

The *Oedipus Rex* moves almost compulsively from beginning to end. There is no fat—not one diversionary action, nor one speech in useless delivery. The play is a continuum of serious events, each causally (synthetically) related to its predecessor. *Oedipus Rex* is an elegant dynamic of consequentiality rather than of sequentiality, such as that which characterizes *The Palm-Wine Drinkard*.[4] It is powerful to us because of the fact that there is nothing at all to adulterate its power. All parts—theme, rhetoric, morality, the unities, the mythoform—work together at their most intense to produce a consummate work. Not least of these is the inexorable forward movement of the right presentation of the mythoform enacting itself not only among the relationships among the characters but also among the constituent actions and dynamics of the diachronic fabric.

The work exists as a nexus of numerous, distinct systems of dialectical (synthetic) oppositions. These, interdigitating and interacting as they constantly do, cause the work to exist as the densest possible actualization of the mythoformal presence in the work, and the more importantly and the more affectingly the mythoform celebrates itself, the more powerful the work. When this concentration is executed in elegant complexity, great and humane imagination, high quality, enormous dignity, and a passionate concern with man and his estates, then such a work becomes a masterpiece. Such is the case with *Oedipus Rex*.

This system of oppositions is comprised of sub-systems, the most important of which may be called structural, not in the current, anthropologically fashionable (and useful) sense of that term but rather in the more ordinary literary sense of meaning that which pertains to that physical shape of the work which is fully though sometimes obscurely given in the work. I am speaking of that perceptible esthetic shape in which the work exists as a spatio-temporal event, and not of any reduction of that work or of its systems to even an elegant and seminal generalization. This is the full structure, that which in large measure generates the work's affecting charge. I shall restrict my remarks to this level—a dimension, in some obscure reaches at least, lying in all probability quite beyond the idiosyncratic control of an author. It is here that we shall see the mythoform normatively at work.

This dynamic revolves about the work's chief process opposition, namely that between innocence and guilt. It is this which structures the whole reverse dialectic of desynthesis of the state of sin in which Oedipus, his house, and his kingdom exist at the play's opening. It is a paradox (which is a relationship between opposites) of the tragedy that by unraveling the mystery, the tragedy itself, in contrast, is raveled up. This is the complement of the dialectic of the work's analysis of Oedipus's guilt. This leads us to the point where we can see that another dialectic is that waged between absolute entropy and growing certitude. Each action diminishes uncertainty and increases certainty. This cluster of oppositions constitutes the chief dialectical dynamic that is primarily generative of the work's compulsive forward drive.

The play begins with Oedipus in an obvious state of innocence (as regards the central issue of the work); soon the contrary estate, that of guilt—absolutely condemned by the gods—is posed. But this estate is anonymous, which is to say that it is not settled upon any particular person. At the work's climax, when we perceive that it is Oedipus who is guilty, he does not assume the mantle of absolute guilt. It is of the nature of synthesis that there should be in guilt an admixture of innocence. We see into his crime. He is factually guilty but morally clean. The interplay between this guilt and innocence, more thoughtful analysis will show, is but another name—a substantive name—for the structural movement of the desynthesis or the unraveling.

A further substantive opposition is formed by the contrast between clutching at the straws of hasty optimism on the one hand and inevitably coming face-to-face with the awful reality of the futility of such an activity on the other. But this opposition, while of importance, is local rather than general, being significantly restricted to this phase and, coming at this precise point, seeming to relax the work's pace a little, while in fact at the same time intensifying it through the exploitation of our more acute knowledge to the contrary.

> Jocasta: What kind of news, sir? From what city do you come?
> Corinthian Messenger: Corinth. And the news I'll tell you will please you surely. It may also grieve. (*RPA: n.b. the oppositions here.*)
> Jo: What kind of news can have such double power?
> C.M.: The citizens of Corinth will make Oedipus their king.
> Jo: What! Does not old Polybus still hold his throne?
> C.M.: No, death holds him now; the king is in his grave.
> Jo: (Excited) What are you saying? Is Old Polybus truly dead, old man?
> C.M.: My lady, if I haven't spoken the truth, why, then—I too deserve to die.
> Jo: (Almost beside herself with relief at the news. She turns to an attendant.) Go at once and tell your master. O oracles of heaven, where is your fulfillment now! So long, so long has Oedipus feared and fled this man, that he might not kill him. Now chance, and not the hand of Oedipus has killed his father. (pp. 47–48).[5]

The dialectic of chorus and cast is a further presentation of the mytho-form. The play begins and ends with a chorus and a chorus concludes each of the six phases of the action. It is the function of these choruses to provide to the actions of the tragedy that counterpoint which is evaluation in terms of the public welfare and morality of the actions committed by the individuated (as contrasted with the choral) actors, chiefly by the protagonist and those significantly interacting with him.

For example, at the end of the dreadful last phase, after blind Oedipus has been led by Creon into the palace, the chorus says,

> Look upon him, all of you who dwell in Thebes.
> Behold, this is Oedipus—he who solved
> the riddle of the Sphinx,
> and was of all men most masterful.
> Upon him fortune smiled, and all men gazed in envy.
> Now, now over him has broken a storm
> of terror and disaster.
> O you who are mortal, look upon life's end
> and on your own.
> Count no man happy until without disaster
> he passes to that last boundary of his life. (p. 77)

One must not think that the chorus stands always in disapproval of the actions of the main character, however. On the contrary, since the role of the chorus is to be oppositional to the individuated actors of the tragedy, the chorus may oppose any one of them. Sophocles does not idealize the public by placing the chorus in an infallible and juridical role. Sometimes it is swayed by its emotions and loyalties. For example, after the bitter disagreement between Oedipus and Tiresias, the chorus says,

> I know
> Zeus and Apollo omniscient
> hold in their minds
> the destinies of men.
> But in this affair
> that a mortal seer
> can win wisdom greater than mine—
> who can perfectly judge this question?
> I know
> one man will excel another
> in skills of augury,
> but till I see
> perfect fulfillment of his word,
> never will I consent
> to reproach the king. (p. 27)

The dialectic of the chorus and the individuated actors is one between the general and the particular, the public and the private. And while in the long run the "general and the public" is bound to be right, in the short run it can make errors of judgment and its attitudes can be wrong.

There is a further dialectic of orders—that between the divine and the mortal. This is a complex and pervasive dynamic in the work. We see it in the opposition of Oedipus to Tiresias; of Jocasta's abiding contempt for prophecy; and most of all in Oedipus's act of pride in presuming that he can escape the fate that Apollo has revealed to be the one that awaits him. Consider the following speech of Jocasta to Oedipus.

> Ah! then absolve yourself of any anxiety in this business. If you will listen to me, Oedipus, you will learn no mortal has the gift of prophecy. And Tiresias is mortal. I will give you quick and clear proof of what I say. An oracle came to Laius, whether from Apollo himself or from his ministers I do not know—a prophecy that if he and I had a son, Laius was fated to die by that child's hand. Now Laius was killed by highwaymen at a place where three roads meet. Those were the facts reported. His son, an infant, lived but three short days. Laius fastened the child's ankles with a pin and had him exposed on a deserted mountain. So! Apollo neither brought it about that he kill his father, nor did Laius experience that terrible thing, though he feared it, of being killed by his own son. Such were the prophecies, but I tell you if a god needs to search out anything—like a king's murder—you can be sure he can do it without a prophet's help. (pp. 38–9)

This opposition gives rise to yet another, thus further enriching the interconnected chain of linked dialectical causalities. We must bear in mind that the Greek audience knew full well the story of Oedipus. Shelley observed that the highest order of suspense lies in knowing what is going to happen and in then proceeding to discover how it is that the inevitable happens. Further, when the audience knows what is going to happen and the actors do not, we have a situation which, as is well known, is called *dramatic irony*. We also have a further oppositional set, and I shall call this one the dialectic of irony.

Our sure knowledge of the impending, inevitable course of events overrides each instance of the tragedy's enactment, coloring with irony all that we behold. Since the play is complex—as I have by now surely suggested—the dialectic of irony is complex as well, pervading the play at every level, throughout the whole dialectical system—not just the structural subsystem I am discussing here. For us, Oedipus's situation grows increasingly intolerable as we know that his hopes are vain and as we see—while he does not—that each moment brings him nearer to his downfall.

So in Jocasta's speech above we see a powerful irony, for we know that contrary to her opinion Apollo *will* have his way. Further, though she dismiss prophecy, yet will it prevail. And Oedipus's assertion "For if I go back to Corinth I must marry my own mother—it is fated—and kill my father, Polybus, who begot me and nurtured me in love" (p. 43), fills us with dread, for we know the truth. The opposition between what we know and what Oedipus and Jocasta presume is a powerful and universally pervasive dynamic of the dialectical structure.

There are further structural dialectics—those between the permanent and the transitory, the real and the transitory, the real and the illusory, the discretionary and the inevitable. I could trace these out, but they would only serve to prove further a point which, in my judgment, is already adequately demonstrated.

As a final note, I should like to indicate that I did not define the existence of the work's five phases merely gratuitously. Indeed, the six phases, each ending with a chorus, also have a dialectical function. This is to be seen when we recognize the function of the phase-terminal chorus, which is not only to evaluate the preceding action but also to provide a brief leveling-off period before the mounting of the action of the next phase. The upward build of the play's action, thus, is not an uninterruptedly rising line of ascent, but rather a series of steps.

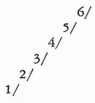

Of these steps, the middle four phases bear common characteristics of relationship for they relate to those phases which are their adjacent environments in the dual of a precurson and successor, while the first phase has only the former role and the last phase only the latter. These movements are dialetical terms, and the progress and resolution of the paly are their relationships.

The final opposition, of course, is that between the distortion of the mythoform in the situation of Oedipus and Jocasta, and the arighting of it by orderly, dialectical processes of the tragedy.

In the analysis of *Oedipus Rex*, we may, with varying degrees of confidence, reach four generalizations.

(1) The first is that in European tragedy the ending is characterized by a defeat of the tragic situation, thus arighting those traditional values which have been threatened. A correlative function of this fact is that although harm comes to the tragic protagonist, yet this downward movement is counterbalanced by the upward movement of the triumph of these traditional values.

(2) The second generalization is that "It is the law of the affecting presence that the greater the concentration of the mythoformal presence

in the work the more importantly and the more affectingly the mythoform celebrates itself and the more powerful the work."

(3) The third generalization suggests that tragedy, as a cultural function, involves the perversion (and to that I would add the denial) of the mythoform by the tragic protagonist.

(4) Finally, in tragedy the mythoform is asserted positively throughout the structure of the work—not in words and actions alone but as a viable and dynamic presence of the structure—thus constituting a normative assertion of itself which all the while maintains the mythoform in its rightness as over and against the substantive awryness of it which the play's explicit actions concern.

It is obvious, I think, that the first and third generalizations may be joined together and that the statement will be to the effect that the cultural definition of a tragedy is that it is a work of affecting presence which enacts a perversion or a denial of the cultural myth; further it does this in such a way that with the defeat of the tragic protagonist a paradoxical terminal situation prevails, taking the hero down but the audience up. In many cases, of course, the protagonist is ennobled by his defeat so that he himself simultaneously exhibits both defeat and victory. If this holds cross-culturally, we can make a firm hypothesis of it. Further, if the other two principles hold as well, we can incorporate them into it, thus reaching an expanded and more useful generalization.

Oba Waja

The foregoing is a compelling reading, from the point of view of a humanistic anthropologist. Yet before we can assert a general proposition to the effect that tragedy is a *cultural* rather than merely a *western* literary form, it is necessary that we examine a work from another culture. For this purpose I have selected Duro Ladipo's *Oba Waja* (*The King is Dead*) as the other work to study. This play, we are told, is based upon a true incident that happened in Oyo in 1946. This particular fact, which perhaps holds little if any significance for the play itself, is nonetheless of considerable interest in terms of attesting to the power of the mythoform (which I shall soon show to be present in the work) which informs an actual life situation in direct, presentational terms quite as readily as it does a drama, with the difference of course that in the play—in contrast to the life situation—the myth presents itself celebratively, which is to say that it enacts the myth in its own terms and for its own sake.

Oba Waja concerns the failure of a certain Yoruba official—indeed a high court official of the King of Oyo, the Alafin—to perform a duty that tradition required of him. This fact would suggest, therefore, that the play is about a conflict between the old and the new—this after all is the determination we have made about so many contemporary African works. Well, this is true—in the most obvious possible sense. Indeed, it is so patent a truism that it is tautologous to remark it. If in saying so much one says nothing at all, then what is one to say about *Oba Waja* and such other works as confront the old and the new? Why simply that at a more fundamental level something far more profound is happening, and that the work has a much greater specific gravity than the mere truistic assertion of the fact of simple acculturation could ever suggest.

It seems that when an Alafin of Oyo dies it is expected, or at least it was not so very long ago expected, that one of the high, court officials, namely the commander of the king's horse, would follow him in death in order that the king might not go unaccompanied into the afterlife. A chorus of market women puts the case this way:

> One hand by itself cannot lift the load on the head
> Ajeje—it is a fact.
> Alafin must not cross the river alone.
> Ojurongbe Aremu, commander of the king's horse;
> Follow in your father's footsteps.
> The forest will be ashamed,
> If the elephant eats and he is not satisfied.
> If the red camwood is used up in the calabash,
> The child cannot anoint its body for the feast.
> If your courage runs out,
> How shall the king confront the gateman of heaven?
> You, owner of crown, born into a big house,
> Ojurongbe Aremu
> Do not allow the world to spoil
> In your own time.
> Will you stay behind to eat earthworms and centipedes?
> Follow your king and
> Share his meal in heaven.
> Commander of the horse,
> Come forth, come forth,
> We are expecting you.
> Today you are the owner of the market,
> Today the town belongs to you.
> Follow the footsteps of your fathers.
> The forest will be ashamed,
> If the elephant eats and is not satisfied.
> The forest will be ashamed. (pp. 58–59)[6]

Praise names with their litany of attributes, are clearly syndetic (additive) means of achieving the constitution of character. They represent an effective way, as does the careful delineation of psychological and historical "causes," to bring a dramatic or a fictive character into existence. The number of attributions accorded a man tends to be an index of his power and importance. Ojurongbe Aremu replies:

> Today I shall accompany my king across the river
> No gate-keeper shall bar his way
> While I am at his side
> Today I shall fly to heaven like the fruit pigeon.
> Today I shall leave you to walk the ground like the hornbill. (p. 60)

However, there is a countervailing view, that held by the wife of the District Officer. She thinks that this sacrificial requirement is a barbarous custom and therefore insists to her husband that he use his authority to prevent Ojurongbe's death. She asks:

> Do you mean to say that in the twentieth century we
> still have human sacrifices in this town—and under
> British rule?
> D.O: This is not a human sacrifice. Nobody will kill
> the man. He will die by simple act of will. (p. 57)

But the wife continues to protest, indeed threatening to take the next boat home unless this death is prevented. The District Officer yields, protesting that "these things are better left alone." Accordingly he intervenes, the people of Oyo saying:

> When Ojurongbe took his title
> He knew he would die like this.
> He knew he would die like his father.
> He knew he would die like his grandfather.
> Let not the world spoil in our time.
> Eeeh, eeeh, eeeh, eeeh!
> The child is weeping. (p. 61)

The D.O. orders the arrest of Ojurongbe, and the people lament:

> The world is spoilt in the white man's time.
> Shall the commander of the horse
> Remain behind to eat earthworms and centipedes?
> And who will give food to the king
> On his way to heaven?
> Alafin, owner of the palace,
> The white man's rule has spoiled our world.
> Vengeance is in your hands. (pp. 61–62)

Ojurongbe has of course lost face with the people, even though he maintains that the white man has overpowered him. Ojurongbe says:

> My head whom I worshipped in the morning,
> My head whom I praised in the morning.
> Why did you allow this to happen in my time?
> The white man rendered my charms impotent,
> He drained the power of my medicine.
> He has deprived me of a glorious death.
> Now I can die of the matchet
> Like a cow slaughtered in the market
> I can bleed to death.
> Now I can burn myself alive
> Smouldering away like a rubbish dump.
> But the glorious road to heaven is closed.   (p. 63)

The dead Alafin manifests himself in order to accuse Ojurongbe, ultimately assuring him that he, the Alafin,

> ... shall not enter the gate of heaven unattended.
> I have chosen my new attendant.   (p. 64)

Ojurongbe's son, who is trading in Ghana, learns of the Alafin's death and rushes home, knowing the mortal obligation upon his father.

> Oh merciless death
> The house of joy collapses when you arrive.
> You break the honeycomb and spill its sweetness   (p. 66)

But Dawudu arrives home to find his father alive, and Dawudu shames him for his lack of resoluteness.

> Ooooh!
> Today a child must carry a father's burden.
> The falling leaf does not stop to rest
> Before it touches the ground.
> The river will never return to its source.
> Today will I face the gatekeeper of heaven
> Preparing the glorious entry of my king!   (pp. 68–69)

Dawudu stabs himself. The chorus of Oyo people let both Ojurongbe and the District Officer know their own responsibilities in this affair. There is now no option left to Ojurongbe but to destroy himself, which he does, saying:

> I shall not carry my head to heaven
> In front of the Alafin.
> Yet I must follow Dawudu.
> Today I shall see the king of the river

And the king of the sun.
Today I shall see my king
Gleaming in the darkness like a red hot sun.   (p. 71)

The work is concluded by the District Officer, the Oyo people, and the women.

Olori Elesin kills himself.

DISTRICT OFFICER: O God!
Can I be blamed for doing justice?
Is kindness my crime?
I was trying to save a life—
And I have caused a double death.
Man only understands the good he does
   unto himself,
When he acts for others,
Good is turned into evil; evil is turned
   into good!

OYO PEOPLE: White man, bringer of new laws.
White man, bringer of new times.
Your work was confounded by Eshu,
   confuser of men.
Nobody can succeed against the will of
   Eshu
The god of fate.
Having thrown a stone today—he kills a
   bird yesterday.
Lying down, his head hits the roof—
Standing up he cannot look into the
   cooking pot.
With Eshu
Wisdom counts for more than good intentions,
And understanding is greater than justice.

WOMEN: Olori Elesin, Commander of the Horse:
You believed the stranger
And the world broke over your head.
You believed in the new time—
As yet we cannot tell
How much of our world you have destroyed
Cross now the river in peace.
Today you shall see the king of the river.
Today you shall face the king of the sun.
Alafin's eyes will gleam in the darkness.
He has become a burning sun, glowing in
   the darkness.

(p. 72)

THE END

With respect to the first hypothesis concerning a work of tragedy's involvement with the cultural mythoform gone awry, and its corollary concerning the bi-valued nature of the ending of such a work, I should remind the reader that I have said that the Yoruba mythoform is compounded, at least in part, upon the premise that reality is constituted not synthetically but syndetically, i.e., accretively. In the particular instance of *Oba Waja*, the point upon which the tragedy devolves is stated by the elders early in the play.

> Shall the owner of the palace cross the river alone?
> Shall he confront the gate-keeper of heaven unaccompanied?   (p. 57)

One can see the significance of this question when he takes the occasion to ask his own question: why should the Alafin *not* go unaccompanied into death? In our culture, for example, the notion of someone's accompanying another to heaven—save in the instance of one with an utterly distraught mind—would never occur to one.

But on the other hand, neither would it ever occur to us to make sacrifices of food, liquor, or material objects to the dead. Aside from our modest and meaningless gifts of flowers, we do nothing for the dead. However, we already know that the institution of the sacrifice is supported or validated by the beliefs that the ancestors continue to intervene in man's affairs, and that their power is subject to growth and diminution, which are directly related to the presence or absence of sacrifices to them. It is an obvious corollary of this position that if they are strong they can intervene more effectively on our behalf—and will be more kindly disposed to intervene in the first place, if they are in a state of maximal power and contentment.

One who has followed my analysis this far will recognize immediately that in the belief that the commander of the king's horses should die in order to accompany the Alafin to heaven we see a clear instance of syndetism. This incrementation of the person of the Alafin, furthermore, is in the interest of his power. For we learn that the Alafin will not face the gate-keeper of heaven on the basis of his moral worth—which may appear to be a product of the dialectic of his life, the synthetic sum-total of his acts—but rather he will gain entry on the basis of augmented power. Since it is not merely a lowly servant or a slave who is to accompany him but a distinguished and powerful member of the court, that increment of power which is owing to the Alafin is great indeed.

What happens in *Oba Waja*, of course, is that this normal, augmentative function of the mythoform is subverted because a weak commander allows the ancient functioning of the culture to be subverted by the actions of the District Officer who does not himself become the villain of the piece; he is merely an instrument of dramatic convenience, though he does come in for some serious and deserved upbraiding from the people of Oyo. While Ladipo could indeed have dwelt at considerable dramatic length on the harm which might come to the people of Oyo from the spirit of the offended Alafin (as Sophocles would have done), his chief interest is not in consequence of faithless and indeed un-Yoruba behavior, but rather in the syndetic aspects of the situation.

The Alafin's spirit persuades us that he shall have his due, and he does: the commander's son performs the syndetic action which the father owed but failed to perform. With this action the state of offense against the mythoform is righted and it may continue to exist in accordance with the dictates of its normal dynamic.

Even the ending of the work is subject to the syndetic imperative, with the result that the expected countermoving forces of the purgation of fear and pity, of victory and defeat occur through the agencies of two characters: Dawudu brings victory for the mythoform while Ojurongbe's apostasy suffers defeat. Dawudu's death itself is a victory for him as a good citizen of Oyo, while Ojurongbe's death, I suspect, brings only minor satisfaction to the viewer. Expressed in the alternative terms, we can say that the ending of the work releases us from pity through Ojurongbe's death and from the terror which was evoked by the suspension of the normal order of the mythoform's suasion over the culture through the sacrifice of Dawudu. We may affirm, then, that *Oba Waja* bears to the mythoform that kind of relationship which we hypothesized and that this hypothesis concerning the nature of tragedy appears therefore to be cross-culturally valid.

May we, then, perform a simple substitution which states that "the work exists as a nexus of numerous distinct systems of syndetic sequences, and that these interdigitate and interact so as to cause the work to exist as the densest possible actualization of the mythoform?" Let us consider the play for a moment in order to ascertain as quickly as possible whether we can or cannot demonstrate this proposition to be true and so confirm the original hypothesis concerning mythoformal concentration in a work.

We should note gross physical details first. The play is nineteen pages long and yet contains five acts. Of course, we realize that *Oba Waja* is an opera and that, owing to the music and dancing, the actual elapsed dramatic time is certain to be considerably greater than this allocation of pages to acts—on the average, fewer than four pages per act. Nonetheless, it is objectively the case that in terms of the story line itself, where the dramatic dimensions of the mythoform's incarnation.are to be perceived (they will also characterize the dance and the music), there simply is not sufficient dramatic "space" for very much elaboration of the mytho-form to occur. Indeed, when we consider the play as a whole, we find that it is relatively simple. There is no system of character complications. As a matter of fact, the characters do not enjoy marked character develop-ment, and the work cannot in any sense be said to be concerned with the psychological dimensions of the protagonists. Ojurongbe is not de-veloped into a fully-dimensioned character even in syndetic terms. He is a type, a role: one who denies the tradition. He has little more dramatic dimension than does the palm-wine drinkard. Nor is there any use made of the mounting of dramatic ironies. And crime is not heaped upon crime to make him even more evil—nor countervailing good upon counter-vailing good so that we might see him as a person in simple error and worthy of salvation. In fact, search as one might, it is not possible to find any system of the assertion of the mythoform save that sole one which constitutes the necessary and sufficient condition for a work of dramatic import to be enacted. It appears then that this hypothesis is wrong. There is not a density but rather a paucity of systems affirming and reaffirming the power of the mythoform.

Yet there is something we have forgotten. This is not merely a syndetic myth, it is a myth of syndetic intensive continuity,[7] where range is in-hibited and where continuity is achieved through the syndetic accretion of small parts into a whole. This last fact explains why there are so many small acts constituting the whole. And if the discipline in terms of which the mythoform exists demands an inhibition of range, then we can hardly expect to find this injunction violated in the creation of an effective tragedy. In fact, what one wishes for in such a circumstance is the clean-est, most straightforward—indeed one should say *elegant*—presentation of the work. It is in this respect that the mythoform for the Yoruba is most eloquently to be incarnated. Accordingly we must count this hy-pothesis in need of significant revision, a revision which will allow for the factor of cultural variability with respect to the understanding given the term *concentration*. We shall have to say that the power with which a mythoform incarnates itself into a tragedy is directly contingent upon the success with which the work in question enacts either a density or a simple elegance of its assertion, depending upon whether the culture in question enacts extension or intension as one of the conditions of the existence of its myth.

Finally, we must inquire whether we can demonstrate that the syndetic myth in its normal function is to be found at the silent levels of the play, for it is on the basis of these results that we must affirm or deny the third proposition about tragedy, namely that the mythoform asserts itself silent-ly within a work of tragedy, acting as a normative factor, countering the substantive message of error.

This inhibition upon the development of an elaborate network of sub-systems of the statement of the mythic power which I have just noted is of course a direct enactment of the intensive aspect of the myth of syndetic continuity. Thus we may see that very quality of the work which may strike the European as a distinct thinness is in fact an eloquent and elegant actualization of the mythoform.

Further, I have already noted the act-density factor which is clearly a syndetic manifestation. Ladipo's achievement through the introduction of so fine a division of the continuity of his work is unquestionably to constitute the whole atomistically. Further, these five acts require four scenes, a fact which further underscores the syndetic achievement of continuity. I should note in passing that this fact of such a high incidence of scene change could under other circumstances be read as an extensive trait—namely under the circumstance of a culture which enacts extension as a condition of the existence of its mythoform. We learn here that the achievement of syndetism may sometimes give the appearance of establishing range. But of course, once we examine the actions that constitute those scenes, we recognize that they reveal naught but the most rigorously maintained intension. We learn further, in other words, that homologous characteristics do not necessarily have the same significance. *Oba Waja*, therefore, exists unrelievedly as a structural enactment of syndetic intension. The fact that it is a dramatic continuity is self-evident from my synopsis of the action.

But there are other manifestations of syndetism as well. The punctuation of the surface of the dramatic continuum into so many acts has the effect not only of atomizing action into its greatest number of phases; it follows that it achieves the same effect with respect to the development of the character of Ojurongbe. In rapid succession we perceive him to be firm, compromised, denying of the traditional values, accused by the dead Alafin, rejected by his people, rejected by his son, robbed of his son, and dead at his own hand. So many significant developments in so short a dramatic space give us an actional continuum almost as dense with events as drumming, which in this as well as in another respect the work suggests.

Nowhere is this particular quality of syndetism more evident than it is in the dialogue itself. Consider these choruses from the opening of the work:

CHORUS: Ye, ye, ye, ye!
The king has gone
the owner of the palace is dead.
Our father returned home,
He entered into a deep forest.
We shall not see him return from there,
Except in our dreams.

ELDERS: We must not see it
It is forbidden.
The king is dead
He has crossed the river of life.
He has crossed the river into darkness.
The owner of the palace
Shall be buried with the beating of gongs.
The sound of the funeral gongs makes us tremble,
When wild animals scatter in fear.
Saworo, ye, ye, saworo.   (pp. 55–56)

The sentences are short and they are simple, each limited to one
assertion. The staccato quality of such speeches is marked. Equally marked
is the fact that there is little variability in the information they contain.
Sentences repeat the same facts, varying only their poetic images. Lineal
movement is achieved by means of lateral diversions—through several
statements of the fact that the king is dead we arrive at the fact that he
will be buried. The significance of this is that it is not the communication
of information which is important but the creation of a dramatic reality.
This is brought about as is the creation of all else in the Yoruba cultural
universe—through syndetic intensive continuity.

Both *Oedipus Rex* and *Oba Waja* enact in their dramatic structures and
in their dramatic actions serious conditions of their respective cultural
mythoforms of synthesis and syndesis. *Substantively* they enact these mythoforms by negations, which is to say that in each play the tragedy results
because the mythoform is specifically denied, ultimately to be set aright.
Operating in the dynamic of counterpoint and arguing the positive sway
of the mythoform, at the same time, the works *structurally* give positive
assertion to the same mythoform.

If one looks for a moment at Aristotle's classic definition of tragedy,[8]
one is impressed to discover how reliable it is—how clearly he perceived
what *is* universal in tragedy. That tragedy arouses emotions of pity and
fear and then purges them is, this study suggests, an action of the tragic
perception of man in his world which is of greater scope than Europe.
Our fear of terror develops from the fact that an individual is corrupting
the basic premise of our existence. If he is a person in a position of great
power, whose actions can have disastrous consequences for all of us, then
the situation is that much worse. This is why Aristotle speaks of a "person
of high estate." We pity such a person, nonetheless, and the tension between these two emotions is a powerful dynamic of tragedy. It is this
tension which is resolved—"purged"—at the work's end, in the condition of final victory (the resolution of fear) and defeat (the resolution
of pity).

So we are finally in a position to propose an anthropologically probable definition of tragedy as a work of affecting presence which enacts at the substantive level a perversion or a denial of the cultural myth, doing so in such a way that with the defeat of the tragic protagonist a paradoxical terminal situation prevails, taking the protagonist down but the audience up. Further, while the spoken language of the play concerns an attempted refutation of the mythoform, the silent "language" of the work—its structures and dynamics—affirms its validity, acting in its silent terms as a profoundly normative assertion. One may conclude that the power of a tragedy is variably dependent on the one hand upon the position of the tragic hero, such that the more serious his deviation and the greater his position, the greater the numbers of innocent others who will be affected; and on the other hand a work's power depends upon the density of substructures which normatively assert the rightness of the mythoform.

NOTES

1. For a full discussion of this theory, see my *Wellspring: On the Source and Myth of Culture* (Los Angeles and Berkeley: University of California Press, 1975).

2. Ibid.

3. Hesiod 308.

4. For a discussion of sequentiality in *The Palm-Wine Drinkard*, see my "The Narrative and Intensive Continuity: *The Palm-Wine Drinkard.*" *Research in African Literatures*, I (1970), pp. 9–34.

5. Charles R. Walker, trans. *Sophocles' Oedipus the King, and Oedipus at Colonus. A New Translation for Modern Readers and Theatergoers* (Garden City: Anchor/Doubleday, 1966).

6. All quotations are from Duro Ladipo's "Oba Waja," in *Three Yoruba Plays*. English adaptation by Ulli Beier. (Ibadan: Mbari, 1964), pp. 54–72.

7. Robert Plant Armstrong, *The Affecting Presence: An Essay in Humanistic Anthropology* (Urbana: The University of Illinois Press, 1971).

8. Samuel Butcher, ed. and trans. *Aristotle's Theory of Poetry and Fine Arts* (4th ed., New York: Dover, 1931), p. 23; Gerald Else, *Aristotle's Poetics: The Argument* (Cambridge, Mass.: Harvard University Press, 1963), p. 221.

> Tragedy, then, is an imitaion of an action that is serious, complete, and of a certain magnitude; in language embellished with each kind of artistic ornament, the several kinds being found in separate parts of the play; in the form of action, not of narrative; through pity and fear effecting the proper purgation of these emotions.

N.B. Because both these works are English translations, I do not consider their diction.

Folklore and Yoruba Theater

OYEKAN OWOMOYELA

The purpose of this essay is not merely to apply a generally accepted opinion—that theater and folklore have a specially close relationship, one to the other—to the Yoruba situation. We know, for instance, that the ancient Greek dramatists relied heavily on folklore for their material, that Shakespeare found European folklore useful, and that the theaters of the East—Japanese, Chinese or Indonesian—also make extensive use of folklore. While in this essay an attempt will be made to show that what was, and is, true of the theaters cited is equally true of Yoruba theater, more importantly, an attempt will be made to disencumber Yoruba theater of the religious and ritual deadweight that threatens to become grafted on to it.

Taking their cues from a certain school of thought that advocates a ritual origin of drama (since Aristotle has supposedly proved this fact with reference to Greek theater), certain writers have claimed that Yoruba theater is a bequest of Yoruba religious instinct. Typical are the following statements by a Yoruba scholar, Joel A. Adedeji:

> Religion is the basis of dramatic developments in Yoruba as in most cultures of the world; disguise is its means, and both depend on artistic propensities for their fulfilment.[1]

> The worship of Ọbàtálá [the Yoruba arch-divinity] has important consequences for the development of ritual drama and, finally the emergence of the theatre.[2]

He further says that "the human instinct for impersonation and ritualistic expression . . . leads to 'developmental drama'."[3]

Another Nigerian, poet-dramatist John Pepper Clark, has earlier written:

> As the roots of European drama go to the Egyptian Osiris and the Greek Dionysus so are the origins of Nigerian drama likely to be found in the early religious and magical ceremonies of the peoples of this country.[4]

He goes on to cite the *egúngún* and *orò* of the Yoruba as "dramas typical of the national repertory."[5]

It is not difficult to see that the views quoted borrow credence from the fact that Aristotle, the first systematic theater historian, had seemingly proved the religio-genic nature of Greek theater and, by implication, of all theater. But the question should be asked whether Aristotle in fact intended to say that the dramatic instinct of the Greeks, or indeed of any other people, resulted from religion. A careful reading of the *Poetics* leads one to believe that Aristotle was primarily concerned with one specific form of theatrical expression—Greek tragedy—which had benefited from the performers and performances associated with the Dionysiac revels. That he would not subscribe to such views as that "Religion is the basis of dramatic developments" is indicated by the following words from the *Poetics*:

> As to the *general* origin of the poetic art, it stands to reason that two causes gave birth to it, both of them natural: (1) Imitation is a part of man's nature from childhood, (and he differs from other animals in the fact that he is especially mimetic and learns his first lessons through imitation) as is the fact that they all get pleasure from works of imitation. . . . and (2) melody and rhythm also. . . , at the beginning those who were endowed in these respects, developing it for the most part little by little, gave birth to poetry out of the improvisational performances.[6]

Thus, two thousand years ago, Aristotle recognized that imitation and impersonation are part of human nature. Whether religion is part of human nature or not is definitely open to debate; what is certain is that the mimetic instinct develops in man very much earlier than any evidences of religious inclination, and before religious indoctrination. Thus, long before children can make any sense of religious beliefs and practices, they evince a sense of mimesis by playing house, and cops and robbers—apart from performing those mimetic activities associated with the learning process.

The evidences adduced by the scholars who believe in a ritual origin of drama to support their claim come in the main from festivals that, while purporting to be religious, incorporate theatrical performances. Depending on the circumstances, the festival cited could be that of Dionysus, or that of *egúngún* among the Yoruba. In any case, the fact that religion and drama can be seen hobnobbing in certain festivals can be very easily explained.

Festivals are social institutions by means of which men satisfy their fun-seeking instincts. They generally take place when the commodities that will ensure their success are in abundance (for example, when the harvest is in) and also when the festivals will not prejudice the performance of activities vital to the life of the community. It follows, therefore, that festivals are generally associated with holidays and periods of community-wide relaxation.

At the end of a hunt, the participants delight to wind down with a feast and a ball; so, at the end of a working season, the community delights to let its collective hair down and have a festival. It can be stated, without the need for a supporting argument, that theatrical sketches are just some of the accretions that festivals incorporate from time to time as they become more elaborate.

The supernatural powers become involved in festivals simply because of man's desire to placate them before and during the revels so that the revellers would be left in peace. To this end, "insurance" sacrifices are offered to the gods at the beginning of the festivals, and at the end, the grateful men return with thanks offerings. Moreover, during the revels, the participants decide to elect their favorite divinity as patron for the same reasons that long ago, certain players elected the King, the Chamberlain, or the Admiral as their patron and called themselves "The King's Men," "The Chamberlain's Men," or "The Admiral's Men." The men in question did not perform plays because they were in the first instance associated with King, Chamberlain, or Admiral, association with whom entailed the performance of plays. Rather, they associated themselves with the notables because they wished to perform plays and thought they could best do so if they enjoyed the protection of such powerful personalities. If the players later included plays about their patrons in their repertoires, that would still be consistent with their strategy.

Therefore, if among the Yoruba we encounter festivals whose designations suggest that they are "in honor of" certain divinities, we should not allow the evidence of the name to befuddle our minds to such an extent that we become unable to determine the relative importance of different festival aspects.

In the Yoruba theater of today (which is often referred to as "folk opera"), we see the culmination of a socio-political development which began around the middle of the nineteenth century in Lagos. It was in 1851 that the British conquered Lagos and put its affairs in the hands of a ruler who would put an end to the hitherto flourishing slave trade. Two years later, a British Consul arrived to take up residence there. With the establishment of British presence, the town became so secure that it began to attract European missionaries, European commercial agents, well-educated freed slaves from the Sierra Leone and the Americas, and ambitious native Africans from the nearby areas. Favored by its situation on the Atlantic coast and by its command of a vast rich hinterland, Lagos soon became a flourishing cosmopolis the direction of whose affairs rested in the hands of a cosmopolitan *élite* class.

The introduction of drama into the city around 1880 was a means of providing evening diversion on the European model for the Lagos *élite*, made up, as we have seen, of expatriates and westernized Africans.[7] As one would expect, the theatrical fare was strictly European, featuring such dramatists as Molière and Gilbert and Sullivan.

In those days, one had to be a practising Christian to be socially acceptable. In fact, the prestige of the Christian establishment was such that the city's life revolved mainly around the different mission houses.[8] It was, therefore, no wonder that the performing groups were invariably connected with one Christian mission or the other. This connection must have eased some practical difficulties because the most readily available performance places were the schoolrooms that were all owned by the missions. The students of certain schools, recognising the social advantages and financial possibilities of theatrical entertainment, had themselves formed dramatic societies either for the purpose of raising money, or just for the love of diversion.[9]

The profound changes that occurred in Lagos after the European powers had divided the continent of Africa among themselves at the 1885 Berlin Conference proved significant for the development of Yoruba theater. In the past, the Europeans in Lagos were there for limited purposes—commerce, or the conversion of heathens—and they were not averse to treating Africans as equals. But now, the emphasis shifted to colonization and the attitude of the resident Europeans underwent a change. They now saw themselves as masters and the Africans as clients and they behaved accordingly. African church officials felt the change most traumatically because the Church was one institution in which native personnel had been put in the fore-front of the campaign, obviously because the European missionary bodies recognized the wisdom of making use of African converts who could function in the inhospitable climate and communicate with the natives. Now, their European colleagues took steps to put all authority in their own hands.

As a result of the friction generated, African groups seceded from the European and American Churches and founded protestant African Churches. The first of these groups broke off under David B. Vincent from the American Baptist mission in 1888.[10]

What is more important is that the Africans began to react against the rigorous suppression of all facets of African culture by the European Christians. They now looked to their culture for reassurance, and as something they could take pride in. According to E. A. Ayandele,

> From 1890 onwards useful researches were made into Yoruba mythology, philosophy of religion and metaphysics of *Ifá* [the Yoruba system of divination]. In 1896 appeared the Reverend Moses Lijadu's *Yoruba Mythology* in which *Ifá* and the legend of creation. . . were examined. . . . Studies of indigenous religion led to the foundation on 12 April, 1901 of "The West African Psychical Institute Yoruba Branch," for the purpose of encouraging the study of comparative religion, philosophy and science, especially the psychic laws known to *Babaláwos* (*Ifá* priests) and secret societies.[11]

As early as 1882, a correspondent of the *Lagos Observer* had made a strong plea for discarding "borrowed plumes" in the form of European or Europeanesque literature in favor of "the legends connected with our race, and . . . the brilliant exploits of our ancestors as handed to us by tradition." By the turn of the century, the African amateur dramatists, mainly drawn from the ranks of the secessionist churches, were performing works mainly on local themes and in the native language—Yoruba.

It was not until 1945 that a professional Yoruba theater group came into existence, and then it came as an offspring of one of the African churches. Ulli Beier has described its development in the following words:

> Theatre in the Yoruba language is mostly a kind of opera, in which the songs are rehearsed, while the dialogue is improvised. In the late twenties and thirties this form was developed in the so-called African Churches, the Apostolic Church and the Cherubim and Seraphim. The bible stories and moralities performed by these church societies soon gave way to profane plays, social and political satires which were played by professional touring companies.[12]

In 1944, Hubert Ogunde presented to the public an expanded version of what he had written as a devotional Service for the Church of the Lord in Lagos. It was a dramatization of the biblical story of the Garden of Eden, the action was simple, and all the lines were sung by dancing performers to the accompaniment of a competent off-stage band. The church had already realized that divine worship enlivened by drumming, clapping, and dancing was more satisfying to the African than the austere and sedate services that characterized "European" worship. The same proved true in the sphere of entertainment, as the enthusiastic public acceptance of Ogunde's "opera" proved. In the next year, he turned professional and gave Nigeria her first professional theater company—the Ogunde Concert Party.

The fact that he called his company a "concert" party is proof that Ogunde acknowledged that he was continuing a tradition that had been long in existence rather than creating something entirely new. (The nineteenth century theatrical activities were often billed as "concerts" because they often formed part of long programs that included songs, duets, magical displays, and such like.)

Moreover, since the missionary schools began presenting plays to parents and friends in the early years of theater, the tradition grew stronger and stronger until it became a fixed part of school activities. In most schools today, "dramatization" is always one of the items on the program of the end-of-year exercise, and Duro Ladipọ, one of the present masters of Yoruba theater, told me he began his career as a dramatist in such end-of-year activities at school. Apart from occasional biblical plays, the fare on these occasions was predominantly extracted from the Yoruba wealth of folk stories. It is not surprising, therefore, that in 1936, a school teacher—E. K. Martin—wrote, "As a means of general entertainment our folklore is never lacking. Folk stories may be . . . dramatized and the songs accompanying them practised and sung in the vernacular."[13] It was precisely this type of dramatization that bridged the gap between the turn of the century when, for several reasons, the theatrical flowering of the late nineteenth century fizzled out, and the time of Hubert Ogunde.

The dependence of Yoruba theater on Yoruba folklore is easily explained. First, it was nationalistic. Reaction to foreign oppression meant, in this instance, return to the native culture. James Coleman wrote:

> The special grievances of the westernized elements [in Nigeria] were crucial factors in the awakening of racial and political consciousness. Much of their resentment, of course, was the inevitable outcome of the disorganization following rapid social change. The desire to emulate Europeans tended to separate them from their traditional milieu. Had they been accepted completely and unconditionally as dark-skinned Englishmen—as, in fact, certain members of the first generation were accepted—and had they been permitted to achieve a social and economic status that was both psychologically meaningful and materially satisfying, the course and the pace of Nigerian nationalism would most likely have been quite different. This did not happen, however, mainly because of the attitudes of many of the European residents and the policies of the British administration in Nigeria.[14]

It was as part of the reaction to those attitudes and policies that the Lagosians gave up trying to emulate Europeans and began to look askance at

European theatrical fare which they eventually replaced with African material. It was to their credit that they did not discard theater wholesale but merely adapted it to suit the new mood.

Secondly, Yoruba theater has depended on folklore as a matter of expediency. Folklore is a vast treasury of theater material. The tales furnish a wealth of plots, the proverbs and such eulogistic poems as *oríkì, ìjálá* and *ewì* provide rich examples of ornamental dialogue, and if we include folkways in folklore, the physical actions connected with certain festivals give to dramatists action ideas that are effective on stage.

Lastly, it is logical that an alien institution that is introduced into a society should, in the course of time, be influenced by the native institution that is its parallel. Theater, being a form of evening pastime, naturally looked to the traditional evening story-telling session for material, the more so because of the political and nationalistic incentives that have already been mentioned.

Today, an accommodation has been effected between the native and the foreign elements of Yoruba experience, and it has resulted in a hybrid civilization at one polar fringe of which is maintained a more or less foreign, and at the other, a more or less native, complexion. Applied to evening entertainment, this situation means that on the one hand, there is a theatrical tradition that is for all practical purposes alien European (as typified by Wọle Ṣoyinka), and on the other hand, there is the continuing tradition of storytelling, particularly in areas that have not been drastically affected by modernization. In the middle of these is the Yoruba "folk opera" of Hubert Ogunde, Kọla Ogunmọla, and Duro Ladipọ.

Wọle Ṣoyinka's drama is world famous and, therefore, there seems to be no reason to dwell on it in this short essay. The uses of folklore among the Yoruba do not differ in essence from those of other traditional societies, and, as a result of international tours by the "opera" artists, their art form is becoming better known internationally.[15] However, to make it easy for readers to compare the traditional evening amusement and the new theater of the Yoruba, I will briefly describe each in its appropriate setting.

For the evening storytelling session, we go to a compound in a ward of Ibadan where we find an extended family that has not been wholly caught up by creeping modernization. Apart from such concessions to progress as the use of electricity, pipe-borne water, and the Rediffusion box that brings a fixed radio program by wire from a local transmitting station, the household remains a redoubt of tradition. After the evening meal, the members of the family gather on a porch and if there is moonlight, the younger members gather in the courtyard to play games like hide and seek.

On the porch, the entertainment begins with riddles. What dines with an *ọba* (paramount chief of a community) and leaves him to clear the dishes? A fly. What passes before the *ọba's* palace without making obeisance? Rain flood. On its way to Ọyọ its face is towards Ọyọ, on its way from Ọyọ its face is still towards Ọyọ. What is it? A double-faced drum.

After a few riddles, the tales begin. A member of the gathering announces the story of a certain man called *Àwòdọ́run*. He lived in a fargone age when men had eyes on their shins and cracked nuts with their behinds. This man—*Àwòdọ́run*—was so nosey that whenever he saw two people conversing or arguing he went and stood by them so that nothing they said would escape him. His parents and friends warned him against such behavior, but all to no avail.

On a certain day, while on his way to the market, *Àwòdọ́run* came upon two men arguing spiritedly. As usual, he hurried to where they stood and listened intently. Before long, the two men decided to press their points by resorting to blows. This new development proved even more exciting to *Àwòdọ́run* who urged them on with encouraging shouts. The combatants fought so hard that soon both fell and died from exhaustion.

At first, *Àwòdọ́run* was alarmed but soon his alarm gave way to anger that the contestants dared die on him and thus deprived him of the benefit of knowing who had won the argument. Deciding that it could not be dismissed as a stalemate and that the two men would, in all probability, continue their argument on their way to heaven, he threw himself down and died, the better to follow them. He would have stayed dead too but for his relatives who came and squeezed the juice of certain leaves into his eyes and thus revived him.

The next tale is of a certain young and beautiful girl who would not accept any man as her husband. Her parents became so angry and worried that they warned her they would turn her out of their home if she did not agree to marry someone soon. She, however, replied that she had not yet seen any man who appealed to her.

On a certain day, she went, as usual, to the market to sell some oil. As soon as she got there, she saw an exceptionally handsome man and immediately decided that she would be his wife. She abandoned her oil and approached the man who told her it was impossible for him to accept her offer. She would not be refused, and she followed him on his way home. As they went, the man sang to her:

Man	El'épo d'èhìn o	Oil seller, please go back,
	Méè ṣ'ọkọ̀ rẹ.	I cannot be yours.

Response	D'ẹhìn o méè d'ẹhìn.	Go back? Not I!
Man	B'ó ò bá d'èhìn wa d'ódò aró.	If you don't You'll cross an indigo river.
Response	D'ẹhìn o méè dẹhìn.	Go back? Not I!
Man	B'ó ò bá d'ẹhìn wa d'ódò èjè.	If you don't You'll cross the river of blood.
Response	D'ẹhìn o méè d'ẹhìn.	Go back? Not I!
Man	El'épo d'ẹhìn o Méè ṣ'ọkọ̀ rẹ.	Oil seller, please go back, I cannot be yours.
Response	D'ẹhìn o méè d'ẹhìn.	Go back? Not I!

As he sang, the young man cast off, piece by piece, the beautiful clothes he wore and, in the end, even his flesh, until he was nothing but a skeleton. The girl saw it all as a trick and still followed him across both the indigo and the blood rivers. Then the young man became a boa constrictor and proceeded to swallow her. Only then did she panic and yell for help. Luckily for her, a hunter heard her cries and came to her aid. He killed the boa and released the girl who there and then agreed to be the hunter's wife.

Many such stories are told until, when it is very late, the gathering disperses to sleep and take up the storytelling tradition the next evening.

For a performance of a Yoruba "folk opera," we need not go outside the city of Ibadan. The Arts Theatre of the University of Ibadan has hosted Ogunmọla's *Palmwine Drinkard* in the past, and it can be recreated here.[16]

The story is of *Lànké* an incurable drunk who follows his dead tapster —*Àlàbá*—to the town of the dead in order to persuade him to come back to earth and resume his palmwine tapping. The "opera" opens on a drunks' carnival hosted by *Lànké*. He exhorts his drunkard friends:

Ẹmu, ẹmu, ẹmu, ẹmu!
Ẹ jẹ k'á m'ẹmu à mu k'ára!
Mo l'ẹ́rú mo n'íwèfà,
Mo l'áya méfà, mo bí mọ méjọ!
Mo l'ówó l'ọ́wọ́, mo ti kọ́'lé.

. . . .

Asán ni gbogbo è l'ójú mi.
Ẹmu, ẹmu, ẹmu, ẹmu!
Ẹ jẹ k'á m'ẹmu à mu k'ára.

Palmwine, palmwine, palmwine, palmwine!
Let's all drink palmwine with all our might!
I have slaves, I have bondsmen,
I have six wives, I have eight children,
I have money, I have a house.

. . . .

That's all vanity to me.
Palmwine, palmwine, palmwine, palmwine!
Let's all drink palmwine with all our might.

The party continues with riddles from the guests. What can you see on
the sea but not on land? The moon and stars. What drops into water and
makes no sound? Needle. A large rock lives in a stream and still com-
plains of thirst? The tongue. What is the two-cent wife that chases a
hundred-dollar wife out of the house? Palmwine, of course! *Lànké* then
recites the *oríkì* of palmwine:

Ẹmu!
Ẹmu ògidì pọnbé!
A bá 'ni w'ọ̀ràn b'á ò rí dá.
Ògùrọ̀ ogidì.
Tí kì í jẹ́ k'ẹni ó mọ̀'ṣẹ́ ara ẹni.
Ìyàwó o kọ́bọ̀-kan àbọ̀.
Tí ńlé onígba-ọ̀kẹ́ s'ígbó.
Akúwáńpá
Ab'itọ́ funfun l'ẹnu.
Ākíìkà!
Ẹni t'áwọn àgbá kì kì kì tí wọn ò le è kì tán,
Wọ́n l'ó sọ baálé ilé
D'ẹni tí ńyọ kóńdó
Lé ọmọ ọl'ọ́mọ kiri.

Palmwine!
Pure undiluted palmwine!
It finds you trouble when trouble is scarce.
Undiluted palmwine!
It screens your mind from pressing problems.
The two-cent wife that chases
The hundred-dollar wife into the bush!
Epileptic
That froths at the mouth.
Truly,

The elders, unable to find your ultimate *oríkì*,
Say you turn a landlord into a raving maniac
That chases children around
With a cudgel.

Soon, the supply of palmwine is exhausted and *Lànké* sends *Àlàbá* posthaste to the top of the palmtree for more palmwine. Unfortunately, the tapster falls from the tree and dies. *Lànké* cannot live without palmwine and there is no tapster like *Àlàbá*. *Àlàbá* must return, so *Lànké* throws himself down and dies and thus begins his pilgrimage to the town of the dead.

Along the way, *Lànké* has many adventures, including an encounter with a white god who asks him to go and capture Death in a net (a feat he successfully accomplishes). But more pertinently, he is instrumental in rescuing a young and beautiful girl from some wicked Spirits determined to kill her. Her name is *Bísí*, and *Lànké* is drinking palmwine at her market stall when her father comes to tell her that complaints have reached him to the effect that she has sent every man who proposed to her away with insults. He warns her that she had better find herself a husband soon, and leaves. A little while later, a well-dressed young man arrives and asks the way to the fish stall. *Bísí* sees him and jumps at him. She has found the man she will marry, she says. The man protests but *Bísí* will not listen. She will follow him home.

On his way home, the man sings to her:

On'íyán d'èhìn l'éhìn mi, tètè d'èhìn o.
Ninikúnni.
On'íyán d'èhìn l'éhìn mi, tètè d'èhìn.
Ninikúnni.
B'ó ò bá d'èhìn o ó d'ódò aró!
Ninikúnni.
B'ó ò bá d'èhìn o ó d'ódò èjè ò ò!
Ninikúnni.

Foodseller leave me and go back home,
Ninikúnni.
Foodseller leave me and go back home,
Ninikúnni.
If you don't you'll cross the indigo river,
Ninikúnni.
If you don't you'll cross the river of blood,
Ninikúnni.

As he sings, he discards his clothes and his flesh, but *Bísí* follows him across the indigo river and the river of blood. They are now in a land inhabited exclusively by all sorts of grotesque Spirits who make it a point to kill any human who discovers their abode and their secrets. *Bísí* is tied up and would have been killed but for *Lànké* who arrives to put a spell on the Spirits and cut her loose.

The "opera" continues until *Lànké* has contacted *Àlàbá* who, even though he cannot leave the town of the dead and return to earth, gives *Lànké* a magic egg that will turn water to palmwine. He returns home with the egg only to wake up and find that his adventure was all a dream. The "opera" ends as it began with the exhortation:

Ẹmu, ẹmu, ẹmu, ẹmu!
Ẹ jẹ k'á m'ẹmu à mu k'ára!

Palmwine, palmwine, palmwine, palmwine!
Let's all drink palmwine with all our might!

When Ogunmọla's *Palmwine Drinkard* is considered in the light of the description of a family evening entertainment provided earlier, it is easy to see that his form of theater is, essentially, Yoruba folklore in a dress more compatible with a new milieu. The *Palmwine Drinkard* may not be typical in all respects of Ogunmọla's work or of the other Yoruba dramatists', but it will not be difficult to take any work by any of the dramatists and prove the same points that this essay has sought to prove.

A more detailed examination of the Yoruba "operas" will undoubtedly reveal borrowings from aspects of Yoruba culture other than the folklore. But that is only to be expected in a work of art whose nature is to pretend to be real life. The cornerstone of Yoruba theater is story, and Yoruba folklore has been, and remains, the most useful and the most important quarry of the dramatists.

REFERENCES

1. Joel Adeyinka Adedeji, *The Alárìnjó Theatre: The Study of a Yoruba Theatrical Art from its Earliest Beginnings to the Present Times* (Ph.D. Thesis, University of Ibadan, 1969), p. 32.
2. Ibid., p. 39.
3. Ibid., p. 66.
4. John Pepper Clark, "Aspects of Nigerian Drama," *Nigeria Magazine*. 89 (June 1966), 118.
5. The *egúngún* are fully masked figures that are supposedly the embodied spirits of dead ancestors. There is an annual festival around June, when the *egúngún* materialize out of secret groves and join humans in a feast during which some of them perform tricks and satirical sketches. Some funeral ceremonies also feature some *egúngún* that represent the deceased at funerary processions. *Orò* is a god of the night that

must not be seen by non-initiates and never by a woman. This institution supposedly came into being early in Yoruba history as a means of preserving Yoruba culture and mysteries in the face of alien influences.

6. *Poetics*, 1448b, 4–24; Gerald F. Else, *Aristotle's Poetics: The Argument* (Cambridge, Massachusetts: Harvard University Press, in cooperation with the State University of Iowa, 1963), p. 124.

7. The first dramatic group was P. Z. Silva's Brazilian Dramatic Association formed in 1880. See Lynn Leonard, *The Growth of Entertainments of Non-African Origin in Lagos from 1866–1920 (with Special Emphasis on Concert, Drama, and the Cinema)* (M.A. Thesis, University of Ibadan, 1967), p. 25.

8. J. F. Ade Ajayi, *Christian Missions in Nigeria, 1841–1891: The Making of a New Elite* (London: Longmans, 1965), ch. 5.

9. Leonard, pp. 19, 23.

10. E. A. Ayandele, *The Missionary Impact on Modern Nigeria, 1842–1914: A Political and Social Analysis* (London: Longmans, 1966), p. 200.

11. Ibid., pp. 264–265.

12. Ulli Beier, "Introduction," in Ọbọtunde Ijimere, *The Imprisonment of Ọbàtálá and Other Plays*, English adaptation by Ulli Beier (London: Heinemann, 1966).

13. E. K. Martin, "The Importance of Our Folklore," *The Nigerian Teacher*, 8 (1936), 14.

14. James S. Coleman, *Nigeria, Background to Nationalism* (Berkeley: University of California Press, 1958), 145.

15. In 1964 and 1965, Duro Ladipọ participated in the Berlin Theatre Festival and the Commonwealth Festival in Britain respectively, Kọla Ogunmọla participated in the 1969 Festival of Negro Arts at Algiers, and Hubert Ogunde toured Britain from 1968–1969.

16. See Kọla Ogunmọla, *The Palmwine Drinkard*, translated and transcribed by R. G. Armstrong, Robert L. Awujọọla and Val Ọlayẹmi. Occasional Publication No. 12 (Ibadan: Institute of African Studies, University of Ibadan, 1968).

YORUBA "OPERAS" IN TRANSLATION

1. Ijimere, Ọbọtunde. [Duro Ladipọ and Ulli Beier] *The Imprisonment of Ọbàtálá* and *Everyman (Èdá)* in Ọbọtunde Ijimere. *The Imprisonment of Ọbàtálá and Other Plays*. English Adaptation by Ulli Beier. (African Writers Series.) London: Heinemann, 1966.

2. Ladipọ, Duro. *Ọba Kò So*. Transcribed and translated by R. G. Armstrong, Robert L. Awujọọla and Val Ọlayemi. (Occasional Publication No. 10.) Ibadan: Institute of African Studies, University of Ibadan. 1968.

3. ───────. *Three Yoruba Plays*. [*Ọba Kò So, Ọba M'Órò, Ọbá W'Àjà*.] Ibadan: Mbari Publications, 1964.

4. ───────. *Mórèmí*. In *Three Nigerian Plays*. Introduction and notes by Ulli Beier. London: Longmans, 1967.

5. Ogunmọla, Kọla. *The Palmwine Drinkard*. Transcribed and translated by R. G. Armstrong, Robert L. Awujọọla and Val Ọlayẹmi. (Occasional Publication No. 12.) Ibadan: Institute of African Studies, University of Ibadan, 1968.

NOTES ON CONTRIBUTORS

J. A. Adedeji is a professor and head of the Department of Theatre Arts at the University of Ibadan and director of the University of Ibadan Theatre. He is currently serving as president of the Nigerian Association of Theatre Artists. His major publications are "The Alarinjo Theatre," "The Adamuorisa Play," "The Yoruba Opera," and "Perspectives of the Nigerian Theatre: 1866–1945."

Robert Plant Armstrong is a professor of anthropology and Master of College V of the Social Sciences at the University of Texas at Dallas. Among his books are *The Affecting Presence: An Essay in Humanistic Anthropology* and *Wellspring: On the Myth and the Source of Culture.* He has also written numerous essays and articles.

Dan Ben-Amos is an associate professor in the Folklore and Folklife Program at the University of Pennsylvania. He is the author of numerous books, among them *Sweet Words: Storytelling Events in Benin* and *Thrice-Told Tales: Folktales from Three Continents,* along with many articles and book reviews. He is on the advisory board of *Genre* and is an associate editor of *Monographs in Folklore and Folklife* and *Research in African Literatures.*

Veronika Görög-Karady is in charge of the Archives de la Littérature Orale Africaine at the Centre d'Etudes Africaines in Paris and of research at the Centre National de la Recherche Scientifique. She is the author of *Stéréotypes ethniques et domination* and many other publications.

Jeanette Harries was an assistant professor of linguistics at the University of Wisconsin from 1966 to 1974. She has written several essays on Berber dialects and a report for the Department of Health, Education, and Welfare entitled *Tamazight Basic Course.*

John E. Kaemmer is an assistant professor of anthropology at DePauw University. He has two contributions in the process of being published: "Changing Music in Contemporary Africa" in *Introduction to Africa* and "Anthropology and Music" in *Logos and Anthropos: Handbook on Anthropology and the Other Disciplines.*

Bernth Lindfors is a professor of English and African literature at the University of Texas at Austin. He has written *Folklore in Nigerian Literature* and has edited several books; he is an editor of *Research in African Literatures.*

Wyatt MacGaffey is a professor of anthropology at Haverford College. He is the author of three books: *Cuba, Custom and Government in the Lower Congo,* and *An Anthology of Kongo Religion.*

Philip A. Noss is director of the Gbaya Translations Center of the Evangelical Lutheran Church of Cameroon at Meiganga, Cameroon. He has written several essays on Gbaya oral literature.

Oludare Ọlajubu is a lecturer in Yoruba at the Department of Linguistics and Languages at the University College in Ilorin, Nigeria. His teaching and research interests are in the area of Yoruba oral literature and traditional institutions. Among his publications are an anthology of Egúngún chants in Yoruba entitled *Akojọpọ Iwi Egúngún* and a collection of essays on Yoruba life and customs entitled *Iwi Aṣa Ibilẹ Yoruba.*

Oyekan Owomoyela is an associate professor of English at the University of Nebraska. He has published several essays on African literature and a book in conjunction with Bernth Lindfors called *Yoruba Proverbs: Translation and Annotation.*

Denise Paulme is director of studies at the Ecole des Hautes Etudes en Sciences Sociales in Paris. Her most recent publication is *La mère dévorante: Essai sur la morphologie des contes africains.*

Alain Ricard is a research associate of the Centre National de la Recherche Scientifique at the Institut de Littérature et de Techniques Artistiques de Masse at the Université de Bordeaux III. He is the author of *Théâtre et Nationalisme: Wole Soyinka et LeRoi Jones* and *Livre et communication au Nigeria,* and he is presently working on a book on popular culture in Togo.

Harold Scheub is an associate professor in the Department of African Languages and Literature at the University of Wisconsin. He is the author of *The Xhosa Ntsomi* and has two books forthcoming on African oral narratives and folktales. He has also published many essays and articles on African oral literature.

Index

Aarne-Thompson Tale Types[1]

Arewa Tale Types[2]

Lambrecht Tale Types[3]

Thompson Motif Numbers[4]

Note: Tale Type and Motif indexing was done by the following: Moyra Byrne, Rachel Cohen, Michael Licht, Craig Mishler, Johnny Saldana, and James Wanless, Jr.
[1]Tale Type numbers are taken from Antti Aarne and Stith Thompson, *The Types of the Folktale: A Classification and Bibliography*, FF Communications, no. 184, 2d rev. ed. (Helsinki, 1964).
[2]Tale Type numbers are taken from Erastus Ojo Arewa, "A Classification of the Folktales of the Northern East African Cattle Area by Types," Dissertation, University of California, Berkeley, 1966.
[3]Tale Type numbers are taken from Winifred Lambrecht, "A Tale Type Index for Central Africa," Dissertation, University of California, Berkeley, 1967.
[4]Motif numbers are taken from Stith Thompson, *Motif-Index of Folk-Literature*, 6 vols., rev. ed. (Bloomington, 1955–1958).

Lambrecht Motif Numbers[5]

[5]Motif numbers are taken from Lambrecht, "Tale Type Index for Central Africa."